# 1 *and* 2 KINGS *for* EVERYONE

Also available in the Old Testament
for Everyone series by John Goldingay

*Genesis for Everyone, Part I*

*Genesis for Everyone, Part II*

*Exodus and Leviticus for Everyone*

*Numbers and Deuteronomy for Everyone*

*Joshua, Judges and Ruth for Everyone*

*1 and 2 Samuel for Everyone*

# 1 *and* 2 KINGS
## *for* EVERYONE

### JOHN GOLDINGAY

Published in the United States of America in 2011
by Westminster John Knox Press, Louisville, Kentucky

Published in Great Britain in 2011

Society for Promoting Christian Knowledge
36 Causton Street
London SW1P 4ST
www.spckpublishing.co.uk

*British Library Cataloguing-in-Publication Data*
A catalogue record for this book is available from the British Library

ISBN 978–0–281–06130–3

1 3 5 7 9 10 8 6 4 2

Printed in the United States of America

# CONTENTS

# Contents

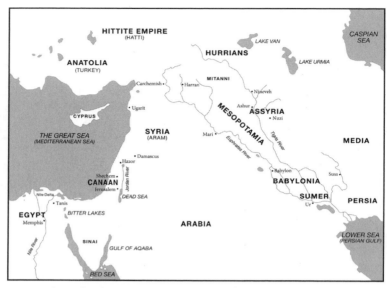

© Karla Bohmbach

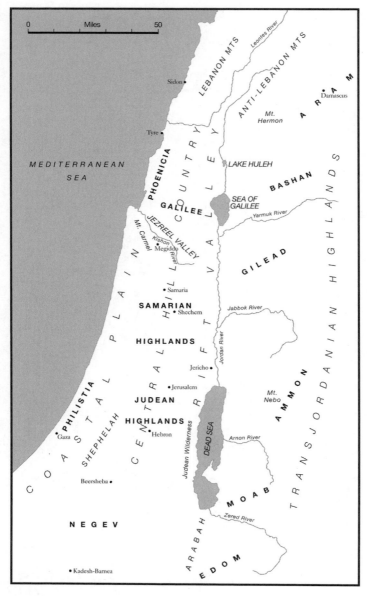

© *Karla Bohmbach*

# ACKNOWLEDGMENTS

The translation at the beginning of each chapter (and in other biblical quotations) is my own. So that you can see more precisely what the text says, I have stuck closer to the Hebrew than modern translations often do when they are designed for reading in church. Similarly, although I myself prefer to use gender-inclusive language, I have let the translation stay gendered if inclusivizing it would make it unclear whether the text was talking in the singular or plural—in other words, the translation often uses "he" where in my own writing I would say "they" or "he or she." Sometimes I have added words to make the meaning clear, and I have put these words in square brackets. Space confines do not allow for including the whole of the biblical text in this volume; where there is insufficient room for the entire text, I make some general comments on the material I have had to omit. At the end of the book is a glossary of some terms that recur in the text (such as geographical, historical, and theological expressions). In each chapter (though not in the introduction) these terms are highlighted in **bold** the first time they occur.

The stories that follow the translation often concern my friends as well as my family. While none are made up, they are sometimes heavily disguised, to be fair to people. Sometimes I have disguised them so well that it took me time to work out who they were describing when I came to read them again. My wife Ann appears in a number of them. The year before I started writing this book, she died after negotiating with multiple sclerosis for forty-three years. Our shared dealings with her illness and disability over these years contribute to everything I write, in ways you will be able to see but also in ways that are less obvious. I thank God for her, and I am glad for her sake though not for mine that she can now sleep till resurrection day.

I am grateful to Matt Sousa for reading through the manuscript and pointing out things I needed to correct or clarify, and to Tom Bennett for checking the proofs.

# INTRODUCTION

As far as Jesus and the New Testament writers were concerned, the Jewish Scriptures that Christians call the "Old Testament" *were* the Scriptures. In saying that, I cut corners a bit, as the New Testament never gives us a list of these Scriptures, but the body of writings that the Jewish people accept is as near as we can get to identifying the collection that Jesus and the New Testament writers would have worked with. The church also came to accept some extra books, such as Maccabees and Ecclesiasticus, that are traditionally called the "Apocrypha," the books that were "hidden away"—a name that came to imply "spurious." They are now often known as the "deutero-canonical writings," which is more cumbersome but less pejorative; it simply indicates that these books have less authority than the Torah, the Prophets, and the Writings. The precise list of them varies among different churches. For the purposes of this series that seeks to expound the "Old Testament for Everyone," by the Old Testament we mean the Scriptures accepted by the Jewish community, though in the Jewish Bible they come in a different order as the Torah, the Prophets, and the Writings.

They were not "old" in the sense of antiquated or out-of-date; I sometimes like to refer to them as the First Testament rather than the Old Testament to make that point. For Jesus and the New Testament writers, they were a living resource for understanding God, God's ways in the world, and God's ways with us. They were "useful for teaching, for reproof, for correction, and for training in righteousness, so that the person who belongs to God can be proficient, equipped for every good work" (2 Timothy 3:16–17). They were for everyone, in fact. So it's strange that Christians don't read them very much. My aim in these volumes is to help you do that.

My hesitation is that you may read me instead of the Scriptures. Don't do that. I like the fact that this series includes much of the biblical text. Don't skip over it. In the end, that's the bit that matters.


## An Outline of the Old Testament

The Jewish community often refers to these Scriptures as the Torah, the Prophets, and the Writings. While the Christian Old Testament comprises the same books, it has them in a different order:

Genesis to Kings: A story that runs from the creation of the
    world to the exile of Judahites to Babylon
Chronicles to Esther: A second version of this story,
    continuing it into the years after the exile
Job, Psalms, Proverbs, Ecclesiastes, Song of Songs: Some
    poetic books
Isaiah to Malachi: The teaching of some prophets

Here is an outline of the history that lies at the background of the books (I give no dates for events in Genesis, which involves too much guesswork).

| | |
|---|---|
| 1200s | Moses, the exodus, Joshua |
| 1100s | The "judges" |
| 1000s | Saul, David |
| 900s | Solomon; the nation splits into two, Ephraim and Judah |
| 800s | Elijah, Elisha |
| 700s | Amos, Hosea, Isaiah, Micah; Assyria the superpower; the fall of Ephraim |
| 600s | Jeremiah, King Josiah; Babylon the superpower |
| 500s | Ezekiel; the fall of Judah; Persia the superpower; Judahites free to return home |
| 400s | Ezra, Nehemiah |
| 300s | Greece the superpower |

| 200s | Syria and Egypt, the regional powers pulling Judah one way or the other |
|------|------|
| 100s | Judah's rebellion against Syrian power and gain of independence |
| 000s | Rome the superpower |

## First and Second Kings

As the name implies, 1 and 2 Kings tells the story of Israel when it was a monarchy, beginning from the accession of Solomon and taking the story through to the termination of the monarchy with the exile. The first eleven chapters of 1 Kings cover Solomon's reign. After his death, in about 970, the nation splits into two. The majority of the twelve clans abandon their connection with the line of David and with Jerusalem and set up their own monarchy in the north. Because they are much the larger unit, they inherit the name "Israel," which can be confusing because that is also the name of the people as a whole. They are also sometimes called "Ephraim" after one of the central clans, so to avoid confusion I refer to them as "Ephraim." The other nation comprises Judah, sometimes with Simeon and/or Benjamin as well. The story of the two nations occupies 1 Kings 12 through 2 Kings17, with their stories being told in an overlapping way reign by reign until the Assyrians invade Ephraim and bring the life of the northern nation to an end, in 722. From 2 Kings 18 through 25 there is thus only the story of Judah to tell; its life as a nation comes to an end in 587 with a similar invasion of Judah by the Babylonians.

Whereas none of the books that precede 1 and 2 Kings come to a proper end (that is, they stop rather than finish and always drive you to turn over the page to the next book), 2 Kings does come to an end in the sense that there is no more of this particular story to tell. When you turn over the page at the end of 2 Kings, you find yourself going back to the beginning of the entire story again in 1 and 2 Chronicles, which starts once more with Adam. (In the Hebrew Bible's order, the effect is the same in that you turn over the page at the end of

2 Kings and find yourself in the prophecy of Isaiah.) This is not really to say that the story achieves closure. It does not do so. After all, it ends up with both kingdoms defeated and their leadership taken off into exile. It leaves open what the future might hold.

It makes sense to assume that the books reached their final form in the decades after the fall of Jerusalem in 587. They do refer to one later event, the release from detention of the Judahite king in Babylon. He is still in exile, but maybe his release is a sign that God has not finished with David's line. The question is, What stance will Israel take to God now, and what stance will God take to Israel?

First and Second Kings tell the story of Israel's life from Solomon to the exile in such a fashion as to acknowledge the ways in which both nations failed to follow after Yahweh, their God. Sometimes they served other gods; sometimes they served Yahweh in ways Yahweh abhorred (notably, by sacrificing their children to God). They invite the people who read the story to acknowledge that the story is true—not merely in the sense that the historical facts are correct but in the sense that they accept responsibility for their wrongdoing over the generations. In effect the story is a kind of confession; it says, "Yes, this is the way we have lived as a people." The only possibility by way of a future for them is thus to face facts and to acknowledge these facts to God. There is no way they can undo those facts or *compel* God to forgive them and give them a new start. All they can do is cast themselves on God's mercy.

Although the books presuppose a context in the exile, they were hardly written from scratch then. They put together material from older written records, stories people told, and theological judgments on the part of the authors. Sometimes as you read the story, you can get the impression that the judgment of exile has not yet happened, and this may indicate that the first edition of the books was produced before Jerusalem fell to the Babylonians, perhaps in the time of King Josiah (see 2 Kings 22–23). At that stage the future was still open; if the people really turned back to Yahweh's ways (as Josiah sought to get them to do), then disaster could be averted. The first edition was then updated after the exile had actually happened.

4

In Jewish thinking, 1 and 2 Kings (along with Joshua, Judges, and Samuel) are "the Former Prophets." That title can have various implications. The books tell us about prophets such as Elijah, Elisha, Jonah, and Isaiah. They give us the background story to the ministry of other prophets such as Hosea, Amos, Micah, Jeremiah, Habakkuk, Nahum, Zephaniah, and Ezekiel. They also are a prophetic kind of history. They are not merely an account of some things that happened in history and not merely a collection of good stories, but a narrative that gives you God's perspective on the history from Solomon to the exile.

# 1 KINGS 1:1–53

## How to Manipulate the Old Man in Order to Get Things Done

¹King David was old, advanced in years. They covered him in bedclothes but he could not get warm. ²His staff said to him, "They will look for a young girl for my lord the king, and she will stand [in attendance] before the king and be his caregiver. She can lie in his arms, and my lord the king will get warm." ³So they looked for a beautiful girl in all the territory of Israel and found Abishag the Shunammite and brought her to the king. ⁴The girl was very beautiful. She became the king's caregiver and ministered to him, but the king did not have sex with her. ⁵Now Adonijah son of Haggith was putting himself forward, saying, "I shall be king." He got ready for himself chariotry and cavalry and fifty men running ahead of him. ⁶His father had never vexed him by saying, "Why have you acted like this?" Further, he was very good-looking, and [his mother] gave birth to him [as David's next son] after Absalom. ⁷He had words with Joab son of Zeruiah and with the priest Abiathar. They supported Adonijah, ⁸but the priest Zadok, Benaiah son of Jehoiada, the prophet Nathan, Shimai, Rei, and David's warriors were not with Adonijah. ⁹Adonijah sacrificed sheep and cattle and fatlings at the Zohelet stone, near En-rogel, and invited all his brothers, the king's sons, and all the men of Judah, the king's staff, ¹⁰but the prophet Nathan and the warriors and his brother Solomon he did not invite. ¹¹Nathan said to Bathsheba, Solomon's mother, "You must have heard that Adonijah son of Haggith has become king without our lord David recognizing it. ¹²Now, go (may I give you counsel) and save your life and the life of your son Solomon. ¹³Go, come to King David and say to him, 'My lord the king, you certainly swore to your servant, "Your son Solomon—he will become king after me. He is the one who will sit on my throne." So why has Adonijah become king?' ¹⁴Now. While you are still speaking there with the king, I myself will come after you and fill out your words."

*[Verses 15–49 relate how they implement this plan and get David to have Solomon anointed as king.]*

⁵⁰Adonijah was then afraid of Solomon. He got up and went and took hold of the horns of the altar. ⁵¹Solomon was told, "Now. Adonijah is afraid of King Solomon. Now. He has taken hold of

the horns of the altar, saying, 'King Solomon must swear to me this very day that he will not kill his servant with the sword.'" [52]Solomon said, "If he becomes a man of worth, none of the hairs on his head will fall to the ground, but if wrong appears in him, he will die." [53]King Solomon sent and they brought him down from the altar. He came and bowed down to King Solomon, and Solomon said to him, "Go home."

I have friends in Kyrgyzstan, where a few weeks ago there were protests against the president and the government on the part of the opposition party and its supporters, citing widespread government corruption and abuse of expense claims. My friends deemed it wise to stay home during the riots that followed; scores of people were killed. Eventually the protesters took over the security headquarters and the state television station; the president and his family left the country; and the former opposition set up a new government. In Britain there were scandals last year over similar matters, and these will be a factor in the way people vote in an election that happens tomorrow. Political corruption is also an issue in the United States. But at least in both contexts we have a system for changing the government every few years and in this way "punishing" politicians. While the system's administration is subject to abuse and there can be controversy about the validity of an election's results, neither country has had a coup lately.

You could say that Israel was more like Kyrgyzstan. God's promise to David in 2 Samuel has established the principle of dynastic succession. God is committed to David's household. In the British monarchy the king's eldest son becomes the next king, and it rather looks as if Adonijah assumes this rule should apply. Of his elder brothers mentioned in 2 Samuel 3, we know that Amnon and Absalom are dead, and by implication Kileab has also died. While Adonijah comes next, God has not laid down that the eldest of a king's offspring should succeed him (or even that it should be a son rather than a daughter), and in the Old Testament God often shows an inclination to defy the regular rule whereby the eldest son is the senior one; for instance, God preferred Jacob to Esau. So there is no presumption regarding who should succeed.

David, too, has taken no action in connection with who should succeed him. It is an aspect of the way he has become more and more irresponsible and feeble as years have gone by. The point is illustrated by the pathetic account of his dotage with which 1 Kings begins. It seems sad not least that this king with many full wives and **secondary wives** cannot get one of them to keep him warm and that his staff assume he needs a nubile girl to do so. It's not clear whether they assume she will be another secondary wife for him, and thus that his not having sex with her is another sign of his feebleness.

Adonijah and his supporters could well argue that in the circumstances someone needs to take decisive action rather than leave the nation with this apology for a leadership, and that as David's eldest son, Adonijah is the person to do so, but he goes about it the same way as Absalom, by accumulating the outward trappings of kingship. He has David and Absalom's good looks, too, and leaders should be good-looking; F. D. Roosevelt in his wheelchair could never have been president if it had been more obvious to people that he had to use a wheelchair. Second Samuel has portrayed the way David failed his sons in not exercising any discipline in relation to them, but the point is here most explicit: he had never vexed Adonijah by challenging him about his behavior. David could confront his enemies but not his sons (like the Old Testament's comments on this subject elsewhere, such observations on discipline likely relate to them as one's offspring as they grow up and become adults, not to small children).

The leadership of Israel is totally divided about who should succeed. Adonijah wins the support of one of David's key officers in the army and one of the two senior priests. The other senior priest and several other figures in the military, along with the prophet Nathan, support Solomon. Adonijah holds a festive banquet to which he invites David's other sons and David's staff, but he pointedly does not invite Solomon and his supporters. (If it seems odd that there are apparently two senior priests, the explanation may relate to the way Jerusalem has become Israel's central sanctuary after David captured it from the Jebusites (see 2 Samuel 5–6). Psalm 110 speaks of David himself having become a priest in the order of Melchizedek, who appears in Genesis 14. In other words, he inherits the position of priest and king in Jerusalem in accordance with the arrangement when the Jebusites lived there. Connecting some dots, it looks as if Abiathar belongs to the priestly line by birth, while Zadok is a former Jebusite priest who is adopted into the native Israelite priestly line.)

Nathan's reporting that Adonijah has become king attributes to the banquet a more concrete importance than the actual account of the banquet did. Adonijah was certainly planning to take over as king, but Nathan is cutting corners in his description of the event's significance. It is not clear why Nathan would support Solomon, though it may simply go back to the story of his birth in 2 Samuel 12:24–25. God had struck down David's first son by Bathsheba; he had then sent Nathan to tell David that Bathsheba's second son was someone God would love. In these stories, the word for "love" often means be committed to and loyal to. So Nathan could connect some dots and conclude that God intended Solomon to be king. A willingness to draw this inference and to attribute to the banquet more significance than it actually had would link with the plan he presents to Bathsheba. It would be quite natural for her to hope her son would end up as king, and not simply for the usual motherly reasons. The transition from Saul to David illustrated how people who might look like rivals for the throne and people who might support such rivals are in a dangerous position during the transition process and afterward. If Adonijah succeeds to the throne, both Solomon and Bathsheba may not live long. So she would be quite willing to "remind" the befuddled David of a promise that (as far as we know) he had never made. Adonijah in turn will know that his number is up when David at last takes the decisive action he needed to take long ago.

Just after I wrote that opening line about my friends in Kyrgyzstan, one of them e-mailed me to say he had been listening to a recording of my classes on iTunes. Someone asked why God uses all these sinful people in the books of Samuel and Kings, and I answered, "Well, he doesn't really have much choice, does he?" My friend told me how he laughed out loud at that comment on the public transit. God works though people's manipulations and failures and fears and plotting. That doesn't necessarily mean we get away with them.

# 1 KINGS 2:1–46

## Coping with the Aftermath

[1] As the days drew near when David would die, he commanded his son Solomon: [2] "I shall be going the way of all the earth. Be strong. Be a man. [3] Keep the charge of Yahweh your God by walking in his ways by keeping his laws, his commands, his rules, and his declarations, as it is written in Moses' teaching, so that you may succeed in everything you do and everywhere you turn, [4] so that Yahweh may establish his word which he spoke to me: 'If your descendants guard their ways by walking before me in truth with all their mind and spirit—there will never cease to be a man for you on Israel's throne.' [5] Further, you yourself know what Joab son of Zeruiah did to me, what he did to the two commanders of Israel's armies, Abner son of Ner and Amasa son of Jether—he slew them and shed the blood of war when there was peace, and put the blood of war on the belt around his waist and the shoes on his feet. [6] Act in accordance with your wisdom, and do not let his white hair go down to Sheol in peace. [7] But the sons of Barzillai the Gileadite: show commitment to them so that they are among the people who eat at your table, because they were close to me when I fled from your brother Absalom. [8] Now. Shimei son of Gera the Benjaminite from Bahurim is with you. He uttered grievous belittling of me at the time I was going to Mahanaim, but when he came down to meet me at the Jordan I swore to him by Yahweh, 'I will not put you to death by the sword.' [9] So now do not treat him as innocent, because you are a wise man and you will know how to act toward him and let his white hair go down to Sheol in blood."

[10] So David slept with his ancestors and was buried in the city of David. [11] The time David reigned over Israel was forty years. In Hebron he reigned seven years; in Jerusalem he reigned thirty-three years. [12] Then Solomon sat on his father David's throne and his rule was firmly established.

*[Verses 13–46 relate how Solomon has Adonijah killed when he gets Bathsheba to ask if he can marry Abishag; he dismisses Abiathar from his priesthood; he has Joab killed even though he was holding onto the horns of the altar in the sanctuary; and he has Shimei killed when he breaks the terms of his parole.]*

As an undergraduate, I often walked past the Martyrs Memorial, standing where Hugh Latimer, Nicholas Ridley, and Thomas Cranmer were burned at the stake in Oxford in 1555 and 1556, caught in the conflict between different Christian groups. Many stories tell of Christians martyred by pagans; stories about Christians being killed by other Christians are more disturbing. We are fortunate to be living in a time when holding the wrong views does not cost you your life as it did a few centuries ago, but it is still the case that when you take sides, you take risks. Over the past year or so, two acquaintances of mine have lost their jobs because they said things about the Bible that clashed with the theological positions of the seminaries where they worked. Holding the wrong political views and backing the losers in an election will also not imperil your life in Britain or the United States, but it will do so in other parts of the world.

So it did in Israel when David came to the throne and when Solomon succeeded him. Indeed, some of the violence involves the continuing effects of events associated with David's accession. Joab is an instance. David had an older sister called Zeruiah, and she had three sons, Abishai, Joab, and Asahel. Joab rose to the position of commander-in-chief of David's army, yet his story shows him to be a person who made up his own mind about things. In the course of the conflict over who would succeed Saul, he killed the commander of the forces supporting Saul, Abner, who had himself killed Joab's brother Asahel in the course of this conflict. Joab killed Absalom, against David's orders, and confronted David over his subsequent preoccupation with Absalom's death. In the course of David's attempts to mend the wounds in the nation after Absalom's coup, Joab lost his position as commander-in-chief to Amasa, another of David's nephews, who had supported Absalom, and Joab also killed him. He then supported Adonijah.

If you're confused, it's OK, you have good reason. Anyway, Joab has a number of strikes against him. Abiathar the priest just has the one strike, his support of Adonijah, but that is enough to take him into early retirement, and thus simplify arrangements at the sanctuary; two senior priests is one too many. The requirement that Solomon take action against Shimei perhaps looks a little mean. The action of Adonijah in seeking to marry David's hot caregiver looks at best stupid. He could hardly complain when Solomon reads his request as resembling Absalom's action in sleeping with David's **secondary wives**. It is tantamount to an announcement that he still aspires to taking David's place.

So the way things work out issues from the stupidity of the people around Solomon, but it also issues from Solomon's own wisdom—at least David urges him to exercise his wisdom in the way he deals with the people David mentions. Solomon needs to be a person who reacts to people's action with insight and makes events work his way, who seizes the opportunities, makes things happen, knows how to get things done. His doing so issues in the happy result that potential threats for his throne all disappear. Yes, Solomon's throne was securely established. Further, it happened without Solomon's own hands getting stained with blood. Other people do his dirty work. Like David, he is Mr. Clean.

How is God involved in all these events? Perhaps God's providential purpose is at work, but the story's silence on this question is loud. That is all the more so when the storyteller reports many statements about God that other people make. David himself appeals to Solomon's wisdom; he does not tell him to do what God says. Adonijah comments that Solomon's accession to the throne is something that God brought about, but does he mean it? Solomon swears a solemn oath before God that he will have Adonijah executed and asks that God may punish him if he fails to do so; what does God think when listening to the oath? Solomon says that killing Joab as he stands before the **altar** will be the means of God's exacting payment for the blood he shed; what does God think? He also prays that God's **peace** may rest on David's successors forever. Does God say yes? When Shimei breaks his parole to pursue two runaway servants who have gone to Gath and Solomon says that his execution will be God's exacting payment for his wrongdoing (namely, his insulting David), is Solomon right? The nearest the storyteller comes to associating God with what happens is to comment that Solomon's dismissal of Abiathar fulfilled God's warning that Eli's descendants would lose their position as priests (1 Samuel 3).

There is quite a contrast between the main body of this chapter, with its account of David's reminders concerning action that needs taking and action that gets taken, and the chapter's opening words (and the earlier portrait of David in his feebleness). David's opening charge to Solomon is reminiscent of Moses' charge to Israel just before the end of his life (Deuteronomy 31), God's charge to Joshua as he becomes leader (Joshua 1), and Joshua's own charge to Israel just before the end of his life (Joshua 23–24). Once again at this crucial moment of transition for the people and for the leader himself, the leader is given a commission to be strong and confident, an exhortation to stick by Moses' teaching, and a promise that God will be faithful to him and that he will be successful. The four charges in fact summarize themes that run through the story from Deuteronomy through 2 Kings and provide keys to understanding the story as a whole. In this context, the phrase "Moses' teaching" refers in particular to Deuteronomy, which provides the key to understanding the story that unfolds through Joshua, Judges, Samuel, and Kings; hence the story can be called a "Deuteronomistic History," a history showing how Deuteronomy's teaching works itself out.

There was another charge to which Solomon was heir, God's charge to David in 2 Samuel 7. It put the emphasis more on God's promises to David and his successor(s) than on God's challenge to obedience; it did not mention Moses' teaching. There, while allowing for chastising David's successor but not for casting him off, God declared that David's household and monarchy would continue in perpetuity. Here David notes that this continuance will depend on his successors' "walking before God in truth." Leaders and people somehow have to hold onto both those ways of seeing the way God relates to us. God is absolutely committed to us, like a father and mother committed to their children. When their children defy them, the parents do not cast them off. Yet the children's responsiveness is indispensible to the ongoing relationship. They cannot assume the relationship will continue satisfactorily if they flout their parents' expectations. They imperil the relationship. The parents and the children live in the tension between these two facts (husbands and wives do the same, but our Western emphasis on the egalitarian nature of the marriage relationship makes marriage a less appropriate image for understanding our relationship with God). That is how the relationship between God and the kings or God and Israel will be.

# 1 KINGS 3:1–15

## What Do You Most Want?

[1]Solomon made a marriage alliance with Pharaoh king of Egypt; he married Pharaoh's daughter and brought her to the City of David until he had finished building his house and Yahweh's house and the walls around Jerusalem. [2]Although the people, however, were sacrificing at the high places because the house for Yahweh's name was not yet built up to that time, [3]Solomon was loyal to Yahweh in walking by his father David's laws. However, given that he was sacrificing and burning incense at the high places, [4]the king went to Gibeon to sacrifice there, because it was the largest high place. Solomon would offer a thousand burnt offerings on that altar. [5]At Gibeon Yahweh appeared to Solomon in a dream by night. God said, "Ask for what I should give you." [6]Solomon said, "You yourself showed great commitment to your servant David, my father, as he walked before you in truth and faithfulness and in uprightness of mind with you. You have kept this great commitment for him and given him a son sitting on his throne this very day. [7]But now, Yahweh my God, you yourself have made your servant king in place of my father David when I am a small boy who does not know how to go out and come back [to get things done]. [8]Your servant is in the midst of this people that you chose, a great people that cannot be numbered or counted because of its size. [9]So you should give your servant a listening mind to exercise authority for your people to discern between good and bad, because who can exercise authority for this massive people of yours? [10]The thing was good in the Lord's eyes, that Solomon had asked for this thing. [11]God said to him, "Because you asked for this thing and you did not ask for long life for yourself or for wealth for yourself or for the life of your enemies but you asked for yourself to be discerning in hearing judgment: [12]right, I am acting in accordance with your words. Right, I am giving you a wise and discerning mind such that there has not been anyone like you before you and that there

will not arise anyone like you after you. [13]What you did not ask I am also giving you, both wealth and honor all your life, such that there has not been anyone like you among the kings. [14]If you walk in my ways by keeping my laws and commands as your father David walked, I will give you a long life." [15]Solomon woke up. Right: a dream. He came to Jerusalem and stood before the Lord's covenant chest and offered whole offerings and sacrificed fellowship offerings and made a banquet for all his staff.

I used to ask a friend of mine from time to time, "What would you like to do?" The question would usually relate to concerts; I would outline possibilities to her, but she would usually ask me to decide. Just last week she protested that this was because she didn't know enough to decide; "It would be like me telling you something about the Old Testament," she said. I saw what she meant, but her hesitation deprived me of the pleasure of our doing something she wanted. I once heard a preacher declare that Jesus' question to Bartimaeus in Mark 10:51, "What do you want me to do for you," is the most devastatingly challenging question a person can be asked. Bartimaeus could reasonably have asked for some change (which was the reason he was by the roadside, like a beggar in the United States sitting by traffic lights where the cars have to stop), but he dares to ask for his sight, and he gets not only this gift of healing but the gift of following Jesus. Just a few verses previously, Jesus has asked two of his disciples the same question, and they have asked to sit on thrones either side of him in his glory. Disciples can have less insight than new converts.

Solomon gets asked the question "What would you like me to do for you?" and provides a model answer in the sense that it is the right answer given the situation he is in; the right answer for other peoples in other situations (such as Bartimaeus) might be different.

Yet the account of God's appearing to Solomon and Solomon's making this request comes in a context that attaches some irony to it. The very first thing we are told about Solomon once he is secure on his throne is that he made a marriage alliance with Pharaoh king of Egypt. There are several reasons why this is a troublesome statement. In Western culture, with our romantic view of marriage, we will be offended that marriage becomes subordinate to politics in this way, though I doubt if there is evidence that the subordination of marriage to politics generates less happy and stable marriages than the subordination of marriage to romanticism. Within the Old Testament, there would be more concern that Solomon is getting sucked into political alliances as a means of ensuring the nation's security and stability; to judge from the Prophets, trusting in political alliances rather than in God will be a main problem through the period covered by 1 and 2 Kings. Within these books, the main problem will be worshiping the gods of other peoples, or worshiping **Yahweh** in the way other peoples did (for instance, using images—or sacrificing children). Bringing foreign wives to live in the city of David will mean making it possible for them to worship their gods there, only a few feet away from Yahweh's own sanctuary, and this development will also encourage a process whereby the Israelites' own worship is influenced by such worship.

The subsequent verses indicate that there isn't an immediate problem, though it hints that there will be a problem in due course. The people were sacrificing at the **high places**, which would be problematic in later years but would be all right if it meant proper worship of Yahweh, such that Solomon himself offered. Although Jerusalem will have had its own sanctuary before David's day, and David had brought the **covenant chest** to Jerusalem so that there was some kind of sanctuary there, apparently the sanctuary at Gibeon just up the road was more impressive and was thus chosen for a significant event. (It is thought to have been located at the village now called Nebi Samwil, "Prophet Samuel," which is visible from Jerusalem.)

It looks as if this act of worship with its gargantuan sacrifice (though maybe the account is hyperbolic) was a special occasion near the beginning of Solomon's reign; hence God's response of appearing to Solomon with that testing question. The terms of Solomon's response are telling. He is concerned with the fact that his job is to exercise **authority** for the people. It is the responsibility David accepted when he was at the peak of his achievement (2 Samuel 8:15), before everything went south. There is no separation of powers in Israel, so that means exercising political, military, and judicial responsibility. In all these connections Solomon knows he needs to be able to discern between good and bad.

You might be surprised that he dares to ask this, because back at the beginning God had told the first human beings to keep off the tree that could convey the knowledge of good and bad (we usually say "good and evil," but the words here are the same). It seems that the issue back then was not that God was against people having this knowledge but that God wanted to decide the terms on which people had access to it. The problem was people's unwillingness to let God be sovereign in respect of it; elsewhere the Old Testament recognizes that this discernment is needed by and appropriate for human beings, and especially kings. Here Solomon knows he needs a "listening mind." Adam and Eve had "listened" to the voice of the serpent; Solomon knows he needs to be listening to God but also knows he needs God's help in order for him to do so, because it's not the human instinct. (Maybe he also knows that he needs to be listening to the people whom he has to govern and for whom he has to make decisions, and to have discernment about them.)

Solomon's words thus clarify what he and God mean by wisdom. The key to wisdom or discernment lies in having a listening mind, in submitting one's thinking to God's way of thinking. The way the "Wisdom books" in the Old Testament such as Proverbs and Job will put it is that reverence for God is the beginning of wisdom, and reverence to God in the Old Testament means listening to God and doing what God says, paying attention to the **Torah** and doing what it says. It's no coincidence that Solomon becomes the patron saint of wisdom in the Old Testament. Comparing the picture of Solomon in this chapter with the picture in the opening chapters of 1 Kings and with the one we will get from some later chapters suggests that the picture here is idealized. It thereby sets before people (and especially before later kings) a vision of what a king is supposed to be. If they want to rule well, they are to be like Solomon in his attitude to knowledge of good and bad, not like Adam and Eve.

So Solomon woke up and realized it was a dream. In Western culture that would mean it was "only a dream." If we asked what it meant, we would give an answer in terms of Solomon's subconscious desires and fears. Traditional cultures realize that dreams can be means of God speaking. To say it was a dream is to open up the possibility that it was a revelation from God, as the opening of the story suggested.

## 1 KINGS 3:16–4:19

### Two Mothers, One Baby

[16]Afterward two prostitutes came to the king and stood before him. [17]The one woman said, "Please my lord, this woman and I are living in the same house. I had a baby with her in the house. [18]On the third day after I had a baby, this woman also had a baby. We were together. There was no one from outside in the house with us, only the two of us in the house. [19]This woman's son died in the night because she lay on it, [20]and she got up in the middle of the night and took my son from by my side while your servant was asleep and she laid him in her arms and laid her dead son in my arms. [21]So I got up in the morning to nurse my son and there—he was dead. But I looked at him closely in the morning, and there—it was not the son that I had given birth to." [22]The other woman said, "No, the live one is my son and the dead one is your son," while the first woman was saying, "No, the dead one is your son and the live one is my son." As they spoke before the king, [23]the king said, "One woman is saying, 'This is my son, the live one, and the dead one is yours,' while the other one is saying, 'No, the dead one is yours, and the live one is mine.'" [24]So the king said, "Get me a sword." They brought a sword before the king. [25]The king said, "Cut the live baby in two and give half to one and half to the other." [26]Then the woman whose son was the live one said to the king (because her compassion welled up for her son)—she said, "Please, my lord, give her the live baby. Don't actually kill it," whereas the other was saying, "It won't be either mine or yours—cut it in two." [27]The king answered, "Give the live baby to her. Don't actually kill it. She is its mother." [28]When all Israel heard the authoritative decision that the king had made, they were in awe before the king, because they saw that there was divine wisdom in him to exercise authority.

⁴:¹King Solomon was king over all Israel, ²and these were his officials: Azariah son of Zadok (the priest), ³Elihoreph and Ahijah sons of Shisha (secretaries), Jehoshaphat son of Ahilud (the recorder), ⁴Benaiah son of Jehoiada (over the army), Zadok and Abiathar (priests), ⁵Azariah son of Nathan (over the prefects), Zabud son of Nathan (priest, the king's adviser), ⁶Ahishar (over the house), and Adoniram son of Abda (over the conscript labor). ⁷Solomon had twelve prefects over all Israel; they would provision the king and his household (a month per year the provisioning would be incumbent on each).

*[Verses 8–19 give their names and their regions.]*

Yesterday was Mother's Day, and I was reading a newspaper story about two mothers with one baby. Its birth mother had got pregnant while she was a single student, and she had decided she didn't want to keep the baby but that she would not have an abortion. While she and the child's father had eventually split up, they had already decided to have the baby adopted by a couple who could not have children of their own. When her son was born, all her instincts were to keep it. She could not imagine how a mother could give up a child and live, but she did so. Yet this is an "open adoption"; the two mothers stay in touch, and from time to time she sees the child she bore. Sometimes she holds him, and her whole body shudders.

I cannot imagine what that experience of motherhood can be like nor imagine what the experience of the two mothers in 1 Kings 3 could have been like. As these women were prostitutes, was their getting pregnant purely an accident, or was it something they half wanted? What on earth were they going to do when their babies were born? Did they plan to help each other, taking turns to look after the babies in the house they shared, and to ply their trade? In a Western context might they have had abortions, and might they have looked forward without enthusiasm or even with dread to the complications motherhood would bring? Did they then find their feelings were quite different when the babies were born? How deep was the pain in the heart of the woman whose baby had died?

How great was the fear of the woman who was in danger of losing her baby, or of watching him be slain? Yet her motherly instincts are her salvation and her baby's salvation. The Hebrew word for "compassion" is actually the plural of the word for the womb. Compassion is the feeling a mother has for the child of her womb. The real mother's compassion saved her child.

Like many a great insight, Solomon's solution to the problem is obvious as soon as he has enunciated it, yet it is a stroke of genius. It is an expression of wisdom because it is uttered in the course of his exercising **authority** for the community. The king's task is to see that decisions get taken in a proper way for people. His vocation does not focus on economics or international relations but on seeing that right gets done.

We may be a bit bewildered that the story concerns two prostitutes and that it makes no comment about issues that raises, as it makes no comment on the deceptive plan of the woman who has lost her baby. The Old Testament often feels no compulsion to make obvious moral points; it assumes its readers can work things out for themselves (though the extra dynamic in this story is its focus on Solomon and his wisdom). Women are often driven into the sex trade by economic pressures, and these two are likely to be women who for some reason have no families and thus no livelihood. Perhaps they are in a position like that of Naomi, Ruth, and Orpah, and their husbands have died, but (unlike those three) they do not or cannot go back to their original families and/or their original homelands. They know there are men who will pay for sex, and however unpleasant it is to service them, doing this makes it possible for them to survive. Given the absence of modern birth control methods, it's not surprising if they end up pregnant. The troubling question the story raises concerns the way Israelite society has developed. As in many traditional societies, especially as urbanization develops, or as with many contemporary Western societies, the exercise of authority by David and Solomon has not produced a healthy society.

The ambiguity of Solomon's leadership reappears in the account of his organization of government. As Israel evolves into a more complex state, his organization of it is another sign of his insight and skill. Like David, he has people in charge of worship, of military affairs, of administration, of labor, and of providing for the needs of his palace. In fact, the list of the offices and the people overlaps substantially with the list for David's reign in 2 Samuel 20. With respect to David and Solomon, the list raises some questions. When the Israelites first floated the idea of having a king, Samuel urged them to think about what it was going to cost them in terms of the way the king would require the services of their people to drive his chariotry, plow his fields, and cook for his palace, and the way he would introduce a taxation system to provide for his staff (see 1 Samuel 8). In small ways his warnings will have been fulfilled in Saul's day and in more significant ways in David's day, but Solomon embodies Samuel's warning more spectacularly. Adoniram's department is a particularly worrying one. The word for conscript labor is often translated "forced labor," and this could be misleading. There is no need to assume we are talking about men with whips standing over people in chains. Some of this conscript labor could involve the ancient equivalent of sitting in front of a computer screen. The point is that we are three stages removed from the Old Testament's vision for work. Ideally work does not involve employment, selling your labor. Work is the family's business; the family works together in order to generate all that it needs for its life. If a family gets into trouble and cannot make ends meet because its land does not produce enough food for one reason or another, then its members may have to become servants in relation to another family until it can get back on its feet again. Again this does not exactly involve selling your labor, though this may be what happens if for some reason you become a day laborer, an employee, but the Old Testament sees being employed as weird. Stage four is when you are forced to do this, whether you want to or not. It was the position of the Israelites in Egypt (from which God had rescued them!) and the position the Israelites imposed on some of the **Canaanites** (though they may have preferred this to either being dead or fleeing). First Kings will make clear that Solomon feels free also to draft Israelites to do the work he wants done.

# 1 KINGS 4:20–5:18
## Everyone under Their Vines and Their Fig Trees

²⁰Judah and Israel were as many as the sand on the sea in number, eating, drinking, and enjoying themselves. ²¹Solomon was ruling over all the kingdoms from the River [Euphrates] to the country of the Philistines as far as the border of Egypt, bringing contributions and serving Solomon all the days of his life. . . . ²⁵Judah and Israel lived in security, each one under his vine and fig tree, from Dan as far as Beersheba, all the days of Solomon. . . . ²⁹God gave Solomon wisdom and insight in very great measure and breadth of mind like the sand on the seashore. ³⁰Solomon's wisdom was greater than the wisdom of all the Kedemites and all the wisdom of the Egyptians. ³¹He was wiser than anyone else, than Ethan the Ezrahite, Heman, Chalcol, and Darda, the sons of Mahol. His name spread among all the nations. ³²He spoke three thousand sayings and his songs were one thousand and five. ³³He spoke about trees from the cedar in Lebanon to the hyssop that grows on a wall. He spoke about animals, birds, moving things, and fish. ³⁴They came from all peoples to listen to Solomon's wisdom, from all the kings of the earth who had heard his wisdom. ⁵:¹Hiram, king of Tyre, sent his staff to Solomon because he had heard that they had anointed him as king in place of his father, because Hiram had always been loyal to David. ²So Solomon sent to Hiram to say, ³"You yourself know of my father David, that he was not able to build a house for the name of Yahweh his God because of the war that surrounded him. . . . ⁶So now, order people to cut cedars for me from Lebanon. My staff will be with your staff, and your staff's wages—I will give it to you in accordance with anything you say, because you yourself know that there is no one among us who knows about cutting logs like the Sidonians." ⁷When Hiram heard Solomon's words, he was very glad. He said, "Yahweh be worshiped today, that he gave David a wise son over this great people." ⁸Hiram sent to Solomon to say, "I have heard the message you sent me. I will do all you want by way of cedar and cypress logs. ⁹My staff will bring them down to Lebanon to the sea. I will be the one who makes them into rafts by sea to the place you specify to me and I will split them up there. You will be the one who takes them and you will do what I want by giving food to my household. . . ."

<sup>13</sup>King Solomon raised conscript labor from all Israel; the conscript labor came to thirty thousand men. <sup>14</sup>He sent them to Lebanon ten thousand a month in shifts. They would be a month in Lebanon and two months at home. Adoniram was over the conscript labor. <sup>15</sup>Solomon had seventy thousand carriers and eighty thousand stonecutters in the mountains <sup>16</sup>apart from the directors of Solomon's prefects who were over the work, three thousand three hundred, supervising the company doing the work. <sup>17</sup>The king ordered them to transport large stones, fine stones, so as to found the house with cut stones. <sup>18</sup>Solomon's builders, Hiram's builders, and men from Byblos shaped and prepared the logs and the stones to build the house.

A few weeks ago my son and his family were visiting, and we spent some great times sitting out in the shade eating bread and cheese and drinking wine while the children played in the pool. The eruption of a volcano in Iceland halted flights back to Europe and confined my visitors to California for five extra days, which didn't trouble them too much and made for some extra, unexpected relaxed and unplanned lunches like that. They reminded me of times we had as a family nearly thirty years ago when my sons were the children, my wife and I were the parents, and my mother and mother-in-law were the seniors. We would sit under the shade of a tree in the garden of a French gite (as the French would call it) or cottage (as Brits would call it) or cabin (as people in the United States would call it) eating bread and cheese and drinking wine, though without a pool to amuse the children. For me there is a picture of heaven there, or at least a picture of old age: sitting under your vine and under your fig tree, eating, drinking, and enjoying yourself.

Yet there is something enigmatic about this story of Judah and Israel under the rule of Solomon. You could say it rounds off the enigmatic nature of the entire story of the three kings who ruled Israel before the nation split into two. In Saul's story, God's dealing with Saul is the mystery. In David's story, David himself is the mystery. In Solomon's story, Israel is the mystery, though the storyteller is something of a mystery, too.

On one hand, there is that idyllic picture of a vast people relaxing under their vines and fig trees. One of its significances is that in Solomon's day God's promises to Abraham and to Israel have been marvelously fulfilled. Israel is indeed as numerous as the sand on the seashore (compare Genesis 22:7). Solomon rules from the Euphrates to Egypt (compare Genesis 15:18). It is not exactly that the vast area to the northeast covering much of modern Syria and Iraq is part of Israel (there are still separate "kingdoms" there) but that Israel has acquired something of an empire in that direction. It controls the destiny, and the economy, of that entire area.

Then there is Solomon's wisdom. There is no doubt that he would need to be an astute guy to administer and control this miniempire. In the Middle East, the kind of wisdom that the story talks about (much of it the kind that is collected in Proverbs) was an indispensible adjunct to such political and economic leadership, and the peoples around had court colleges for training people involved in the administration. It would almost be a necessity for Solomon's wisdom to exceed that of these other peoples if his wide rule was to be effective. We do not know anything about the Kedemites or the other wise people who are mentioned. We do know that peoples such as the Egyptians generated collections of insight comparable to that in Proverbs. If you ask how Israel's was superior, then you could say it was in the more systematic way it interwove a concern about fairness and a concern about God with its interest in what works. Presumably any contribution Solomon made lay not so much in composing sayings (presidents don't write their own speeches) as in promoting and endorsing such work.

One application of Solomon's wisdom, then, lay in devising a system for getting the subject peoples in those areas Solomon controlled to pay taxes (to use our term for "bringing contributions"). First Kings 4:22–28 goes on to describe the quantities of provision that Solomon's administration required, such as a hundred sheep and goats *per day*. The king and other decision makers and public servants do well off the backs of foreign peoples, though the same applies to ordinary people. Did the Israelites enjoying themselves under their vines and fig trees think about the price these other peoples paid for their pleasant life? When I sit in the shade with my glass of two-dollar-a-bottle wine (I have cheap tastes), I don't think too much about the vast army of immigrant vineyard workers whose poorly paid labor makes it possible for me to do so. Actually I have never thought about it until this moment.

It wasn't just those economically subordinate peoples who paid the price. The Israelites themselves paid taxes. Each of the twelve prefects whom Solomon had appointed was responsible for raising enough income from the area under his control to provide for the king and his household for one month. The story adds that Solomon had thousands and thousands of chariots and horses, and it was those taxes that paid for the horses' provisioning. Did the Israelites sitting under their vines and fig trees think about the price they paid for their security any more than we do? Did they just shrug their shoulders about it? Did they ask whether there was something un-Israelite about it? When Deuteronomy 17 lays down some rules for kings, it includes that they mustn't accumulate horses or wealth. It also declares that they mustn't accumulate wives, which is a sign of status (so David and Solomon are both in trouble). Deuteronomy hadn't been written by Solomon's day, and this prohibition likely indicates that Israel's theologians had indeed reflected on Solomon's leadership style and lifestyle and concluded that there was something un-Israelite about it.

Solomon's plans for building the temple contain more ambiguities. God had approved of David's plan to build a temple, albeit reluctantly. Solomon is in a position to do so, and he is able to take advantage of his mutually beneficial relationship with Hiram as king of the next-door empire, to the northeast; it was in Hiram's interests to stay on friendly terms with Solomon. Once again this involves huge cost to Hiram's people and Solomon's people, who have no choice but to provide the labor for the work and thus neglect their own farms, and directly or indirectly to provide the provisions for the thousands of workers involved—again from the produce of their farms, which was often barely enough for their own needs. Maybe they were happy about that. When I look at a wondrous building such as Lincoln Cathedral or Durham Cathedral, I wonder about the cost to ordinary people of the work involved in it. Maybe they were glad to pay the cost of making something beautiful for God.

# 1 KINGS 6:1–38

## Temples and Churches

¹In the four hundred and eightieth year in relation to the Israelites' leaving Egypt, in the fourth year in the month Ziv (that is, the second month) in relation to Solomon's reign over Israel, he built the house for Yahweh. ²The house that King Solomon built for Yahweh was sixty cubits long, twenty cubits wide, and thirty cubits high. ³The portico in front of the hall of the house was twenty cubits long (to the width of the house), ten cubits wide (to the front of the house). ⁴He made narrow latticed windows for the house. ⁵Against the wall of the house (the walls of the house round the hall and the inner sanctuary) he built a lower story around and made side rooms. . . . ⁷When the house was built, it was built of stone finished at the quarry. Hammer, chisel, or any other iron tools did not make themselves heard in the house while it was being built. . . . ¹¹Yahweh's word came to Solomon: ¹²"This house that you are building: if you walk by my laws and act by my rules and keep my commands, walking by them, I will substantiate with you my word that I spoke to your father David. ¹³I will dwell in the midst of the Israelites and I will not abandon my people Israel." ¹⁴So Solomon built the house and finished it. . . . ¹⁶He built twenty cubits from the sides of the house with boards of cypress from the floor to the walls—built inside the house an inner room, for it, the holiest place. . . . ¹⁹Thus he prepared an inner room in the midst of the house, on the inside, to put there Yahweh's covenant chest. . . . ²²The entire house he covered in gold, until the entire house was complete, and the entire altar belonging to the inner room he covered in gold. ²³In the inner room he made two cherubs of olive wood, ten cubits high. . . . ³⁷In the fourth year Yahweh's house was founded, in the month Ziv, ³⁸and in the eleventh year, in the month of Bul (that is, the eight month), the house was complete in relation to all his instructions and decisions. So he built it over seven years.

The little church building where I worship each Sunday holds only fifty or sixty people, but it divides into three parts. The congregation sits in the main body of the church; there is a little step up to the choir stalls; and finally there is another little step and a rail separating off the area where the altar or holy table is. That is not the only traditional way to build a church; some have a more open plan. Yet it is the pattern of most of the larger churches in England with which I was familiar and where I was a pastor. In one of those churches I remember an old lady who felt that her place was in the main body of the church and who was certainly very hesitant to go beyond that second step into the railed off area. It was as if it was a very holy place. You could say she had reacted in a way that corresponded to the message the architecture of the church gave her.

It's a message that goes back to the temple Solomon built. The main body of the church, where the congregation gathers, is equivalent to the temple yard, where the Israelites gathered. The choir stalls are the equivalent to the first part of the stone structure, the hall, also referred to as the holy place, with a portico. Only priests go there. The area where the holy table stands is equivalent to the inner room, the holiest place or holy of holies. The basic shape corresponds to that of many **Canaanite** sanctuaries and royal palaces. That's partly because it follows the logic of any house, or in particular of a palace. There is a public area where people are welcomed into the king's presence, the equivalent of a yard or a lounge; there is the hall where the king would meet with his staff; and there are the king's private quarters. Even though it is kings who are responsible for the temple's building, they have no more rights there than ordinary people. The arrangement of the temple thus keeps the king in his place. It is not a royal chapel.

Like the idea of having a temple, the plans for the temple don't come from God. Typically, God goes along with what seems natural to the people who want to relate to God. The plan of the temple thus compares with the plans of many Canaanite temples. It's quite small. A cubit is about half a yard or half a meter, so its size is not so different from that of our little church that seats fifty or sixty people. That's no problem for us, because that's the usual size of our congregation. It would seem a problem for *the* temple in Jerusalem, until you realize that the temple was not designed as a place to accommodate the entire worshiping congregation. The actual temple building was not a meeting place for the entire community but a house for God. Sometimes it seems regrettable that we use the word "church" to denote a building as well as a people, but there is a certain appropriateness to it. The church building is a place for the church people to meet. In the Old Testament, the actual temple building isn't a place where the congregation meets for worship. You could say it is a kind of shrine, though the Old Testament doesn't use a word like that to describe it; it doesn't even call it a temple. When the word *temple* comes in English translations, it renders either the ordinary Hebrew word for a house or the one for a palace, the word you would use for a splendid royal residence. The temple is a house for God, a palace for the divine King. It's a house because it's a dwelling. It's a palace because it's paneled with cedar and decorated with carvings and covered in gold (some hyperbole may be assumed here). That same word for "palace" is also used for the main "hall" of the building.

Around the main hall of the temple are side rooms that would be used for storage, preparation, and so on. Outside the temple is a big open area, which compensates for the smallness of the temple itself. Stories in the Old Testament and in the Gospels describe how large crowds could gather in the temple area. As a result of its enlargement by Herod the Great, in New Testament times it was as big as a football field, as it is today. It was not so big in Old Testament times, but it was still big enough for any assembly that could be imagined. The climate in Jerusalem being more like that of Southern California than that of Britain, at a time of year like that for the temple dedication in September–October, you could plan for events without worrying about whether it might rain, though you might get caught out if you had a big gathering in January (see the story in Ezra 10).

Three other comments in the story of the temple building are worth noting. One is the date, four hundred and eighty years after the exodus. That sounds like a symbolic date; one generation is forty years; the total period is thus forty generations; and the figure is approximately the one you gain by counting up the dates in the Old Testament from the time of Moses to Solomon, though historically those dates overlap. So this isn't the kind of date you can make the basis for writing our kind of history (you can't work out from Solomon's date, about 960 BC, that the exodus must have happened about 1440). It's more like the account of Jesus' genealogy at the beginning of Matthew, which tells of fourteen generations from Abraham to David, fourteen from David to the **exile**, and fourteen from the exile to Jesus. You can compare that account with the lists of generations in the Old Testament that Matthew was using and see that his version works only because he is selective in what he includes in order to devise an account that symbolizes the careful way in which God's sovereignty is at work in the story. The dating in 1 Kings is similar. As well as making a link with the exodus, it may also make a link with the temple's destruction and/or its restoration, which happened four hundred and eighty years or so later. So Matthew's structuring of Israel's story is very similar to that in 1 Kings, and both make the same point, that God's sovereignty is at work in the events the account relates.

The second comment concerns the silence. In general, the Old Testament is much more interested in noise than in silence. Noise makes it possible to praise God and to pray, and noise on God's part is an indication that God is acting in response to prayer and in a way that deserves praise. So it is striking when occasionally the Old Testament commends silence as a mark of awe, respect, and anticipation (compare Zephaniah 1:7; Habakkuk 2:20; Zechariah 2:13).

The third comment is the reminder about the terms of God's living among the Israelites. It might seem to raise metaphysical questions; how can the creator God live in a small, humanly made house? In considering that question, God is more interested in some moral or relational considerations. God has no problem about living among the Israelites as long as they live the way God expects. That's symbolized by the presence of the **covenant chest** in the inner room, the holiest place.

## 1 KINGS 7:1-8:9

### Temples and Palaces

¹His house he built over thirteen years, and he completed his entire house. ²He built the Lebanon Forest house, its length a hundred cubits, its width fifty cubits, and its height thirty

29

cubits, [with] four rows of cedar columns and cedar beams on the columns. . . . ⁷He made the portico for the throne where he would issue judgment (the Judgment Portico). It was covered in cedar from floor to floor. ⁸His house where he lived, [in] the courtyard within the portico, was made in the same way. He would make a house for Pharaoh's daughter, whom Solomon married, like this portico. . . . ²¹He set up the columns at the portico of the hall. He set up the right-hand column and named it "He-establishes" and set up the left-hand column and named it "In-him-is-Strength." ²²On the top of the columns was lily work. So the manufacture of the columns was complete. ²³He made the Sea, cast, ten cubits from rim to rim, circular all round, five cubits in height; a line of thirty cubits would go all round it. . . . ⁵¹When all the work that King Solomon had done for Yahweh's house was finished, Solomon brought in the holy things of his father David. The silver, the gold, and the accoutrements he put in the treasury of Yahweh's house.

⁸:¹Then Solomon assembled the elders of Israel, all the heads of the clans and the ancestral leaders of the Israelites, before King Solomon in Jerusalem, to bring up Yahweh's covenant chest from the City of David (that is, Zion). . . . ⁶The priests brought Yahweh's covenant chest to its place in the inner room of the house, the holiest place, under the cherubs' wings, ⁷because the cherubs spread their wings toward the chest's place, and the cherubs covered the chest and its poles from above. ⁸The poles extended so that the ends of the poles were visible from the holy place in front of the inner room, but they were not visible outside. They have been there until this day. ⁹There was nothing inside the chest except the two stone tablets that Moses put there at Horeb when Yahweh sealed [the covenant] with the Israelites, when they left Egypt.

Joe, who is remodeling my bathroom, has just arrived at our apartment. There was nothing really wrong with my bathroom that made it need remodeling, any more than there was anything wrong with the kitchen when he remodeled it in the fall, but then remodeling isn't usually based in need. My son had looked a bit askance at the bathroom a couple of years ago and rolled his eyes in the way children do at their parents and commented that really I needed to do something about it to maintain the value of the property (I don't think he was simply concerned about its value to him and his brother after I die). I remembered how, as I grew up, I thought it a bit pathetic that my parents were still using the same dining furniture that they bought when they married; now I am doing the same thing. How do you decide what level of updating and comfort and luxury is appropriate when many people in the world don't have a bathroom at all? Similar questions arise at a less personal level. In the context of a huge state financial deficit, this week our governor has proposed a budget that cuts help to poor people and cuts expenditure on low-cost community health centers. How do we balance such needs with expenditure on prestige buildings or symbolic projects?

Intriguingly interwoven with the story of the temple building is the brief account of Solomon's spending thirteen years building his house; he spent seven years building God's house. Is that a sign that God's house had priority, that he focused on the work and got it done, or that he gave rather a lot of attention to his own house? Solomon's palace is much bigger than God's. What of the other impressive state buildings he also constructed? The Lebanon Forest house is apparently so called because it had so many pillars of cedar from Lebanon that it seemed like a forest; it would be a hall to use for state occasions. What of the house for his Egyptian wife? One recalls once more that ultimately it is ordinary people who pay for such projects. At least as pressing are the questions raised by the way the temple, the royal palace, and the state buildings adjoin one another. That opens up the positive possibility that the faith celebrated in the temple can be taken seriously by the king and embodied in the way politics and economics operate. It also opens up the possibility that the faith celebrated in the temple becomes subordinate to the power of the king and the way he sees the state's political and economic needs. So eventually there will not only be a foreign queen living near the temple and sanctuaries for foreign gods located near the temple but also shrines to foreign gods within the actual temple complex because politics requires it.

With the reference to the hall we return to the account of the temple itself. Outside it are two especially impressive pillars. They are not part of the structure; they don't hold the building up. They seem to symbolize what their names refer to, the fact that God establishes the world by his strength; it is therefore secure. If you thought your world looked insecure, looking at the temple reminded you of an aspect of the good news concerning the God whose name dwelt there.

If you turned around from looking at these pillars, one thing you saw was "the Sea," a huge basin (five yards or meters in diameter, two-and-a-half in height, fifteen in circumference). Its impressiveness was enhanced by the fact that it stood on twelve bulls made of bronze. Associated with it were ten bronze water carts. Providing the water to fill the Sea would be a huge logistical challenge; the temple is on the top of a hill, and the water supply is near the bottom. So perhaps these fulfilled a function in this connection. Alternatively they may have been used to transport the water from the Sea to points in the court where it was needed. From a practical point of view, presumably the point of the Sea was to hold water for the many acts of cleansing that were required by the worship of the temple. Exodus 30 is specific that the equivalent of the Sea in the wilderness dwelling was for the priests to cleanse their hands and feet in connection with fulfilling their priestly duty, but water would also be required for other washing rites in connection with sacrifices.

Yet the height of the Sea would work against its ease of use in this connection, and the basin's strange name would also suggest a symbolic significance, not least as it stood over against those pillars. For Middle Eastern peoples the sea was often an embodiment of dynamic and threatening power; the sea could overwhelm the land if it chose to. Thus they told stories about creation involving the gaining of control over the sea. This Sea constituted a visual reminder of the assertion on the pillars, that the world is established by God's strength. While the Old Testament sometimes speaks of creation in these terms, it also tells of God's victory over the Reed Sea, a victory that asserted God's power over all that could threaten to overwhelm Israel. So the basin contained the sea in more than one sense. It held a vast quantity of water, and it also suggested that the sea was under control.

The Sea stood in the courtyard, along with the main **altar** on which animals were burnt and offered to God, so the people could take part in making the offerings. Within the hall, where people did not go, were the altar on which priests burned incense, the table on which was set the "presence bread" that suggested the people's grain offerings and/or God's provision for the people, and ten lamp stands.

At the back of the hall was the inner room, the holiest place, where a priest went just once a year in connection with the need to purify it. There two gold-plated **cherubs** stood, imaginary figures that are part animal and part bird that symbolize the creatures that transport God's throne through the heavens and to the earth. They thus point to the presence of the invisible God, enthroned above them. In turn they stand over and protect the **covenant chest**, which becomes the only artifact within the inner room. Its presence there underlines questions about the relationship between the covenant that goes back to Sinai and the way Israel has become a state like any other. Will the state be willing to shape its life by what the two stone tablets say (the Ten Commandments)? Answer: no, actually.

## 1 KINGS 8:10–30

### Will God Really Dwell on Earth?

[10]When the priests came out from the sanctuary (the cloud was filling Yahweh's house [11]and the priests were not able to stand and minister in the face of the cloud, because Yahweh's splendor was filling Yahweh's house), [12]then Solomon said, "Yahweh has said he would dwell in the thundercloud. [13]I have indeed built a stately house for you, a place for you to live forever." [14]The king turned his face and blessed the entire congregation of Israel as the entire congregation of Israel was standing. [15]He said, "Yahweh be worshiped, the God of Israel who spoke by his own mouth with my father David, and by his hand has fulfilled it: [16]'From the day I brought my people Israel from Egypt I did not choose a city from all the clans of Israel to build a house for my name to be there, but I chose David to be over my people Israel.' [17]It was in my father David's mind to build a house for the name of Yahweh, the God of Israel, [18]but Yahweh said to my father David, 'Because you had it in your mind to build a house for my name, you did well when it

was in your mind. ¹⁹Yet you yourself will not build the house. Rather, your son, who came out of your loins—he will build the house for my name.' ²⁰Yahweh has established his word, which he spoke. I have arisen in place of my father David. I sit on the throne of Israel as Yahweh spoke, and I have built the house for the name of Yahweh the God of Israel. ²¹I have set a place there for the chest where Yahweh's covenant is, which he sealed with our ancestors when he brought them out of Egypt." ²²Solomon stood before Yahweh's altar in the presence of all the congregation of Israel and spread his palms to the heavens, ²³and said, "Yahweh, God of Israel, there is no God like you in the heavens above and on the earth beneath, who keeps covenantal commitment with your servants who walk before you with all their minds. . . . ²⁷Yet will God really live on earth? There—the heavens, the highest heavens, would not contain you, still less this house I have built. ²⁸But turn your face toward your servant's plea and prayer for grace, Yahweh my God, by listening to the cry and the plea that your servant is making before you today, ²⁹so that your eyes are open toward this house night and day, toward the place of which you have said, 'My name will be there,' so that you hear the plea that your servant makes toward this place. ³⁰When you listen to the prayer for grace by your servant and your people Israel which they make toward this place, and when you listen in the place where you sit, in the heavens: listen and pardon."

An hour or two ago I was sitting not at my desk, as I am now, but in my recliner chair, where I start off the day with my coffee, reading the Bible just for my own benefit and praying for people, and I sometimes picture God sitting on the sofa on the other side of the room; I did so this morning to remind myself that God was with me. The picturing is an exercise in the imagination, but the presence is a reality. Yesterday in church as I sang hymns or said the creed or gave people bread and wine, I didn't feel I had to summon up that reality; it was built into what we were doing ("Where two or three gather in my name, I am there among them," Jesus says in Matthew 18:20). While my coffee was brewing this morning, I mixed the dough for the bread I shall bake later, and God was there, too, not least making the dough rise (I just checked it). I didn't think about God's presence then, but it was nevertheless a reality. Here at my desk God had better be present, too, or this writing won't be much use to you, and obviously I think about God, though in a more third-person way than when I was in my recliner. I don't talk to God very often except for saying thank you when something nice happens.

In other words, what it means for God to be present with us can vary a lot. First, it varies on God's side. There is a big difference between God's being present with people when they are sick, to comfort them, and God's making them better. It also varies on our side; we have to distinguish our subjective sense of God's presence and the objective reality of God's presence. We're inclined to talk as if "God's presence" simply means "our sense of God's presence." Actually God's presence may be real when we don't feel it, and we may feel that God is present when actually God has not shown up or has departed.

Solomon's prayer deals with some of the mystery and the paradox involved in thinking about God's presence with us. It starts from something that is presented as objective reality: a cloud filled the house. A cloud is a common symbol of God's presence. It's a useful symbol, because it is both a sign of God's being present (within or above or behind the cloud) but also a practical means of protecting people from the overwhelming, blinding, electrifying effect of being in God's presence (in Los Angeles we have smog that similarly protects us and makes it possible to look at the sun as it goes down). The words for cloud and thundercloud are ones that can be used for ordinary clouds, but they more often refer to this kind of cloud that both signifies and conceals God's presence. Hebrew has other words that it uses more frequently for ordinary cloud.

Exodus and Deuteronomy talk about a column of cloud accompanying the people on their journey from Egypt, about God being in a cloud or thundercloud (that is, an even more impressive, thick cloud) at Sinai and speaking to the people from there, then about a cloud covering the dwelling that God commissioned the Israelites to make for God. That same cloud and thundercloud is present in the temple in such a way as to signify that God's presence continues to accompany the people. I don't know how literally the story means us to take this picture. Perhaps we are to picture the priests withdrawing from the temple because they knew God was coming there, so that speaking of the cloud is a metaphor. However we are to understand that language, God certainly became present there. Henceforth Israel could know they could come to the temple court and offer their sacrifices there and know they did so before the God who was present in the sanctuary.

Talking about the temple as a place where God will live could imply that the Israelites had unsophisticated ideas about God, but Solomon himself later makes explicit his awareness that the idea of God's dwelling in a house on earth is silly. Nor did the Israelites naively think that God lived in the sky, as if you would find God if you shot a rocket high enough—or if they did think so, they were ignoring what their Scriptures told them. The entirety of the heavens could not contain God, Solomon comments. That's why the idea of building a house for God is a silly idea.

So why is Solomon building one? He speaks of building a house for God's name. It is a way the Old Testament often seeks to square the circle of affirming that God was really present in the midst of Israel while recognizing that this was an unsophisticated idea. The name of a person stands for the person. When people who know me say "John Goldingay," it summons up an impression of who I am. It reminds them of my characteristics and nature. It's almost as if I am there. When Christians whisper or shout "Jesus," it brings home to them the reality of his presence. That's especially so with the name of God, **Yahweh**, and with the name Jesus, because the name expresses something of the nature of the person. Jesus means "savior." The name Yahweh suggests "the God who will be there with you" (see Exodus 3:11–15). The temple will be the place where Israel proclaims the name of Yahweh and calls on the name of Yahweh. Israel will know that the proclaiming of this name signifies that in whatever sense the great God of the heavens and the earth can be in a humanly constructed building, that great God is indeed there, receives people's praise and offerings there, and hears and responds to their prayers there.

It remains an idea that raises questions. In his act of praise Solomon notes that after bringing the Israelites out of Egypt,

God never chose a city where Israel could build a house for God's name. We expect the sentence to continue, "but now God has chosen a city," Jerusalem, but he never makes such a statement. Instead, he refers to God's choice of David. He is perhaps wise, because the person whom the story has credited with the choice of Jerusalem is David, not God. God had chosen David, and God has evidently gone along with David's choice of this city, as God went along with David's idea of building a temple. The city thus became God's choice, and subsequent parts of Israel's story will refer to Jerusalem as the city God chose. But Solomon's own words incidentally preserve the ambiguity of the entire temple-building project. God did not originally choose either the city or the temple.

## 1 KINGS 8:31–40

### A Few Things You Can Pray For

[31]When a person wrongs his neighbor and [the neighbor] takes up an oath against him to swear, and the oath comes before your altar in this house, [32]may you yourself listen in the heavens, and act, and decide for your servants, by declaring the guilty person to be guilty, bringing his conduct on his head, and by declaring the innocent person to be innocent, giving to him in accordance with his innocence.

[33]When your people Israel take a beating before an enemy because they wrong you, but they turn to you and confess your name and plead and ask for grace from you in this house, [34]may you yourself listen in the heavens and pardon your people Israel's wrongdoing and restore them to the land you gave their ancestors.

[35]When the heavens shut themselves and there is no rain because they wrong you, but they plead toward this place and confess your name and turn from their wrongdoing because you afflict them, [36]may you yourself listen in the heavens and pardon the wrongdoing of your servants, your people Israel, when you had shown them the good way they should walk in, and give them rain on your country that you gave your people to possess.

[37]When famine happens in the country, when epidemic happens, blight, mildew, locust, caterpillar; when their enemy

besieges them in the country, in their settlements—any trouble, any disease; [38]any plea, any prayer for grace that there will be by any person from all your people Israel who acknowledge, each one, the trouble of his own spirit and spreads his hands toward this house, [39]may you yourself listen in the heavens, the place where you live, and pardon, and act, and give to the person in accordance with all his ways as you know his spirit (because you yourself alone know the spirit of all human beings), [40]so that they may revere you all the days they are living on the face of the land that you gave our ancestors.

I just had a phone call from the rector of the church where I am to preach on Sunday. It will be Pentecost, and I thought they were asking me just because they wanted a guest preacher for that festival, but she had apparently forgotten, or forgotten to tell me, that the church is also celebrating the hundredth anniversary of its moving from being a mission to being a parish (the time when it had ceased needing financial support from the diocese and became able to support itself financially). In a sense she now wants the church to move from being a parish to being a mission—that is, to being outward-looking in mission. That (she told me) will be the theme of the church's prayers on this Sunday. Surely that is a great theme for a church's anniversary celebration, and hardly a prayer God could resist.

Which is my segue into Solomon's prayer, a prayer about prayer. What can you pray about and expect God to answer?

You can pray for God to be involved in seeing that justice is done and that disputes are resolved fairly. The first prayer concerns a situation when one person claims to have been wronged by another person (maybe his wheat field caught fire, and he believes that the other person set it on fire), and there are no witnesses to help decide who is in the right. One of the people can lay an oath on the other—that is, make him swear he didn't do wrong. Superficially this resembles the oath Western courts conventionally require, but Solomon takes God's involvement more seriously. The temple becomes the place where you take the oath, so that you take it before God in quite a strong sense. That obviously puts psychological pressure on people, but Solomon presupposes something bigger than that.

He asks the God who is in the heavens to pay attention to the oath that is taken in the divine dwelling on earth, and he presupposes that God will then act. The answer will come not in the form of a voice from heaven or a conviction on the part of a priest or a shrewd insight on the king's part (as happened in the case of the two mothers with one baby) but in the way God makes things work out in trouble for the guilty person and blessing for the innocent person.

Several of the prayers concern when things go wrong for the people of God. Maybe they experience defeat, maybe there is no rain, maybe there is a famine or an epidemic. Typically of the Old Testament, Solomon doesn't assume that every such reversal issues from the people's wrongdoing, but he assumes that it is true of some such reversals. When they have one of those experiences, it is thus appropriate to ask the question about whether it is divine chastisement, not simply to assume that it is "just one of those things." Solomon's prayer assumes that God is involved in the world and is not just an absentee landlord. Maybe the experience makes them face ways in which they have been doing wrong in relation to God (perhaps they have been praying to other gods, or making images of God, or attaching God's name to things that have nothing to do with God, or ignoring the Sabbath—just to consider the first four commandments). Given that they had turned away from God, their task is then to turn back—the literal meaning of the verb commonly translated "repent." Given that they had not been acknowledging that **Yahweh** is God, their task is to "confess" God's name again. Then they can "plead" with God. It's a common word for prayer, implying that we stand before the judge and plead our case. Of course, as wrongdoers we have no rights; we cannot plead for justice. All we can do is plead for mercy. That's implicit in the verb "ask for grace" that goes along with "plead," because talk in terms of "grace" also presupposes that we have no rights but that we know God is gracious.

Then the people who pray before the earthly temple may hope that God will listen in the heavenly temple, and they may hope that God may "pardon." Whereas "forgiveness" is something people who are equals offer one another, "pardon" is what a king or president gives to a subject. Using this word not only recognizes that we have no rights and are making no excuses. It recognizes the power differential between us and God. It also recognizes the obligation on the part of the one in power to bear in mind an obligation not to undermine standards of justice or make it seem as if people can get away with wrongdoing or imply that doing wrong does not matter. It recognizes all this, yet it can still hope for pardon. The people may also hope for restoration to their land. God in some sense "removed" David's wrongdoing (though the story did not say that God pardoned or forgave him) but did not restore things to the way they had been before. Solomon invites people to believe that God restores as well as pardons.

The prayer concerning what we might call natural disasters makes an unexpected shift to talk about such troubles affecting individuals. Sometimes it is simply an individual family that runs out of food or an individual person who experiences some illness. Like the Psalms, Solomon's prayer keeps a balance between the corporate and the individual. The Psalms sometimes constitute prayers for the community to pray when it experiences trouble and comes to the temple to bring its reversals to God; they sometimes constitute prayers for an individual to pray when he or she experiences trouble; when that happens, the individual comes to God (maybe with members of the family) to bring the trouble to God. Israel knew that God was involved both in the life of the community and in that of the individual. Solomon refers to the way God knows how this trouble relates to the person's spirit (literally, "heart"), which has various implications. God can tell how our troubles affect us in our spirits and can tell whether there is something wrong in our attitude to God or to other people that lies behind the trouble that has come to us. It is both good news and solemn news that God knows our spirits.

Both the good side and the solemn side link with the fact that the aim and result of God's being involved in answering their prayers will be that they revere God all their days. While it is misleading to think of this as involving a negative fear of God, both the Old and New Testament assume that reverence for God recognizes the seriousness of the fact that God is God and we aren't, and they assume that this recognition affects our

attitudes and also our lives. Reverence for God issues in doing
what God says. It also relates to the fact that God can look into
our spirits. God is not limited to what we say and do. Yet Solomon's prayer implies another aspect to the dynamic whereby
we are led into reverence and obedience. God knows what is in
our hearts in the sense that God knows the pressures and the
pains we live with; and even when God sees sin in our hearts,
God is one who pardons. That might make us take God's pardon for granted. Solomon's prayer rather believes in a different
dynamic, that appreciation for God's love and grace issues in
that reverence.

## 1 KINGS 8:41–66

### A Few More

[41]"Further, the foreigner who does not belong to your people
Israel who comes from a distant country for the sake of your
name ([42]because they will hear of your great name and your
powerful hand and extended arm) and comes to plead toward
this house, [43]may you yourself listen in the heavens, the place
where you live, and may you act in accordance with all that the
foreigner calls to you, so that all the peoples of the earth may
acknowledge your name so as to revere you like your people
Israel and acknowledge that your name is proclaimed over this
house that I have built.
[44]When your people go out to battle against their enemy by
the way you send them, and they plead with Yahweh in the
direction of the city you have chosen and the house I have built
for your name, [45]may you listen in the heavens to their plea and
their prayer for grace and exercise authority for them.
[46]When they wrong you (because there is no human being
who does not do wrong) and you are angry with them and
you give them up before an enemy and their captors take them
captive to the country of the enemy, far or near, [47]and they turn
their spirit in the country where they have become captive and
turn and pray for grace from you in their captors' country . . .
[49]may you listen in the heavens, the place where you live, to
their plea and their prayer for grace, and exercise authority for
them, [50]and pardon your people who have wronged you, for
all the acts of rebellion they have committed against you, and

41

give them compassion before their captors so that they may have compassion on them, [51]because they are your people, your possession, which your brought out of Egypt, from within the iron furnace, [52]so that your eyes are open to your servant's prayer for grace and to your people Israel's prayer for grace, and so that you listen to them every time they call to you, [53]because you yourself set them apart for yourself as a possession from all the peoples of the earth, as you declared by means of your servant Moses, when you brought our ancestors out of Egypt, Lord Yahweh."

[54]When Solomon had finished making to Yahweh all this plea and prayer for grace, he got up from before the altar from bowing down on his knees with his hands spread to the [55]heavens, and stood and blessed the whole congregation of Israel:

[56]"Yahweh be praised, who gave a place of rest to his people Israel in accordance with all that he spoke. Not one word failed of all his good declaration that he made by means of his servant Moses. [57]May Yahweh our God be with us as he was with our ancestors and may he not abandon us, [58]by inclining our spirit to him so that we walk in all his ways and keep his commands, laws, and rules that he commanded our ancestors. [59]May these words of mine that I have made as a plea before Yahweh be near Yahweh our God day and night so that he may exercise authority for his servant and for his people Israel according to each day's need, [60]so that all the peoples of the earth may acknowledge that Yahweh is God; there is no other. [61]And may your spirit be wholehearted with Yahweh your God so as to walk in his laws and keep his commands this very day."

[62]The king and all Israel with him were offering sacrifices before Yahweh. [63]Solomon offered fellowship sacrifices, which he offered to Yahweh: 22,000 oxen and 120,000 sheep. So the king and all the Israelites dedicated Yahweh's house. [64]That day the king consecrated the middle part of the court that was in front of Yahweh's house, because there he made the burnt offering, the grain offering, and the fat parts of the fellowship sacrifices, because the bronze altar that was before Yahweh was too small to hold the burnt offering, the grain offering, and the fat parts of the fellowship sacrifices. [65]So at that time Solomon and all Israel with him kept the festival (a great congregation from Lebo-Hamath to the Egypt Wash) before Yahweh our

God for seven days, then seven more days, fourteen days. [66]On the eighth day he let the people go, and they praised the king. They went to their tents, celebrating and in good spirit because of all the good that Yahweh had done for his servant David and for his people Israel.

I can still picture myself sitting in Sunday School as a little boy of nine or ten, and I can still hear the voice of the stern Sunday School superintendent exhorting us to bow our heads, put our hands together, and close our eyes to pray. I suspect I can still remember this because I was in trouble with regard to some aspect of these instructions, or perhaps because I was talking to someone else as the instructions were given and got into trouble for it. That in itself probably indicates that the instructions were wise ones.

The close of Solomon's prayer indicates that his posture was very different, with a rationale of its own. Praying involves laying flat on the ground. Sometimes the Old Testament speaks of licking the dust, meaning you have your face right on the ground, as if you were trying to eat the dust. That is the appropriate posture before a king, from whom you are asking favors; it is therefore a telling posture for one who is himself a king. Yet it can't imply lying flat all the time, because apparently it also allows for having one's hands stretched out to God in the heavens, with your palms open because they demonstrate their emptiness and your need that God should fill them. That, too, would be a posture that a suppliant adopted to a king. Having bowed down as an act of obeisance, a suppliant would also look to the king, and in prayer your eyes would be open in appeal to God, like a servant looking to a master (Psalm 123).

Solomon's prayer involves some bold requests, so the dramatic nature of his posture is appropriate. His first requests include two that relate to the experience of having been defeated by enemies, and in a moment he will come to one that relates to Israel itself taking on enemies; he will then come to the experience of being taken into captivity by enemies. It would therefore be easy for the prayer as a whole to have an exclusivist cast, to have no thought for anyone outside Israel. But the Old Testament can't be like that for more than a few pages at a time.

It knows that **Yahweh** is God of the whole world, not just of Israel. So Solomon's fourth request, the one that occupies the center of his prayer, starts from the assumption that foreigners will come to this house that Solomon has built because they have heard about Yahweh. It asks Yahweh to treat such individual foreigners the same as Israelites, so that the world as a whole may come to revere Yahweh in the same way that Israel does. His closing blessing expresses the broader longing that all the nations may come to acknowledge Yahweh.

Solomon's prayer closes with what may seem in the context another implausible act of imagination, and an initially unpleasant one. Here we are at a highpoint in the entire Old Testament story, and Solomon starts talking about the people going so wrong in their relationship with God that God will get angry enough to let them be taken off into **exile**. Excuse me?

It's one of the points in the narrative when it helps to remind ourselves that the story as a whole is told not just as a piece of history but as a message for some people; and the people for whom it is told are those who have gone through that experience of exile. The books of Kings tell the story down to the exile, and thus they tell it for people in the time of the exile. It's a time when they could easily be quite depressed about their situation. The story invites them to face some facts but also to hear some good news. The bad news is that they are in a mess as a result of relying on their own religious and political insight rather than relying on and responding to Yahweh. The good news is that this does not mean the story has to be at an end. They can turn around and ask for grace.

Once again it is significant that this word for prayer starts from the assumption that we have no rights or claim on God in a situation such the one the exiles are in. Indeed, let's face it (the prayer says), there is no human being who avoids doing wrong. Sometimes the Old Testament pictures God as surprised by Israel's wrongdoing; yes, God is saddened by it. It is not what God hoped for. In contexts such as the present one, it is quite realistic about us as the people of God (it's not talking about people in general, though this truth would also apply in that connection). We all go wrong. But that's not the end of the world. God is gracious, and therefore Israel can appeal to

God's own character, appeal to God to exercise **authority** on its behalf, to act decisively for them, even though they have no right to ask for such action. Israel can ask for pardon even though they have no right to it (but then, you never have a right to pardon). Or with even more chutzpah, Israel can appeal to God's own action and interests and commitments. God had entered into an association with them and made them a personal possession and brought them out of Egypt. Like Moses, Solomon argues that God can hardly give up on working with them now.

One concrete element in this prayer is for their captors to show compassion to them. It might seem a particularly implausible request. It is then fun to find Daniel 1:9 reporting that God did exactly this for Daniel as a captive in **Babylon**, and to find Nehemiah 1:11 reporting that Nehemiah also prayed this way in **Persia**; it came about for him, too.

# 1 KINGS 9:1–28

## Desires and Choices

[1]When Solomon had finished building the house of Yahweh and the king's house and every fancy of Solomon's that he desired to fulfill, [2]Yahweh appeared to Solomon a second time, as he had appeared to him at Gibeon. [3]Yahweh said to him, "I have listened to your plea and your prayer for grace which you have made before me. I have consecrated this house that you have built by putting my name there forever. My eyes and my mind will be there always. [4]As for you: if you walk before me as your father David walked, with his whole mind and with uprightness, by acting in accordance with all I have commanded you, you will keep my laws and my rules, [5]and I will establish your royal throne over Israel forever as I spoke to your father David, saying, 'There will not cease to be for you a man on Israel's throne.' [6]If you all and your descendants do turn from following me and do not keep my commands, my laws that I have put before you, and you go and serve other gods and bow down to them, [7]I will cut off Israel from the face of the ground that I gave them, and the house that I have consecrated for my name I will throw out from my presence. Israel will

become a byword and a taunt among all the peoples. [8]This house will be a ruin. Anyone who passes by it will be appalled and will whistle and say, 'Why did Yahweh act like this toward this country and this house?' [9]and they will say, 'Because they abandoned Yahweh their God who brought their ancestors out of Egypt, and took hold of other gods and bowed down to them and served them. That's why Yahweh brought upon them all this trouble.'"

[10]At the end of the twenty years during which Solomon built the two houses, Yahweh's house and the king's house, [11]since Hiram king of Tyre had helped Solomon with cedar and cypress wood and with gold, all he desired, King Solomon then gave Hiram twenty cities in Galilee. [12]Hiram came from Tyre to see the cities that Solomon had given him, but they were not substantial in his eyes, [13]and he said, "What are these cities that you have given me?" He called them Kabul, as they have been called until this day. [14](Hiram had sent the king 120 talents of gold.)

[15]This is the account of the conscript force that King Solomon raised to build Yahweh's house and his own house and the Millo and the wall of Jerusalem, and Hazor, Megiddo, and Gezer [16]when Pharaoh king of Egypt had come up and captured Gezer, set it on fire, and slain the Canaanites who lived in the city, and given it as a dowry to his daughter, Solomon's wife. [17]So Solomon built Gezer, Lower Beth-horon, Baalat, and Tamar in the wilderness, within the country, and all the storage cities that Solomon possessed, the chariot cities and cavalry cities and the fancy that Solomon had for building in Jerusalem, Lebanon, and all the country that he ruled. [20]The entire people that survived of the Amorites, Hittites, Perizzites, Hivites, and Jebusites, those who were not born of the Israelites ([21]their descendants who survived them in the country, whom the Israelites were not able to "devote") Solomon raised as a conscript serf force, as it is until this day. [22]Of the Israelites Solomon did not make anyone a serf, because they were soldiers, his staff, his commanders, his officers, his chariot commanders, and his cavalry.

*[Verses 23–28 add some further detail, including Solomon's building of a fleet at Elat.]*

In connection with 1 Kings 7 I mentioned the work Joe is doing on my bathroom. Yesterday he finished the work. The fixtures look as if they were designed in the twenty-first century rather than somewhat before; the rusty cupboards are gone; the door shuts properly; the sink drains properly; the fan works silently instead of clattering; and my bathtub is all shining white instead of stained. I just need to go and buy a new shower rail and bath mat. I can stand and look at it and almost feel a bit like God in Genesis 1 and say, "That's good." Joe does the same, having more right to feel a little like God. For me as the person who will use the bathroom every day, however, the enjoyment will soon fade. It's like buying a new outfit. After a short while, you need another fix of newness. You don't fulfill your desires in such a way as not to need to fulfill more desires.

Solomon has now fulfilled every fancy on which he has set his desire. The word *fancy* first appears in Scripture to describe Shechem's fancy for Dinah (Genesis 34); it can be used for things that God fancies, too, so it's not a word that can't be redeemed, but it's a worrying word. The story uses it again in connection with some other building projects outside Jerusalem that involved turning **Canaanites** into a conscript labor force. We noted in connection with 1 Kings 4 that "conscript labor" does not mean "forced labor" in the sense of chain gangs overseen by men with whips, but it's nevertheless a worrying expression. It's accompanied by the word *desire*, another word that can be used of God, but another worrying word (it was the word Joab, David's general, used in 2 Samuel 24 in connection with David's desire to take a census). Later in the Old Testament, the book of Ecclesiastes will take Solomon as its poster child in discussing the emptiness of the things that people assume will make life worthwhile. He is the man who could fulfill all his fancies and desires; but what did it do to his relationship with God and with people, and did it get him anywhere? Not for nothing does Ecclesiastes imagine Solomon reflecting on his achievements as architect and builder and conclude, "There was nothing very valuable about it."

So that opening verse begins to raise such questions in our minds, but it doesn't answer them. Instead it segues into the report of a kind of sermon that God preached to Solomon, challenging him about his commitment to God. He needs to take his father David as his model. This might seem a surprising idea. Solomon would know what a mess David made of the second half of his reign. But there was one crucial thing that David stuck by. He was always faithful to **Yahweh** rather than to other gods. That will be one connection in which the story makes explicit its judgment that Solomon goes astray. It will be his equivalent to the David-Bathsheba-Uriah affair.

I refer to God's message as a kind of sermon on the assumption that it is a contribution by the compilers of Kings; it tells us the kind of challenge they believe lay before someone like Solomon in the kind of position he was in, and the kind of challenge that leaders and people face in their own day. I don't imagine it corresponds to anything that God actually said to Solomon, but I assume God was happy to have these compilers express the challenge that way. It's the kind of thing God could have said, the kind of challenge Solomon did face, and the kind of challenge people in their day did face. (If you can't believe that God could have acted in this way in inspiring Scripture, then remember that like other things in this commentary, it's just scholarly opinion, and you can disagree with it.)

In turn the sermon gives way to some anecdotal accounts of Solomon's relations with Hiram king of Tyre, the other big player in the Levant in this period, and of Solomon's dealing with the indigenous peoples of Canaan. So what is Solomon doing giving away cities in the promised land, for goodness' sake? It might also come as a surprise to find that there are so many of these indigenous people to deal with if you thought Joshua **devoted** them all, but reading between the lines of the book of Joshua makes clear that Joshua did no such thing, and so does the present chapter. In the short term the Israelites had to coexist with the Canaanites, who were bigger than they were. In due course, the power relationship changed, and the Israelites are now big enough to make the Canaanites work for them. Is that OK? Even if we are glad they didn't get annihilated, is there something wrong with this picture?

First Kings leaves it to us to work out. Sometimes an Old Testament story does offer us an explicit evaluation of the actions people take and the lives they live; for instance, after David has Uriah killed, it comments that the thing David had done displeased God (see 2 Samuel 12:1). Sometimes it leaves you to work things out; this chapter is an example. The practical reason is the way a book like 1 Kings came into being as its authors or compilers strung together material they took from various sources, such as state records and stories people told, and interpretive material they created. Surprisingly, you might think, they make little effort to turn the material into a neat whole, and apparently God was happy with that because it means we have to do the work in understanding what God might make of the story that the books present to us. Maybe God was making allowance for the fact that we learn more effectively this way than we do when we are simply given all the answers. We can't necessarily be clear about some of the judgments that should be passed on Solomon, but that hardly matters; those questions are between God and Solomon. We are the people whose judgment we have to consider in light of his story.

## 1 KINGS 10:1–29

### Enter the Queen of Sheba

[1]Now the queen of Sheba heard report of Solomon in connection with Yahweh's name, and she came to test him with hard questions. [2]She came to Jerusalem with very substantial goods, camels carrying spices, very much gold, and precious stones. When she came to Solomon, she related to him all that was in her mind, [3]and Solomon told her about all the subjects she raised. There was no subject concealed from the king about which he did not tell her. [4]When the queen of Sheba saw all Solomon's wisdom, the house he had built, [5]the food on his table, the seating of his staff, the standing of his ministers and their dress, his drinks, and the whole burnt offerings he used to make at Yahweh's house, there was no longer any breath left in her. [6]She said to the king, "The account I heard in my country about your affairs and your wisdom was true, [7]but I did not believe the accounts until I came and saw with my eyes. Now. Half of it had not been told me. You have more wisdom and goods than the report I heard. [8]The good fortune of your people! The good fortune of these staff of yours who stand continually before you listening to your wisdom! [9]May Yahweh your God be worshiped, the one who delighted in you in setting

you on Israel's throne in Yahweh's love for Israel in perpetuity. He made you king to exercise authority in accordance with what is right."

*[Verses 10–22 note the gifts the queen brought Solomon and the gifts he gave her. It goes on to itemize Solomon's income in terms of gold and to describe how he made gold shields, a gold-covered throne, and goblets.]*

[23]King Solomon exceeded all the kings of the earth in wealth and wisdom. [24]All the earth was seeking audience with Solomon to listen to the wisdom that God had put in his mind, [25]and they would each bring his gift: gold and silver objects, robes, weapons and spices, horses and mules, the amount specified as due for each year. [26]Solomon assembled chariotry and cavalry. He had one thousand four hundred chariots and twelve thousand cavalry. He put them in chariot cities, and with the king in Jerusalem. [27]The king made silver [as common] as stones in Jerusalem, and cedars [as common] as the sycamore-fig trees in the foothills. [28]Solomon's horses were exported from Egypt and from Que; the king's merchants would get them from Que for a [set] price. [29]When a chariot came up, it was exported from Egypt for six hundred silver [shekels], a horse for one hundred and fifty, and thus they would be exported by means of [the merchants] to all the Hittite and Aramean kings.

The news yesterday reported on one of the unbreakable rules of capitalism: whatever regulations are put in place to control capitalism, people will find a way around them. Interestingly, one of its examples was the Old Testament ban on lending at interest, which the church long affirmed. In the Middle Ages, traders found a way around it by arranging for loans to be paid back in a different currency from the one in which they were made. In the decade that led up to the great recession that we have been going through as I write, financiers have been finding their own way around the regulations that existed (which is one reason why we are in a mess), and we can be sure that as governments put in new controls in the aftermath of a recession, they will do so again. In one sense there are no rules of economics. In another sense, this is one such rule.

Once Solomon is a ruler like other rulers, he works by the same rules as other rulers. Evidently Sheba joins Tyre and Israel as one of the great trading powers of the day. Tyre sits on the Mediterranean coast north of Beirut, having a great harbor and thus being in a position to control sea trade to the west as well as the Lebanese timber trade. Sheba was traditionally identified with Ethiopia, which at least gives the right geographical impression; it is another sea power to the south, on the Red Sea, from where it is able to trade in gold, silver, and spices between Asia and Africa to the east and south and the countries to the north. So the monarchs of Tyre and Sheba are careful to maintain good relationships with one another, sealed by impressive "gifts." Like personal gifts at Christmas and at weddings, these are symbolic as well as substantial; they arise out of relationships and express them (woe betide you if you get the gift exchange wrong). The passage doesn't imply a love relationship between the king of Israel and the queen of Sheba; for both sides, these conversations all have dollar signs, not Cupid's arrows, floating over them.

In a sense it's a mystery how Solomon belongs in this company. Jerusalem is on top of some mountains and not on an important trade route (consider where Israel's airport is), and it has no natural resources. Indeed, it would not be surprising if the entire portrait of Solomon and his empire contains much hyperbole. When Barak Obama decided to run for president of the United States, no one would have given him a chance of succeeding, but he did so because he possessed wisdom, insight, and shrewdness. One might suspect that any empire Solomon possessed came into being through the exercise of the one asset his story emphasizes—wisdom or insight or shrewdness. You want to know how to build an empire? You want the answers to tricky questions of economics? You want to know how to build trade relations to mutual advantage? You want to know how to organize things at home so you have a sophisticated system for collecting taxes and well-organized military bases? Solomon is your man.

Once Barak Obama became president, it became clear that for all his commitment to a new politics, he needed to be able to recognize the rules of the old politics. We don't get the impression that Solomon sensed any tension between the kind of politics that might be at home in Israel and the kind that might be at home among other nations. At the end of her eulogy, the queen of Sheba comments that God has put him on the throne to exercise authority in accordance with what is right. Second Samuel 8 comments that his father did exercise authority in that way, but 1 Kings never makes such a comment about Solomon. We noted that Ecclesiastes takes Solomon as its poster child in portraying the man who has everything and is thus in a position to testify to its meaninglessness. Psalm 72 takes Solomon as its poster child in its prayer that God may make the king someone committed to exercising authority in this way (and it promises that he will then receive the recognition of other monarchs as Solomon here does) but it then carries a great irony. It is not a prayer God granted in Solomon, as was the case with most kings.

Once more the story's judgment is unstated or understated; alongside the comment on the way to exercise authority, we recall the **Torah**'s explicit ban on importing horses from Egypt (Que, in Turkey, to the north, would actually be the main place where horses came from; it was the chariots that would come from Egypt). And once more, there is a big difference between various elements in the story. In chapter 9 there was a message of God to Solomon, there was anecdote, and there were lists of achievements and people, and similar features appear here. In noting the difference between these, I don't just mean that there is a difference in the teaching of the different parts but that there is a difference in the kind of writing that they are. It's a little like the difference between news items, interviews with individuals, and opinion pieces on television. All these can be true; they are still different in the kind of statement they make and the process that generates them. Before they became part of one television program, they had different origins and different status.

We noted in connection with Solomon's prayer that it's often worth bearing in mind that the first audience of the books of Kings as we have them lived in the time of the **exile**. That's when the books were put together. They weren't written from scratch then. Indeed, if they had been, they might have flowed better than they do. They were put together a little like a television news or magazine or documentary program, combining various kinds of archival material with contemporary comment. When people in the ancient world wrote history, they could be happy combining material of varying origin in this way, not willing to sacrifice useful archival material or stories that had a long history of being told in the community with expressions of their own perspective, sometimes put into the mouth of key players. When God inspired Israelite history writers, God inspired them to write a great example of the kind of history that was at home in their culture, which would then communicate as God's word with the people for whom it was written.

# 1 KINGS 11:1–43

## Wives and Adversaries

[1]Now King Solomon loved many foreign women (and Pharaoh's daughter), Moabite, Ammonite, Edomite, Phoenician, and Hittite, [2]from the nations about which Yahweh had said to the Israelites, "You will not have sex with them, and they will not have sex with you, then they will turn your spirits after their gods." To them Solomon attached himself in love. [3]He had seven hundred consorts and three hundred secondary wives, and his wives did turn his spirit. [4]In Solomon's old age, his wives turned his spirit after other gods. His spirit was not at one with Yahweh his God like the spirit of his father David. [5]Solomon followed Ashtoret the god of the Phoenicians and Milcom the abomination of the Ammonites. [6]Solomon did what was displeasing in Yahweh's eyes and did not fully follow Yahweh like his father David. [7]At that time Solomon built a high place for Chemosh the abomination of Moab on a hill facing Jerusalem and for Molech the abomination of the Ammonites. [8]He did so for all his foreign wives who burned incense and sacrificed to their gods. [9]Yahweh was angry with Solomon because his spirit turned away from Yahweh the God of Israel who had appeared to him twice [10]and had commanded him about this matter, not to follow other gods. He did not observe what Yahweh had commanded. [11]Yahweh said to Solomon, "Because this has been your attitude, and you have not observed my covenant and my laws, which I commanded

you, I will tear the kingship right away from you and give it to your servant. [12]Yet in your days I will not do it, for the sake of my servant David; from the hand of your son I will tear it away. [13]Yet the entire kingship I will not tear away; one clan I will give to your son, for the sake of my servant David and for the sake of Jerusalem, which I chose."

[14]Yahweh raised up an adversary for Solomon, Hadad the Edomite; he was of the Edomite royal family. . . . [23]And God raised up for him as an adversary Rezon son of Eliada, who had fled from his master Hadadezer, king of Zobah. . . . [26]Now Jeroboam son of Nebat, an Ephraimite from Zeredah, whose mother's name was Zeruah (she was a widow), a servant of Solomon, raised his hand against the king. [27]This was the way he raised his hand against the king. When Solomon built the Millo, he secured the breach in the city of his father David. [28]This Jeroboam was an able man and Solomon saw the work the young man was doing, so he appointed him over all the conscript labor in the household of Joseph. [29]At that time he went out of Jerusalem, and the prophet Ahijah from Shiloh met him on the road. [Jeroboam] was wearing a new coat. The two of them were alone in the open country. [30]Ahijah grasped the new coat that [Jeroboam] had on and tore it into twelve pieces. [31]He said to Jeroboam, "Take yourself ten pieces, because Yahweh the God of Israel has said this: 'Right. I am tearing the kingship from Solomon's hand and giving ten clans to you. . . . [36]To his son I will give one clan so that my servant David will have control permanently before me in Jerusalem. . . .'" [40]Solomon sought to put Jeroboam to death, but Jeroboam set off and fled to Egypt to Shishak king of Egypt and was in Egypt until Solomon's death. . . . [43b]Then his son Rehoboam reigned as king instead of him.

When my sister was abandoned by her husband just after the birth of their son, she moved back to live with our parents for a while to find a way of getting her life back together, and eventually met a nice young man (also called John, as is her son, so it became a bit complicated at family gatherings). The only snag was, he had not been used to going to church. Now, we had been brought up at church to commit ourselves to live by Paul's exhortation in 2 Corinthians 6 not to be yoked together with unbelievers. It's like a mule and an ox; it can't work properly.

So a few eyebrows were raised at this relationship, and they included mine, though I had to bear in mind the fact that my sister's first husband had been brought up in the same church as we were, so the allegedly equal yoke didn't work out too well. Anyway, the two of them married (I think I may have been the best man); John came to know Christ; and they have lived happily together for thirty or forty years. My sister and I are plotting for John to look after us in our dotage (he is younger than we are), so I hope he doesn't read this book.

The rationale for that rule that we were offered as teenagers overlapped with the rationale in 1 Kings, though here some other considerations combine to make the ignoring of it problematic. At first sight a rule about not marrying a non-Israelite looks like an ethnic one, and no doubt in the ancient Middle East it was the norm to marry within your ethnic group as is the case in Western society. At the same time, there are many examples of people not doing so, such as Ruth the Moabite and Uriah the Hittite, as there are in Western society, and no one in Israel seems to mind. In Israel the crucial consideration is not ethnic but religious. It is explicit that Ruth has committed herself to **Yahweh** and implicit that Uriah has done so (his name means "Yahweh is my light"). In a later period when Ezra makes Israelite men break up their marriages with foreign women, it is for religious, not ethnic, reasons, and it is religious considerations that make Solomon's marriages objectionable.

A second factor usually influences considerations of whom one marries. In Western culture we simply take for granted that people marry for love and nothing else; logically, then, when they fall out of love, they divorce. While the Scriptures occasionally allow for a link between love and marriage, notably in the Song of Songs, they recognize that marriage is about many things other than love. One is that it sets up a relationship between families or larger groups. Solomon marries all these women to cement relationships with the people they come from. And you might think this is a rather splendid reason for marriage. To think that my marriage might mean there was no more war between (say) my people and the Moabites or the Ammonites or the Edomites. . . . But there's no reason why it shouldn't develop into a romantic relationship; arranged marriages do so.

Not that there is much chance in Solomon's case, however, given the numbers of wives involved. There is a huge irony about attaching Solomon's name to the Song of Songs, since he may have been wise enough to sponsor and give his name to it as expressions of wisdom, but he can hardly have had any personal clue about the kind of relationship it speaks of. Solomon indeed "loved them," even "attached himself in love to them," but this has nothing to do with what in our culture we would mean by love. He made a commitment to them, and he kept that commitment. The relationships were polygamous, but they did not involve adultery. His sexual relationships with a number of wives and **secondary wives** took place within a social and moral framework. Admittedly it's difficult to imagine him actually having sex with all thousand of them, at least not very often. And that shows that marriage isn't much about sex either, as married couples will often comment (perhaps ruefully).

Alas, part of the commitment was to make it possible for them to worship their gods, which meant erecting places for such worship within sight of the central sanctuary for the worship of Yahweh, the home that Solomon erected for Yahweh. That was itself an abomination. Perhaps it was part of the deal that he should sometimes join them in worship of their gods, part of the cementing of relationships with these other peoples. But it wasn't something to which Yahweh felt like turning a blind eye. So whereas 1 Kings for the most part leaves the judgment concerning Solomon's social and political policies to its readers, it takes no chances over evaluation of his religious policies. It is these that are central to its account of why the **exile** happened, and it sees Solomon as responsible for the first great steps toward that disaster (even as his prayer in chapter 8 opens up the possibility of turning to God when it does happen). Ashtoret and Molech look like deliberate reworkings of the names of the goddess Ashtarte and the god Milcom or Melek (the word for "king"), combining its consonants with the vowels of the Hebrew word for "shame." Milcom, Chemosh, and Molech are more explicitly identified as abominations. They were pretty abominable when worshiped by foreigners (people sacrificed

children to Milcom) but much more abominable when Israelites turn their backs on Yahweh to worship them.

Like David, Solomon is arguably a much worse character
than Saul, but once again, God is caught by commitments it is
impossible to go back on and has to compromise. While trouble begins for Solomon in his lifetime, and his marriage policy
turns out not to have worked too well, the sin of the father will
be visited in a more far-reaching way on the son (though as
usual, this comes true only because the son also deserves it).

## 1 KINGS 12:1–32

### The Chance to Be a Servant Leader

[1]Rehoboam went to Shechem, because all Israel came to
Shechem to crown him king. [2]When Jeroboam son of Nebat
heard of it while he was still in Egypt, where he had fled from
King Solomon (Jeroboam had settled in Egypt), [3]they sent and
summoned him. He came to Rehoboam with all the assembly
of Israel and declared to Rehoboam: [4]"Your father—he made
our yoke heavy. You—now lighten your father's hard servitude
and the heavy yoke he put on us, and we will serve you." [5]He
said to them, "Go away for three days, then come back to
me." So the people went away. [6]King Rehoboam took counsel
with the elders who had been standing in attendance on his
father Solomon while he was alive: "How do you counsel me
to give a response to this company?" [7]They declared to him,
"If today you will be a servant to this people, and answer them
and speak good words to them, they will be your servants all
your days. . . ." [10]But the young men who had grown up with
him declared to him . . . : "Speak like this to them: 'My little
finger is thicker than my father's waist. [11]So now, if my father
imposed a heavy yoke on you, I myself will add to your yoke.
If my father flogged you with whips, I myself will flog you with
scorpions. . . .'" [15]The king did not listen to the company [of
elders] because it was a turn of affairs from Yahweh to fulfill the
word Yahweh had spoken by means of Ahijah the Shilonite to
Jeroboam son of Nebat. [16]When all Israel saw that the king had
not listened to them, the people gave word back to the king:
"What share do we have in David? We have no part in the son
of Jesse. To your tents, Israel. Now see to your own household,

57

David." And Israel went to its tents, ¹⁷though the Israelites living in cities in Judah—Rehoboam reigned over them. . . . ¹⁹So Israel rebelled against David's household, as it has done until this day. ²⁰When all Israel heard that Jeroboam had returned, they sent and summoned him to the assembly and made him king over all Israel. No one followed the household of David except the clan of Judah alone.

*[Verses 21–24 relate how Rehoboam made plans to attack the rebel clans, but God sends him a prophet to tell him not to do so.]*

²⁵Jeroboam built up Shechem in the mountains of Ephraim and lived there; he went out from there and built up Penuel. ²⁶Jeroboam said to himself, "The kingship will now return to the household of David; ²⁷if this people go up to offer sacrifices in Yahweh's house in Jerusalem, this people's spirit will go back to their master, to Rehoboam king of Judah. They will slay me and go back to Rehoboam king of Judah." ²⁸So the king took counsel and made two gold calves, and said to [the people], "It is too much for you to go up to Jerusalem. Israel, there are your gods who brought you up from Egypt." ²⁹He placed one in Bethel and put one in Dan, ³⁰and this thing became an offense.

*[Verses 30b–32 relate how Jeroboam also set up the rest of an alternative worship system, including a priesthood and a fall festival.]*

One of my faculty colleagues was asked to become director of the chapel in the seminary, and she loved to relate how she needed to go and talk to the provost of the seminary (vice principal in Brit-speak) about her role, and how his opening words were something like "How can I serve you?" When my rector arranged for the replacing of the notice board outside the church, alongside the names of the ministers he put not words such as "rector" but "servants." Both are great ideas for leaders to live by. We live in a culture that is excessively preoccupied with the nature of leadership, and one of the clichés that we use to try to safeguard against the toxicity of this preoccupation is to talk in terms of "servant-leadership." Claiming that we just want to serve people can be another excuse for exercising power over them, but it doesn't need to be that.

The Scriptures usually talk more about leaders as servants of God than as servants of their people, but the story of Rehoboam provides a great instance of the second kind of talk, though it is finally a sad one. It is an idea that comes out of nowhere. We haven't seen much indication that Saul, David, or Solomon were concerned with serving people, and we have seen that Solomon was too busy building great buildings and collecting the money to pay for them to worry too much about that.

The beginning of a new king's reign (or the inauguration of a new administration or the opening of a new parliament) is a moment when people in power have to win their people's confidence. In the Middle East it was often a time when kings issued edicts outlining the kind of social policies they were committed to. In Israel, the dynastic principle was established (that is, the king should be a descendant of David), but this need not mean that the king must be the son of the last king or that it should be his eldest son. Solomon was not David's oldest living son, and in later years things did not always work this way. So Rehoboam might not be able to take his position for granted.

His going to Shechem links with the fact that the union of north and south in Israel was always a fragile one. David had been accepted in the south long before he had been accepted in the north. Solomon had been inclined to milk the resources of the north. Rehoboam could perhaps take the south for granted; he had more winning of confidence to do in the north. It is always tempting for people in power to rely on power and to try to achieve things by force, to think that they need to show that they are people you can't mess with. Yet in this situation, from a purely pragmatic angle, to present yourself as the people's servant was a good idea. How can one explain Rehoboam's stupidity? I can see God behind it, says the narrator of the story. Rehoboam's stupidity will contribute to the fulfilling of God's plan. The situation parallels that in Egypt, when Pharaoh's attitude to Moses was stubborn, when Pharaoh encouraged himself to be stubborn, and when God encouraged him to be stubborn. You can look at what happens from different angles and see both the reality of human freedom and decision making and the reality of divine sovereignty and the fulfilling of the divine will. You can also see God operating in an interventionist way as well as making use of decisions people make for themselves; so when necessary God sends a prophet to keep

Rehoboam on the course God wants if he shows an inclination to act contrary to the way God wants.

Jeroboam's action reminds one of the exodus story, too. When the book of Exodus was written, and it came to the story of the gold calf that Aaron made, it seems to be nudging the reader to see the parallel with Jeroboam's action. The people as a whole had felt the need for something that would represent the presence of God for them, and they got Aaron to make the calf to fulfill that function. They were not necessarily turning away from **Yahweh**, but they did feel the need of something that would suggest Yahweh's presence. Jeroboam feels the same need, and he uses exactly the same words as are put on Aaron's lips, that these are "your gods [or your God] who brought you up from Egypt." A difference is that his reason is political. He sees that his state will be likely never to have a proper sense of its independence if his people always have to traipse off to Jerusalem for a festival, and the addition of some images of the kind he devises will make up for the novelty of his sanctuaries over against Solomon's splendid temple (largely built with **Ephraimite** labor and resources). There are two problems here. One he shares with the Israelites in Aaron's day. Even if he and Aaron might describe their images as images of Yahweh, Yahweh's view is that an image is such a silent and static thing that it can't actually represent Yahweh (who speaks and acts a lot). In effect, it is bound to be an image of a different god. So that is one reason why "the thing became an offense." The other problem he shares with David and Solomon. For all these kings, religion has become the servant of the state. Its job is to buttress the position of the state. There is a lot to be said for separation of church and state, not to protect the state but to protect the church.

His building up of Shechem makes sense; it is the obvious place for a capital city, at a crossroads between north and south, east and west, and the place where Rehoboam had gone to be crowned in Ephraim; Nablus, the center of the northern half of the West Bank today, is nearby. Penuel is east of the Jordan, so his building up of this city also makes sense, because it gives him a major center in that region.

# 1 KINGS 12:33–13:32

## Prophets, and When to Ignore Them

<sup>33</sup>On the fifteenth day of the eighth month [Jeroboam] went up onto the altar he had made in Bethel, which he devised out of his own mind, and held the festival for the Israelites, but when he went up onto the altar to burn an offering, <sup>13:1</sup>there: a man of God came from Judah by Yahweh's word to Bethel, when Jeroboam was standing on the altar to burn an offering. <sup>2</sup>He cried out against the altar by Yahweh's word: "Altar, altar, Yahweh has said this: 'Now. A son is to be born to David's household, Josiah by name. He will sacrifice on you the priests of the high places who burn offerings on you. People will burn human bones on you.'" <sup>3</sup>That day he gave a sign: "This is the sign that Yahweh has spoken: 'Now. This altar is to be split apart and the ash on it is to pour out.'" <sup>4</sup>When the king heard the message from the man of God that he cried out against the altar at Bethel, Jeroboam put out his hand from above the altar, saying, "Seize him!" but his hand which he put out against him shriveled and he could not bring it back to himself, <sup>5</sup>while the altar split apart and the ash from the altar poured out in accordance with the sign the man of God gave by Yahweh's word. <sup>6</sup>The king spoke out and said to the man of God, "Will you entreat the favor of Yahweh your God and plead for me so that I can bring back my hand to myself." The man of God entreated Yahweh's favor, and the king's hand came back to him and became as it was before. <sup>7</sup>The king spoke to the man of God: "Do come with me to my house and have something to eat, and I will give you a gift." <sup>8</sup>The man of God said to the king, "If you gave me half your household I would not come with you; I will not eat bread or drink water in this place, <sup>9</sup>because so I was commanded by Yahweh's word. . . ."

<sup>11</sup>But an old prophet was living in Bethel. . . . <sup>14</sup>He went after the man of God and found him sitting under a terebinth. . . . <sup>15</sup>He said to him, "Come with me to my house and I will give you food to eat. . . ." <sup>18</sup>[The prophet] said to him, "I am also a prophet, like you, and an aide spoke to me by Yahweh's word, saying, 'Bring him back with you to your house and so that he can eat some food and drink some water.'" He was lying to him. . . . <sup>20</sup>As they were sitting at the table, Yahweh's word came

61

to the prophet who had brought him back, [21]and he cried out to the man of God who had come from Judah, "Yahweh has said this: 'Because you rebelled against Yahweh's word and did not observe the command that Yahweh your God gave you, . . . [22b]your corpse will not come to your ancestors' grave. . . .'" [24]When he went, a lion met him on the road and killed him. . . . [28][The prophet] went and found his corpse thrown on the road, with the donkey and the lion standing by the corpse. The lion had not eaten the corpse nor mauled the donkey. [29]The prophet lifted the corpse of the man of God and laid it on the donkey and took it back. So it came to the old prophet's city for it to be mourned and buried. [30]He laid the corpse in his own grave and they mourned over it, "Oh, my brother!" [31]After burying him he said to his sons, "When I die, bury me in the grave where the man of God is buried; lay my bones by his bones, [32]because the word that he cried out by Yahweh's word against the altar at Bethel and against all the houses [of God] belonging to the high places in the cities of Samaria will definitely come true."

When I look back over the leadership of the various bosses I have had (present company excepted, in case he reads this) and reflect on my own time as a boss, I can see various ways in which proven ability and divine guidance played a part in their appointment, and I can recognize ways in which their leadership was successful or not. One boss had proved himself in a different context but didn't do so well in ours; another had proved himself in a less responsible position and also did well as the person at the top; and one person did well in a less responsible position but turned out not to be up to the top job. In all the cases, appointment bodies were seeking God's guidance, but sometimes the appointments were mistakes. Was God not involved? Did they not listen to God enough? Was God limited by the talent available?

Prophets are really tiresome, and it is their destiny to be ignored. In Israel's history, they start coming into their own when there are kings. For Saul and David, they are ambiguous figures; they initiate the process whereby Saul and David become kings, and they confront them about the way they fulfill their role. They have the same function in relationship with Jeroboam. It was a prophet who initiated the process whereby Jeroboam became king, though one might guess that this would have happened anyway. Unlike Saul and David, before Jeroboam's designation by Ahijah he had already proved himself the stuff of which leadership is made and the kind of person who either might have aspirations to the kingship or might be drafted by his people; Solomon's attempt to kill him shows that he could see that this was so. So sometimes God takes someone with no leadership ability and makes him a leader, as happened with Saul and with earlier leaders; God doesn't need to use people with leadership ability because God isn't dependent on people's ability. Sometimes God takes someone who is too young to have had a chance to show leadership ability and takes a chance on how things will turn out, as happened with David. The results are then ambiguous. Sometimes God lets human willfulness and plotting take their course, as happened with Solomon. The results are again ambiguous, though with a different profile.

Sometimes God harnesses human ability, as happens with Jeroboam. It is striking that the story has no comment on whether God wanted Rehoboam to be king, as was the case in respect of Solomon, though both of them do have the one qualification that Jeroboam lacks in that they are descendants of David. Perhaps that is all they need; God doesn't mind which descendant of David reigns. For there to be a king who is not a descendant of David, there would need to be a prophetic word parallel to the ones that designated Saul and then David. Yet the reason for recounting the prophetic word back in chapter 11 (and the one in 12:21–24) did not relate to **Ephraim**'s need so much as to the readers' need. It shows us that what happens in Ephraim is the fulfillment of God's word of judgment in light of Solomon's reign. In terms of the reduction of oppression in Ephraim, Jeroboam's reign is an improvement on what Solomon did and on what Rehoboam planned, but in terms of relationship with God, ironically Jeroboam's reign is hardly an improvement on Solomon's.

Hence a man of God confronts Jeroboam with a prophecy, as prophecy initiated his reign. Now, I am not sure how literally we are to take the story of what happened at Bethel. I have no doubt that God could do the kind of thing that is described, but the revealing of the name of the king who will eventually kill the priests who minister at this sanctuary (which will happen three centuries later) seems particularly odd in light of the way the Old Testament usually describes God as acting. But as is often the case, the significance of the story is not much affected by whether we come to the right view about whether it is more a piece of history or more "just a story." It declares that Jeroboam could be the means of God's judgment being exacted on the line of David, while also being liable to God's judgment for the way he himself subordinated religion to politics and in his religious policy ignored the real truth about the kind of person God is.

What takes place between the two anonymous prophets later in the story arouses similar questions about whether it really happened. Both prophets are ambiguous figures, like those kings. One would suspect that a Bethel prophet is a suspicious figure. What stance has he been taking to Jeroboam and his actions? Has he been supporting the regime, or at least colluding with its policies? Is that why God has to send a prophet from Judah (there being no one in Ephraim to use)? If so, the story implies that at least he learns a thing or two through what happens. A contrast emerges from consideration of the Judahite prophet himself. He risks his life to confront Jeroboam yet then loses his life because he relaxes and is insufficiently suspicious of someone who says that he has a word from God, that a divine **aide** has appeared to him. It would be inappropriate to infer that we should always trust what we think God has said to us rather than what someone else says is a word from God (one significance of expressing something in a story is to describe something that has happened without implying that it regularly happens). Indeed, the opposite will often be the case. But gullibility doesn't pay.

## 1 KINGS 13:33–14:20

### When the Apostate King's Son Gets Sick

³³After this act Jeroboam did not turn from his wrong way but again made priests for the high places from all parts of the people. Any who desired, he appointed to become priests of the high places. ³⁴By this act Jeroboam's household became

an offense, to its ruin and destruction from upon the face of the ground. <sup>14:1</sup>At that time Abijah, Jeroboam's son, got sick. <sup>2</sup>Jeroboam said to his wife, "Will you set off, disguise yourself so people will not recognize that you are Jeroboam's wife, and go to Shiloh. Now. The prophet Ahijah is there. It was he who declared over me that I would be king over this people. <sup>3</sup>Take ten loaves of bread in your hand, and some cookies and a jar of honey, and go to him. He will tell you what will happen to the boy." <sup>4</sup>Jeroboam's wife did so. She set off and went to Shiloh and came to Ahijah's house. Ahijah couldn't see, because his eyes had gone, through his old age, <sup>5</sup>but Yahweh had said to Ahijah, "Now. Jeroboam's wife is coming to inquire something of you in relation to her son, because he is sick. You are to speak such and such things to her. But she will be pretending to be a stranger." <sup>6</sup>So when Ahijah heard the sound of her feet as she came through the door, he said, "Come in, wife of Jeroboam. Why on earth are you pretending to be a stranger? I am sent to you with a tough message. <sup>7</sup>Go and say to Jeroboam, 'Yahweh the God of Israel has said this: "Because I elevated you from the midst of the people and made you ruler over my people Israel <sup>8</sup>and tore the kingship from the household of David and gave it to you, but you have not been like my servant David who kept my commands and followed me with all his spirit by doing only what was upright in my eyes, <sup>9</sup>you have been more wrong in your actions than all who were before you. You have gone and made other gods and images for yourself, to provoke me. Me you have thrown behind your back. <sup>10</sup>Now. I am therefore bringing trouble to the household of Jeroboam. I am going to cut off for Jeroboam those who urinate against a wall (bond and freed) in Israel. I am going to burn up after the household of Jeroboam as one burns dung, until it is finished. <sup>11</sup>The person who belongs to Jeroboam who dies in the city the dogs will eat; the person who dies in the open country the birds in the heavens will eat. Because Yahweh has spoken.'" <sup>12</sup>So you, set off and go home. When your foot comes to the city, the child will die. <sup>13</sup>All Israel will mourn over him and bury him, because he alone of those who belong to Jeroboam will come into a grave, because in him something good has been found in relation to Yahweh the God of Israel, in the household of Jeroboam. <sup>14</sup>Yahweh will raise up for himself a king over Israel who will cut off the household of Jeroboam. This is the day.

Even now. [15]Yahweh will strike Israel down like a reed that sways in the water and will uproot Israel from this good ground that he gave to your ancestors, and scatter them beyond the River [Euphrates], because they have made Asherah columns that provoke Yahweh."

*[Verses 16–20 relate how Jeroboam's wife takes the message home; the child dies, and eventually Jeroboam dies and his son Nebat succeeds him.]*

Last night a friend of mine was blowing a fuse concerning the sermon at her church a couple of Sundays ago. The preacher was talking about Jesus' healing of the man who had been lying sick by the Pool of Siloam for thirty-eight years and suggested that he had no business lying there for that long. It sounded as if he had not taken responsibility for his healing. My friend blew a fuse because someone close to her is chronically ill, and she knows that a person can't necessarily just decide to get better. As the husband of someone who was sick for forty-three years, I echo that point. What makes a preacher say something so stupid? Part of the answer (we reflected) is that there is something frightening about being sick or having someone near us sick. It makes us feel helpless. We are no longer in control, and control is important to us. Advertisements play on this when they urge us to take control of our asthma or arthritis, even of our cancer.

In a traditional society like ancient Israel, the prospect of being in control is much lower. My son was recently diagnosed with diabetes, but he has a regimen of diet and injections and lives a normal life. A century ago, his illness would have killed him. When Jeroboam and his wife realize that their son is ill and is evidently not getting better, what are they to do? When their child becomes ill, the king and queen are no better off than ordinary people (indeed, we will discover that they are worse off). All they can do is turn to God. Logically enough, they do so by turning to the prophet at Shiloh who had delivered the original message that Jeroboam was destined to be king. The trouble is that they know from the prophet who came to Bethel that they are in trouble with God. With some naiveté they try to circumvent this problem for their son's sake. Abijah's mother is to take a gift with her, which would be natural—prophets live from people's gifts, like pastors. Saul knew he needed to take a gift when he went to ask Samuel about his lost donkeys. The couple will assume not only that Ahijah may be able to tell them their son's prognosis but that he may be able to tell them how they might avert any threat to his life—for instance, what offering they might make to God. In other ways, though, it looks as if they have some rather primitive ideas about prophets—prophets may be able to look into the future but not be able to see what is going on in the present. They discover they are wrong.

It is not explicit whether they have asked themselves whether the illness is in some way a message to them, though it is likely that they would be aware of that question. When bad things happen in people's lives, they are inclined to ask, "Why has this happened to me?" and the Scriptures recognize that illness does sometimes result from wrongdoing (see 1 Corinthians 11:27–32), so it is a proper question. Ahijah knows how profound, far-reaching, and disastrous is the answer to their question. His having been God's means of designating Jeroboam as ruler of **Ephraim** as part of bringing God's judgment on Solomon doesn't mean he is committed to Jeroboam's support. The only person he is committed to is God, and God's message to Jeroboam is now the same as the message to Solomon. It may seem astonishing that Jeroboam should be seen as a worse sinner than anyone before him, but he has institutionalized alien worship in Ephraim, and neither God nor prophet can see him as someone who actually worships **Yahweh**. People can think they are worshiping God but be offering worship that is so alien to who God is that they aren't worshiping God at all. In addition, he has erected **Asherah** columns, that is, objects that were used in connection with the worship of the **Canaanite** goddess of that name. His leadership is ultimately going to mean disaster for his people. (I apologize for the uncouth term the prophet uses to describe men in v. 10; I thought for some time about cleaning up the Bible here, as translations usually do, but I decided to leave it as it is.)

The Old Testament is more hardheaded than Western thinking about the way the destiny of children is tied up with that of their parents. It emphasizes that human courts are not to let children be punished for their parents' sins, but it recognizes that God did not create humanity in such a way that these destinies can easily be separated. We know that sending a mother or father to prison punishes their children, but we do it anyway, and God does something equivalent. If Jeroboam is to be punished for his action, the interweaving of the destiny of children with that of their parents means his children will be punished too. There is a converse. The worst way you can hurt parents is by hurting their children. So when God wants to punish David, God brings about the death of his son (2 Samuel 12). And when God wants to punish Jeroboam, God brings about the death of his son. Admittedly there is a distinctive feature to a story such as this that makes it less threatening to ordinary people. The problem for the family of David and of Jeroboam is that their father is the king. A look at royal families in the modern world shows the price royal children may pay for their position. The future of Israel is now tied up with its kings, and therefore with its kings' children, and they pay a price for this fact.

The story does imply that the boy seemed likely to die anyway. God does not need to intervene to make this happen. God needs only to decline to intervene to heal him. God's actual action is to give his death new meaning for his parents. But the Old Testament is indeed hardheaded in not feeling a need to protect God from responsibility for the child's death. The positive side to it is that his death is not merely chance, random, and unintelligible. Nor does the story assume it is inevitable. Often the point about prophecy is to make itself not come true. If someone repents in response to a prophet's word, that word need not come true. But there is no talk of repentance here. The boy apparently stands in less need of repentance than some people one could name, and the story adds one final note of pathos. There is a sense in which he is fortunate. The fate of people who live on will be worse.

# 1 KINGS 14:21–15:24

## Meanwhile in Judah

[21]Now Rehoboam son of Solomon had become king in Judah. Rehoboam was forty-one when he became king, and he reigned

seventeen years in Jerusalem, the city Yahweh had chosen to put his name there out of all the clans of Israel. His mother's name was Naamah, an Ammonite. ²²Judah did what was displeasing in Yahweh's eyes and aroused stronger passions in him than anything that their ancestors had done by the ways they had come short. ²³They too built for themselves high places, columns, and asherim on every high hill and under every flourishing tree, ²⁴and there were also hierodules in the country. [The Judahites] acted in accordance with all the abhorrent practices of the nations that Yahweh dispossessed before the Israelites.

²⁵In the fifth year of King Rehoboam, Shishak king of Egypt came up against Jerusalem. ²⁶He took the treasures of Yahweh's house and the treasures of the king's house; he took everything. He took the gold shields that Solomon had made, ²⁷so King Rehoboam made bronze shields instead of them and committed them to the control of the commanders who were over the outrunners guarding the gate of the king's house. ²⁸Whenever the king came to Yahweh's house, the outrunners would carry them, then return them to the outrunners' chamber.

*[First Kings 14:29–15:8 summarizes Rehoboam's reign and the three-year reign of his son Abijam.]*

¹⁵:⁹In the twentieth year of Jeroboam, king of Israel, Asa began to reign as king of Judah. ¹⁰He reigned forty-one years. His mother's name was Maacah, daughter of Abishalom. ¹¹Asa did what was right in Yahweh's eyes, like his ancestor David. ¹²He expelled the hierodules from the country and removed all the idols that his father had made. ¹³In addition, Maacah his mother—he removed her from being queen mother, because she had made a monstrosity for Asherah. Asa cut down the monstrosity and burnt it in the Kidron wash. ¹⁴He did not remove the high places. Otherwise Asa's spirit was wholehearted with Yahweh all his days. ¹⁵He brought into Yahweh's house the things his father had consecrated and the things he had consecrated, silver, gold, and utensils.

¹⁶There was war between Asa and Baasha king of Israel all their days. ¹⁷Baasha king of Israel went up against Judah and built up Ramah so as not to let anyone belonging to Asa king of Judah go out or come in. ¹⁸So Asa got all the silver and gold that was left in the treasuries of Yahweh's house and the treasuries

of the king's house and put them into the hand of his staff, and King Asa sent them to Ben-hadad son of Tab-rimmon son of Hazion of Aram, who lived in Damascus, saying, [19]"[Let there be] a covenant between me and you [as] between my father and your father. Now. I have sent you a gift of silver and gold. Go and break your covenant with Baasha king of Israel so that he may pull back from me."

*[Verses 20–24 summarize the rest of his reign.]*

A couple of weeks ago a student asked me with some anxiety whether there was any evidence that any of the events in the Old Testament actually happened. Were there any records from surrounding peoples that people such as Abraham or Moses or Joshua or David even existed? I had to tell him that the answer to that second question is "No." I don't myself think that this is very worrying, any more than that it is worrying that Roman records make no mention of the execution of someone called Jesus from Nazareth. Israel was an undeveloped people that had no means of leaving records of its own until much later, and it was a small-fry people that the big powers of the day had little reason to refer to.

Shishak's expedition in the time of Rehoboam is actually the first event in Israelite history that we can definitively correlate with external records; it also makes it possible to be more concrete about the dates of events in Israel in relation to a Western dating system. The invasion took place in about 926 BC. Shishak is the Hebrew version of a name that was something like Shoshenq in Egyptian. We have already read that Jeroboam took refuge with him when he was on the run for his life from Solomon. In the context of ongoing hostility between **Judah** and **Ephraim,** Shoshenq might have been invading Judah in support of Jeroboam, who would be his underling, but he would also be on the lookout to extend his empire and add to his resources. Shoshenq erected an inscription on the wall of the temple at Karnak in Egypt in which he gave an account of many places in **Canaan** where he asserted his authority on this occasion, and he also erected a monument in Megiddo in Israel, which still survives.

The account of Shishak and of Asa's alliance with Ben-hadad introduces us to the way the history of Ephraim and Judah for the subsequent centuries will be interwoven with the history of the peoples around. Here are the two parts of the people of God trying to find a way of living in the world. The issues this raises are illustrated by the way Asa sets about making a **covenant** with Ben-hadad. While the Hebrew word for "covenant" is also the word for a treaty or a contract, there is something odd about the people who are in covenant with God having to survive by making alliances with other peoples in this way. Yet the story presupposes an even odder piece of background to Jeroboam's relationship with Shishak and Asa's relationship with Ben-hadad: the two parts of the people of God are in an ongoing state of conflict with each other. The seeds sown by Solomon and watered by Rehoboam are bearing horrible fruit. To put it another way, the indigenous religion of the land (the religion of the Canaanites) continued to be a dominant factor in the life of Judah as in the life of Ephraim. The reference to "hierodules" makes the same point. The word literally means a holy person, but in passages such as this it denotes a person involved in religious observances that the Old Testament sees as idolatrous. In other contexts it implies they were seen as immoral, and translations use words such as "sacred prostitutes," but we don't really know what that would mean. They may simply be people who have functioned as ministers of deities other than **Yahweh**, so for Israelites to be so involved implies unfaithfulness to Yahweh and thus something analogous to sexual immorality.

Through the rest of the books of Kings the story will be structured by the reigns of the kings, and as well as describing particular incidents the story will make comments of a general and formulaic kind about the religious policies that characterize each reign. Because the Old Testament does not have a system of absolute dating, the way it will spell out the chronology is by interrelating the dates of the kings of the two countries, though translating this information into our kind of dates is complicated, and there are variant accounts of how this chronology works out. One reason is that while a king was still in the prime of life, he could make his designated successor co-regent to ensure that the succession would eventually happen smoothly. The years of a king's reign would thus overlap with his predecessor's.

Old Testament judgments are uniformly negative about the kings of Ephraim because the very existence of the nation depended on its setting up for itself an unorthodox form of worship. Thus that horrible fruitfulness is also evident in religious affairs. That was also so in Judah, where the religious policy of Rehoboam and Abijam doesn't look so different from that of Jeroboam. That Rehoboam was the son of one of Solomon's foreign wives is hardly a coincidence. At the same time, the fact that Rehoboam's wife Maacah erected a "monstrosity" (some sort of aid to worship that the storytellers view as totally incompatible with true faith in Yahweh) shows that you don't necessarily gain anything by having a mother of pure Israelite blood. The scandal of Rehoboam's reign is highlighted by Jerusalem's being the place where Yahweh had chosen to put his name. There is an implication that events there were actually more scandalous than when people in Ephraim did the same thing.

The judgments on the kings of Judah are more mixed than those on the kings of Ephraim. One complication here is that in later times it became customary to view the **high places** as inherently unorthodox, but in the time of a faithful king such as Asa, they could be places where proper worship was offered to Yahweh. Asa's faithfulness to Yahweh contrasts with the unfaithfulness of his father Rehoboam and his brother Abijam, who immediately preceded him and apparently died young. The things Asa brought into the temple might have been things that had been gained in war and were dedicated to God in recognition that God had made the victory possible. His need to depose his mother from the position of queen mother reflects the power that was recognized to reside in that position.

# 1 KINGS 15:25–16:34

## Two Weeks, Three Kings in Ephraim

²⁵Nadab son of Jeroboam had become king over Israel in the second year of Asa king of Judah, and he reigned over Israel for two years. ²⁶He did what was displeasing in Yahweh's eyes and walked in the way of his father, in the offenses he caused

Israel to commit. ²⁷Baasha son of Ahijah, of the household of
Issachar, plotted against him, and Baasha struck him down at
Gibbethon of the Philistines; Nadab and all Israel were laying
siege to Gibbethon. . . . ²⁹When he became king, he struck down
all Jeroboam's household; he did not let any soul belonging
to Jeroboam survive until he had destroyed it, in accordance
with Yahweh's word which he spoke by means of his servant
Ahijah the Shilonite. . . . ¹⁶:¹Yahweh's word came to Jehu son of
Hanani against Baasha: ²"Because I elevated you from the dirt
and made you ruler over my people Israel but you walked in
the way of Jeroboam and caused my people Israel to offend,
provoking me by their offenses: ³Now. I am going to do away
with Baasha and his household and make your household like
the household of Jeroboam son of Nebat. ⁴The person who
belongs to Baasha who dies in the city the dogs will eat, and the
person who belongs to him who dies in the open country the
birds of the heavens will eat. . . ."

⁸In the twenty-sixth year of Asa king of Judah, Elah son of
Baasha became king over Israel in Tirzah, for two years. ⁹His
servant Zimri, commander of half the chariotry, plotted against
him; he was in Tirzah getting drunk in the house of Arsa, who
was over the household at Tirzah. ¹⁰Zimri came in, struck him
down, and killed him. . . . ¹²Zimri destroyed all Baasha's household, in accordance with the word of Yahweh that he had spoken
to Baasha by means of the prophet Jehu. . . . ¹⁵In the twenty-
seventh year of Asa king of Judah, Zimri reigned for seven
days in Tirzah when the company was camped at Gibbethon
of the Philistines. ¹⁶The company encamped heard, "Zimri has
plotted, and furthermore struck down the king," and all Israel
made Omri, the army commander, king over Israel that day in
the camp. ¹⁷Omri and all Israel with him went up from Gibbethon and besieged Tirzah. ¹⁸When Zimri saw that the city was
taken, he went into the citadel in the king's house and burned
the king's house with fire over himself. So he died. . . . ²¹Then
the people of Israel divided in half. Half the people followed
Tibni the son of Ginath, making him king, and half followed
Omri. ²²But the company that followed Omri was stronger than
the company that followed Tibni son of Ginath; Tibni died and
Omri became king. . . . ²⁴He acquired the mountain of Samaria
from Shemer for two talents of silver, and built up the mountain
and called the city he built by the name of Shemer, the owner

of the mountain, "Samaria...." ²⁷The rest of the acts of Omri which he did, and the power that he showed: these are indeed written down in the annals of the kings of Israel.... ²⁹Ahab son of Omri became king over Israel in the thirty-eighth year of Asa king of Judah. Ahab son of Omri reigned over Israel in Samaria for twenty-two years.... ³³ᵇAhab did more to provoke Yahweh the God of Israel than all the kings of Israel who were before him. ³⁴In his time Hiel the Bethelite built up Jericho. At the cost of Abiram his firstborn he initiated it, and at the cost of Segug his youngest he set up its gates, in accordance with Yahweh's word that he spoke by means of Joshua son of Nun.

Yesterday, as usual, we began our faculty meeting by sharing topics for prayer, and then as it happened I had to try to pray a prayer that covered them all. The sharing referred to someone's health needs, to someone who had lost a job, to someone whose daughter-in-law had just got her PhD, to posts we were trying to fill, to a clash between Israelis and Palestinians that had just taken place (one of the people present was about to go to Israel), to the tension between North Korea and South Korea (one of the people present was Korean), and maybe to other things I can't now remember. In my prayer I thanked God for being the God of all these aspects of our lives and concerns.

The stories in the books of Kings reflect this wide range of God's concerns and involvements and in particular draws our attention to God's involvement in political affairs, though the books often leave open the nature of that involvement. They are thereby tantalizing, though also strangely encouraging: in apparently not always knowing how God is involved, they show that they are in the same position as we are.

After telling us about Jeroboam as king of **Ephraim,** they have focused on his contemporaries in **Judah:** Rehoboam, Abijah, and Asa. Now they backtrack slightly to Jeroboam's successor, Nadab, who came to the throne early on in Asa's reign, and then go on to cover Baasha, Elah, Zimri, Omri, and Ahab. In fact, the story is going to focus for a long time on events in Ephraim, and in particular on the reign of Ahab. That's partly because it lets itself focus on the work of prophets in Ephraim, especially Elijah and Elisha. It's also because the history of

Ephraim is more tumultuous, as the story of these five kings shows, and because Ephraim is much bigger than little Judah and is a bigger player on the international stage. This is itself partly because of its location; Judah is more mountainous and more isolated than Ephraim.

Yet once again the story isn't very forthcoming about how God is involved in all that, though perhaps we are invited to draw our own conclusions about the sequence of coups in Ephraim. One implication of the story is that Judah was fortunate to have the dynasty of David firmly established in Jerusalem; there could be conflict about which descendant of David would reign, but to the very end of Judah's story there wasn't much prospect of some nobody replacing a descendant of David. In Ephraim, however, dynasties changed. Nadab reigns two years and is assassinated by Baasha, who does take steps to make his throne secure by killing everyone belonging to Nadab. But his son is assassinated after two years, while his assassin reigns only a week, and Omri succeeds only after further internal conflict. Omri then gets only half-a-dozen verses in the story, mostly occupied by the usual generalized judgments about his being a bad guy. It does refer to his considerable achievement in founding Samaria as Ephraim's new capital; the city will eventually give its name to the whole area of "Samaria." Further, it refers to the power he exercised. The story does use that expression about some other kings, but in Omri's case there is special significance to the use of the word. **Assyrian** annals often refer to Omri. The records of the Moabites relate how he oppressed them for a long period. Politically, he was a significant figure in the development of Ephraim. But 2 Kings isn't very interested in all that. If you want to know about it, it says, you can go and look in the state records. (Historians would give their right arm to be able to do so; alas, any records of that kind perished millennia ago.)

As far as 1 Kings is concerned, the key question continues to be how faithful the kings are to **Yahweh**. By implication, the apostate origins and foundation of Ephraim's existence mean it is no coincidence that its history is so chaotic. Sometimes the book can note concretely how this works out. Baasha's slaughter of Jeroboam's household fulfills God's message of judgment given to Jeroboam's wife. In turn, God gives another prophet, Jehu, a message of judgment concerning Baasha's household, though this is not because of his violence (there are other passages in the Old Testament that would suggest disapproval of that violence, even though it was God's own means of bringing judgment). Further, this judgment does not fall directly on Baasha, who manages to reign for twenty-four years, but on his son. One usually cannot predict how God's warnings or God's promises will find fulfillment. The fulfillment often comes about through an interaction between policies God wants to implement and political realities. God doesn't often intervene to make things happen that wouldn't ever happen, humanly speaking, but uses the potentials of human commitment, ambition, faithfulness, and wickedness. On the other hand, the consistency of God's involvement is suggested by the words God gives Jehu about the dogs and the birds. With some irony God repeats the message given to Jeroboam in 1 Kings 14:11. Baasha has been the means of that message coming true, but now his own household will see the same message fulfilled in its own life.

The reign of Omri's son Ahab will be the background for the rest of 1 Kings. His representing a new low in the story of Ephraim is implicit in the note about Hiel, which implies that he sacrificed his sons as a kind of enacted prayer for the success of his building venture.

# 1 KINGS 17:1-24

## The Personal and the Political

[1]Elijah the Tishbite from the settlers in Gilead said to Ahab, "As Yahweh lives, the God of Israel before whom I stand [in attendance], during these years there will be no dew or rain except at the word from my mouth." [2]Yahweh's word came to him: [3]"Go from here. Turn east and hide in the Cherith wash, which faces the Jordan. [4]You will drink from the wash, and I have ordered ravens to fill you there." [5]He went and acted in accordance with Yahweh's word.... [6]Ravens were bringing him bread and meat in the morning and bread and meat in the evening, and he drank from the wash. [7]After some time

the wash dried up because there was no rain in the country. [8]Yahweh's word came to him: [9]"Arise, go to Zarephat, which belongs to Sidon, and live there. Now. I have commanded a woman there who is a widow to fill you." [10]He arose and went to Zarephat, came to the city gate, and there: a woman who was a widow was gathering wood there. He called to her, "Could you get me a little water in the vessel so I can drink?" [11]When she went to get it, he called to her, "Could you get me a piece of bread in your hand." [12]She said, "As Yahweh your God lives, I have nothing baked, only a handful of flour in a jar and a little oil in a jug. So here I am collecting a couple of pieces of wood so that I can come and fix it for myself and my son, so we can eat it and die." [13]Elijah said to her, "Don't be afraid. Come, act in accordance with your word, only make me a small loaf from there first and bring it out to me, and afterward make some for you and your son. [14]Because Yahweh the God of Israel has said this: 'The jar of flour will not be used up and the jug of oil will not fail until the day Yahweh gives rain on the face of the ground.'" [15]She went and acted in accordance with Elijah's word, and she and her household ate for some time. . . .

[17]After this, the son of the mistress of the household became sick. His sickness grew very serious, until no breath remained in him. [18]She said to Elijah, "What is between you and me, man of God? You have come to me to draw attention to my waywardness and to cause my son to die." [19]He said to her, "Give me your son." He took him out of her arms and took him up to the upper room where he was living and lay him on his bed [20]and called to Yahweh and said, "Yahweh my God, are you really going to bring trouble on the woman with whom I am residing, by causing her son to die? [21]He stretched out over the boy three times and called to Yahweh, "Yahweh my God, may this boy's breath return to his body!" [22]Yahweh listened to the voice of Elijah, and the boy's breath returned to his body and he came alive. [23]Elijah took the boy and brought him down from the upper room into the house and gave him to his mother. Elijah said, "Look, your son is alive." [24]The woman said to Elijah, "Now I acknowledge that you are a man of God. The word of Yahweh in your mouth is truthful."

I have just deleted an e-mail from a student in whose life I saw something of a miracle a few months ago. She had been diagnosed as having a brain tumor and was hastily scheduled for an emergency operation to try to remove it. The surgeons were not sure this would work, though her mother said on the eve of the operation, "There are so many people praying about this tumor, it doesn't have a chance." This was of course whistling in the wind. Prayer doesn't work like that. But when the surgeons opened up the woman's head, they couldn't find a tumor, and they are still scratching their own heads about it. That doesn't prove that a miracle happened; they are still assuming that there is some "natural" explanation. But it's hard for those of us who were involved to believe that what happened was pure chance.

It's equally impossible to prove that a miracle happened to this boy; maybe the "miracle" lay in the coincidence of timing in connection with Elijah's action and the boy's spontaneous recovery or coming back to life. It's not quite clear whether the boy was near death or had actually died; in the latter case, it would be better to call this a resuscitation than a resurrection, because he is not raised to a new kind of life in the way Jesus will be. Either way, you won't find his mother taking the possibility that his recovery is a coincidence any more seriously than my student's mother can. Further, it is a neatly matter-of-fact, human story. No angels appear, and no bolts from heaven, or even ravens and miraculously lasting flour and oil. It's easy enough to picture it happening and to imagine the human emotions the story describes.

Typically of the Old Testament, the personal and the political interweave in the story. Its background lies in events in the last verses of the previous chapter. In the manner of Solomon, Ahab encourages political relationships with Tyre, the big power to the northeast, by marrying one of the king's daughters, Jezebel. This requires him to facilitate the practice of her faith and thus the erecting of an **altar** to the **Master** and an **Asherah** in the new capital his father had built. It is in light of Ahab's political and religious policies that Elijah declares there is going to be a drought. It is hardly possible to imagine a bigger catastrophe. If there is no rain, nothing grows, people have nothing to eat, and they die. Further, there is some logic about an Israelite prophet declaring that there will be a catastrophe taking this particular form. Whereas there are situations in which the most important practical thing **Yahweh** can do for Israel is protect and deliver it from its enemies (the exodus and Reed Sea story illustrate that), in the regular course of life when the political situation is more settled, the most important practical thing Yahweh can do for Israel is to make sure the country gets the rain it needs. The question is, can Israel trust Yahweh to do so? People such as the local **Canaanites** and their relatives to the northeast, the **Phoenicians**, where Jezebel came from, believed that the Master was the one who did so. By facilitating the worship of the Master in Samaria because it is his wife's faith, Ahab was giving the impression that this might be the case, and other passages make clear enough that many (most?) Israelites were at least prepared to hedge their bets by praying to the Master as well as to Yahweh.

As Yahweh's servant, therefore, Elijah declares that there will be neither rain nor dew (through the summer months dew is also key to the harvest) except when he says so. This sudden declaration is remarkable in a number of ways. Elijah appears like a bolt out of the blue. Indeed, prophecy of this kind appears out of the blue; the power he assumes has no precedent. We know nothing of his background except that he comes from the other side of the Jordan. Who he is as a person does not matter; what happens is that he is a **man of God**, someone taken hold of by God. We know nothing of his call. We hear nothing of God's telling him to say there will be a drought; it is he who says it. He is almost like one of the supernatural divine **aides** who speak as if they are a kind of incarnation of God. In fact, at the close of the story the woman declares not that she now knows that Yahweh is God but that she now knows that Elijah is a man of God who truly speaks a reliable word from God. To recognize Elijah is to recognize Yahweh.

During the drought, God will provide for Elijah by means of an isolated stream he will live near and by means of the help of some scavengers, but a wash (a stream in a valley or ravine that can get very full in the rainy season) can dry up in the summer, and can certainly do so during a drought. No doubt God could have specially provided Elijah with water, but instead God takes him all the way from the southeast of **Ephraim** to the far northwest and beyond Ephraim into the very territory of Jezebel and her father. If you believed in gods who had their own territories, then there is no doubt that this is the Master's territory. So Elijah's being the means of Yahweh's providing for a needy person there carries the conflict into enemy territory and demonstrates that Yahweh is truly God in Phoenicia as well as in Ephraim. The widow's providing for him implies a recognition that he is someone who stands for Yahweh and that this counts for something.

The need to bring her son back to life would make it possible to extend the point. Canaanites and Israelites were also inclined to assume that the Master was the lord of life and death, the one who decided whether children were born and whether people lived or died. There in the Master's territory Elijah demonstrates that it is Yahweh who has that power. Yet the story does not make that point and at this moment focuses on the personal rather than the political or religious. Here is a woman who has committed herself to Yahweh's servant, letting this foreigner with his strange God use her spare room because he needs somewhere to live. She has pain in her heart and the usual human instinct to think that God is punishing her when things go wrong in her life. Will God really have her son die? Actually the answer is, yes God often will do so. But this time God does not, which encourages Israelites to be open to the possibility that the God who definitely can do miracles of this kind might do one for them.

## 1 KINGS 18:1–18

### On Rendering to Caesar and Rendering to God

[1]After a long period, Yahweh's word came to Elijah, in the second year: "Go and appear to Ahab, and I will give rain on the face of the ground." [2]So Elijah went to appear to Ahab. Now the famine was severe in Samaria, [3]and Ahab had summoned Obadiah, who was over his household. (Obadiah was someone who revered Yahweh deeply. [4]When Jezebel cut off Yahweh's prophets, Obadiah had got a hundred prophets and hid them, fifty people to a cave, and provided them with food and water.)

5Ahab said to Obadiah, "Go through the country, to all the springs of water and all the washes. Perhaps we will find grass so we can keep the horses and mules alive and not be left without animals." 6They divided the country between them to go through it. Ahab went on his own one way; Obadiah went on his own the other way. 7Obadiah was on the way, and there: Elijah met him. [Obadiah] recognized him and fell on his face, and said, "Is this you, my lord Elijah?" 8He said to him, "It's me. Go and say to your lord, 'Elijah is here.'" 9He said, "What wrong have I done that you are giving your servant into the power of Ahab, to kill him? 10As Yahweh your God lives, there is no nation or kingdom to which my lord has not sent to seek you out. When they say, 'He is not here,' he makes the kingdom or nation swear that it cannot find you. 11Now you are saying, 'Go and say to your lord, "Elijah is here,"' 12and when I go from you, Yahweh's spirit will carry you somewhere I don't know, and when I come to tell Ahab and he doesn't find you, he will slay me. Your servant has been revering Yahweh from his youth. 13My lord has surely been told what I did when Jezebel slew Yahweh's prophets and I hid a hundred of Yahweh's prophets, fifty people to a cave, and provided them with bread and water. 14Now you are saying, 'Go and say to your lord, "Elijah is here,"' and he will slay me." 15Elijah said, "As Yahweh Armies lives, before whom I stand [in attendance], I will appear to him today." 16So Obadiah went to meet Ahab and told him, and Ahab went to meet Elijah. 17When Ahab saw Elijah, Ahab said to him, "Is it you, troubler of Israel?" 18He said, "I have not troubled Israel. Rather, you and your father's household have, by forsaking Yahweh's commands and following the Masters."

Two friends of mine work in a Middle Eastern country where it is illegal to seek to get people to come to believe in Christ. Their own position is secure because they work in the expatriate church in the capital, and it is OK for them to minister to Christians there and OK for Christians to worship Christ there. It is OK for Westerners, that is, though three local believers were killed for doing so and/or for allegedly speaking about Christ to other people; in a way, one hopes that this allegation was true. But my friends would be expelled if they were discovered to have been seeking to lead local people to faith in Christ.

Somehow they have to "render to Caesar what is Caesar's and to God the things that are God's," and in so doing be as "clever as snakes and as harmless as doves" (see Matthew 10:16; 22:21).

Elijah and Obadiah have to do so, and they exemplify two ways of handling this obligation as both of them seek to bring about radical change in **Ephraim**. It is not the case that only one of the two ways is right; both ways may be effective, and which you adopt may reflect your own personality as well as your vocation and your assessment of the tactical situation. Elijah (as the story is about to show) is a man who makes no compromises, gives in to no fears or pressures, and takes no prisoners. Obadiah is a similarly loyal and committed servant of **Yahweh Armies.** His name actually means "one who serves **Yahweh**" (there is a prophetic book associated with an Obadiah, but this seems to be another prophet of the same name who lived later). But he tries to be a servant of Yahweh who works via the structures and the political realities. Elijah has simply declared that God's judgment is coming and has walked out on Ahab. To judge from the way be behaves in this present story, he has not got out merely because he is concerned for his own safety. He is quite ready to confront Ahab. It was as a **man of God**, a man who mediates God's word and God's action, that he abandoned Ahab. It signified that God had done so. Ahab's reason for trying to hunt Elijah down relates to that fact. Paradoxically, Ahab both recognizes and does not recognize that Elijah has supernatural power, the power to stop the rain. He doesn't submit to Elijah and his God, but he also wants to stop Elijah from exercising that power.

In contrast, Obadiah has stayed on in Samaria, working in a very responsible position as palace administrator while seeking still to be someone who "reveres Yahweh," someone who can call Elijah his "lord" while also calling Ahab his "lord." In one sense that is an easier stance; in another sense it is a tougher one. He is a kind of double agent. He is a member of Ahab's court and draws his pay from there, and he is involved in trying to mitigate the effect of the drought on Ahab and his administration—the drought that his God has caused. (When the story speaks of Ahab's and Obadiah's undertaking a mission each on his own, it will mean they are separate from each

other; they will have a group of other people with them.) Bu
he hides scores of prophets when Ahab wants to capture them,
which requires quite some organizational skills as well as some
bravery. It also opens another window on a scene we would not
otherwise have guessed at. There are hundreds of prophets in
Ephraim, though Jezebel has had many of them killed. These
will perhaps be prophets who offered counsel and brought
God's word to ordinary people in the ordinary situations of
their lives, a little like Elijah himself in his relationship with the
widow at Zarephat. We will discover more about them from
the Elisha stories.

It is the second year—presumably the second year of the
drought. Yahweh and Elijah have offered evidence that Yahweh is God and that Elijah is Yahweh's prophet by declaring
that there would be no rain. There has been no rain. But if you
were looking for a reason not to listen to Elijah, you could say
that was a coincidence. So now God says the opposite. When
Elijah's word again comes true, the evidence will be harder to
evade. In other words, the reason rain will come is not that
God thinks that enough is enough or that God has compassion
for the people (though no doubt God does). The story is about
showing who is God here. It is humorous for us but no joke for
Obadiah that in this connection Elijah wants Obadiah to risk
blowing his cover. There is an incidental insight here on the
way prophecy works. In our own day, sometimes people make
pronouncements about a disaster that has happened, declaring
that it is an act of God's judgment on wrongs in the society—
characteristically the wrongs that were these people's "favorite"
ones. Elijah's judgment is more impressive. He doesn't say after
a drought has come that it was an act of God's judgment. He
says there will be a drought, and there is. One reason is that
he is not merely predicting a drought. He is commissioning it.
He makes it happen. That is what he can do as a man of God.
Which is indeed why Ahab needs to silence him.

There is another piece of background that underlies the
story. We often picture Israel in Elijah's day simply as a nation
that had descended from the Israel of Moses' day, though we
allow for the "conversion" of some individuals such as Rahab
and Ruth and maybe for the submission of some people like the

vho tricked Joshua into giving them green cards. In
loesn't require much reading between the lines of
a Joshua to Kings to see that the people who came
...an from outside have assimilated thousands and
thousands of people who were in Canaan already. The problem
is that the assimilation easily goes the other way. Throughout
the story, the faith of Canaan threatens to overwhelm the faith
of Moses, and archaeological investigations confirm that fact
in the evidence they have unearthed of religion as it was practiced in Israel. To most Israelites, for a prophet such as Elijah to
urge them to worship Yahweh alone would seem like a religious
revolution.

Revolutionaries are troublemakers, and this is what Ahab
calls Elijah, but of course that is exactly how Elijah sees Ahab.

## 1 KINGS 18:19–46

### There Are Times When You Have to Choose

[19]"Now. Send to gather all Israel to me at Mount Carmel, with
the four hundred and fifty prophets of the Master and the four
hundred prophets of Asherah who eat at Jezebel's table." [20]So
Ahab sent to all the Israelites and gathered the prophets to
Mount Carmel. [21]Elijah came near to all the people and said,
"How long are you going to dither between two positions?
If Yahweh is God, follow him. If it's the Master, follow him."
But the people did not answer him a word. [22]Elijah said to
the people, "I am the only prophet of Yahweh who is left. The
Master's prophets are four hundred and fifty. [23]So two bulls
are to be given to us. They can choose one bull for themselves,
divide it up, and put it on the wood, but not make a fire. I will fix
the other bull and put it on the wood, but not make a fire. [24]You
will call in your god's name; I will call in Yahweh's name. The
God who answers by fire—he is God." All the people answered,
"What you say is good." [25]Elijah said to the Master's prophets,
"Choose one bull for yourselves and fix it first, because there
are many of you. Call on your god's name but do not make a
fire." [26]They took the bull they were given and prepared it and
called on the Master's name from morning to midday, saying,
"Master, answer us," but there was no sound, no one answering.

They jumped on the altar that had been made. [27] At midday Elijah mocked at them: "Call in a loud voice, because he is a god, because he is talking or away or on a journey or perhaps asleep, and he will wake up." [28] So they called in a loud voice and slashed themselves in accordance with their custom with swords and spears until blood flowed over them. [29] After midday passed they prophesied until [the time for] presenting the [evening] offering, but there was no sound, no one answering, no paying attention.

[30] Then Elijah said to all the people, "Come near me." All the people came near to him, and he repaired Yahweh's demolished altar. [31] Elijah took twelve stones, in accordance with the number of the twelve clans of the sons of Jacob (to whom Yahweh's word had come, "Israel will be your name"). [32] He built the stones into an altar in Yahweh's name and made a trench, like a receptacle for two seahs of seed, around the altar. [33] He laid out the wood and cut up the bull and put it on the wood. [34] He said, "Fill four jars with water and pour it over the burnt offering and over the wood...." [36] At the time for presenting the [evening] offering, the prophet Elijah came near and said, "Yahweh, God of Abraham, Isaac, and Israel, today may it be acknowledged that you are God in Israel and that I am your servant and that by your word I have done all these things. [37] Answer me, Yahweh, answer me, so that this people may acknowledge that you Yahweh are God and that you yourself have turned their spirit back." [38] Fire from Yahweh fell and consumed the burnt offering, the wood, the stones, and the dirt, and licked up the water in the trench. [39] All the people saw and fell on their faces and said, "Yahweh, he is God. Yahweh, he is God." [40] Elijah said to them, "Seize the Master's prophets. None of them must escape." They seized them, and Elijah took them down to the Kishon wash and slaughtered them there. [41] Elijah said to Ahab, "Go up, eat and drink, because the rumbling sound is rain...." [46] Yahweh's hand came on Elijah. He hitched up his clothes and ran ahead of Ahab until he came to Jezreel.

The soccer World Cup is about to start in South Africa, and I have just had a letter about it from a friend in Lebanon. Lebanon doesn't have a team playing in the World Cup, so people in that country choose a foreign team to support and then fly its flag from their cars. My friend is from the United States, but the

United States hasn't decided to be a world-class soccer nation either, but his wife is Korean by birth, so for them the decision was easy. They have bought a big Korean flag for their car. Now, as it happens I am also reading a book about the Middle East titled *The Media Relations Department of Hizbollah Wishes You a Happy Birthday*. This book also tells of choices that people in Lebanon have to make, and in a sense these choices may also be easy—or rather, people may not feel they have much choice about which community to belong to and whose orders to take. Yet the consequences of the choices may be a matter of life and death. In some situations the decision about what religion to follow may not seem a costly one, particularly in a Western context where religion is a matter of people's private lives.

The **Ephraimites**' decision in 1 Kings 19 was tougher, more like that of the Lebanese today. (Ironically, Lebanon was the region where Jezebel came from.) Indeed, for the Ephraimites it was a matter of life and death. The beginning of the present story may seem to have made it obvious which decision they need to make. Elijah had said there would be a drought because people had turned away from **Yahweh**, hadn't he? There is a drought, isn't there? It's a no-brainer. Yet when you are inside a situation, decisions may look more complicated. That's true for individuals; it may be obvious to someone else what I should do in particular circumstances, but it may not be obvious to me. The same may apply to communities. When the United States was agonizing over health care reform, in general terms the kind of reform that was needed was obvious to the rest of the world, but not to the people of the United States. You have to get inside someone's thinking to see why something that is self-evident to some people is not at all self-evident to others. Elijah is urging Israel to trust in Yahweh alone for its health care, its harvest, and its security. This is counterintuitive and countercultural.

Furthermore, there are all those other prophets whose ministry the people are used to. The story opens yet another window on a reality we would not have guessed. As well as hundreds of prophets of Yahweh, Ephraim has four hundred and fifty prophets who serve in the name of the **Master** and almost as many who serve in the name of **Asherah**. They all have royal patronage and support; they eat at Jezebel's table. It is easy to think of prophets as by definition servants of Yahweh, but the Old Testament recognizes that prophecy is a phenomenon Israel shares with other peoples and with the devotees of other religions. When you needed to know how some sickness might turn out or what to do about it, or what had happened to an animal you had lost, or how long a drought might last, there were hundreds of people with prophetic gifts who might be able to discover what the Master or Asherah had to reveal about such a question.

So Ephraimites have two options. They can look to Yahweh, or they can look to the Master and Asherah. Elijah requires them to make up their minds. It's a matter of guesswork why the contest takes place on Mount Carmel, the long mountain ridge that runs southeast to northwest from the heartland of Ephraim to the Mediterranean. Maybe the point is that this is border territory between Ephraim and **Phoenicia**, Jezebel's territory. Related to that possibility is the fact that Elijah has to build up Yahweh's **altar** there, which suggests it has been torn down—perhaps because Phoenician-style worship has taken over in that region.

In a sense Elijah makes it easy for the people. With scatological delight he demonstrates that the Master's prophets cannot meet his challenge, but he can. In the summer the Master seemed to die; when the rains came in the fall, it was a sign that he had come back to life. The prophets' gashing of themselves then identifies with the dying Master and seeks to bring him back to life. One recalls the sarcastic description of the **Babylonian** gods as needing to be carried by their devotees; I thought God was supposed to carry you, Isaiah 46 comments.

I wish Elijah hadn't killed all those other prophets. Maybe God feels the same; the story doesn't say that God told Elijah to do so, nor does it directly express an opinion on his doing so. I also wish Jesus didn't talk about people going to hell and didn't say that his twelve students were going to judge the twelve Israelite clans and didn't talk about Jerusalem falling again, and I wish Jerusalem hadn't fallen again in AD 70. In judging, the Twelve will act as Jesus' representatives, and implicitly it is as God's representative that Elijah executes the prophets, as it was

as God's representative that he had declared that there would
be a drought and then that there would be rain. He acts as a
"**man of God**," with scary power and authority. (He would
need some strange power in order to execute four hundred
prophets). It wasn't usually what prophets or anyone else did, as
it wasn't what God usually did. This was a extraordinary occasion, like the slaughter of **Canaanites** in Joshua or the slaughter
of Ephraimites when Samaria fell or the slaughter of Judahites
when Jerusalem fell, of which we will read later in this book.
There are occasions when God says, "That's it" and takes desperate action. It was one of those occasions. Like Jesus' warnings about hell, the story is meant to leave us horrified and to
make us face the possible consequences of making the wrong
choice about whether to follow the real God, who has made
himself known to us.

The close of the story has Elijah continuing to manifest the
supernatural power of a man of God. He knows rain is coming.
He runs back to Jezreel quicker than Ahab can drive there.

## 1 KINGS 19:1–21

### The Low, Murmuring Sound

[1]When Ahab told Jezebel all about what Elijah had done and
all about the way he had slaughtered all the prophets with the
sword, [2]Jezebel sent an aide to Elijah saying, "May the gods
do thus and may they do more if this time tomorrow I do not
make your life like the life of one of them." [3]He was afraid, and
he arose and went for his life, and came to Beersheba which
belongs to Judah. He left his boy there, [4]and he himself went
a day's journey into the wilderness. He came and sat under
a broom bush and asked for his life, that he might die. He
said, "It's too much. Take my life now, Yahweh, because I am
no better than my ancestors." [5]He lay down and slept under
a broom bush. And there—an aide was touching him and
saying, "Get up and eat." [6]He looked, and there—by his head
a loaf baked on coals and a jar of water. He ate and drank, and
lay down again. [7]Yahweh's aide came back a second time and
touched him and said, "Get up and eat, because the journey is
too much for you." [8]He got up and ate and drank, and went in

the strength of that food forty days and forty nights as far as God's mountain, Horeb.

⁹He came to a cave there and spent the night there. Then: Yahweh's word came to him. He said to him, "What are you doing here, Elijah?" ¹⁰He said, "I have been very passionate for Yahweh, the God of Armies, because the Israelites have abandoned your covenant. Your altar they have demolished; your prophets they have slaughtered with the sword. I am the only one who is left, and they are seeking to take my life." ¹¹He said, "Come out and stand on the mountain before Yahweh." And there—a great, strong wind was passing by, splitting mountains and breaking up crags before Yahweh (Yahweh was not in the wind), after the wind an earthquake (Yahweh was not in the earthquake), ¹²after the earthquake a fire (Yahweh was not in the fire), and after the fire a low murmuring sound. ¹³When Elijah heard it, he wrapped his face in his coat and went out and stood at the cave's entrance. And there—a voice came to him and said, "What are you doing here, Elijah?" ¹⁴He said, "I have been very passionate for Yahweh, the God of Armies, because the Israelites have abandoned your covenant. Your altar they have demolished, your prophets they have slaughtered with the sword. I am the only one who is left, and they are seeking to take my life." ¹⁵Yahweh said to him, "Go, return by the way you came, to the Damascus wilderness. When you come there, anoint Hazael as king of Aram. ¹⁶And Jehu son of Nimshi you are to anoint as king over Israel, and Elisha son of Shaphat from Abel Meholah you are to anoint as prophet in your place. ¹⁷The person who escapes Hazael's sword, Jehu will kill. The person who escapes Jehu's sword, Elisha will kill. ¹⁸But I have left in Israel seven thousand, all the knees that have not bowed to the Master and every mouth that has not kissed him."

¹⁹So he went from there and found Elisha son of Shaphat. He was plowing with twelve pairs [of oxen] ahead of him; he was with the twelfth. Elijah went over to him and threw his coat over him. ²⁰[Elisha] abandoned the animals and ran after Elijah and said, "I'll just kiss my father and mother and follow you," but he said to him, "Go back, because what have I done to you?" ²¹He went back from following him, took the pair of oxen, and slaughtered them. With the equipment of the oxen [as firewood] he cooked them [as] the meat, and gave it to the people, and they ate. Then he arose and followed Elijah and ministered to him.

I am inclined to think that nothing I do in seeking to fulfill my vocation achieves anything. My vocation is to help people understand the Old Testament and let their thinking and their lives be shaped by it. I am passionately committed to this task and want to carry on seeking to fulfill it rather than retire and spend more time cycling on the boardwalk, but I am inclined to think I totally fail. It is not because I am incompetent but because the odds are stacked so high by the church's ignoring of the Old Testament, especially in our culture over recent decades. Nothing I can do, like writing all these commentaries or having four or five hundred students in my classes every year, can make a significant difference. This raises the question of why I continue seeking to fulfill this vocation, and I guess the answer is contained within the question. It is my vocation.

So in my microscopic way I identify with Elijah when he comes to the conclusion that his work as a prophet is a total failure; and the way God deals with me overlaps with the way God speaks to Elijah. From time to time God gets some graduate to e-mail me to describe how she has been running a Bible Study on (say) Psalms in light of the way we studied them in class, and how it has revolutionized the way the group members pray. Elijah is inclined to see things as bleaker than they are and to think that he is the only prophet (or the only person?) loyal to **Yahweh** who is still left. Is it the case that he knows how to stand up to a man like Ahab but not a woman like Jezebel?

Whether that's so or not, he runs for his life. It would take some days to get to Beersheba, the effective southern boundary of Judah. Has his young assistant had enough when they get there? Elijah has not had enough. Does he know where he is going? Is he just running like a maniac? After another day, for the first time he stops for breath, and for the first time he talks to God. God does not respond to his desperation except by providing him with sustenance. At some point he becomes set on traveling through the wilderness for another week or so to get to where God had long ago appeared to Moses. It is the only occasion in the Bible when someone makes such a pilgrimage. God intends to deal with him there and sustains him so as to be able to do so. On almost any theory of the location of Mount Sinai or Mount Horeb (both names are used in the Old

90

Testament) it wouldn't take a literal forty days to get there, but it sounds like a symbolic number, and it was the time Moses himself spent on Mount Sinai.

God appears to him there and gently points out that he is not the only person left. Perhaps not gently. The way God speaks to Elijah first involves wind, earthquake, and fire, then a low murmuring sound. The King James Version has "a still, small voice," but the expression is more elusive than that phrase implies. The story does not say that God is in the quiet sound though not in the earthquake, the wind, and the fire. The point the story makes in this connection is that you shouldn't identify God with earthquake, wind, and fire, which it might be tempting to do. Old and New Testament will continue affirming that God is the God of earthquake, wind, and fire, and for Elijah these reaffirm the power and might of his God, which he was in danger of forgetting (likewise Old and New Testament will not subsequently picture God as characteristically speaking through a still, small voice). He gets the reassurance that God is still the kind of God who appeared to Moses and the Israelites at Sinai.

Having established that fact, God has a new, threefold commission for Elijah. One aspect of it is that he is to anoint a new king of **Ephraim** in place of Ahab. This is not very surprising. Ahab has clearly tested God's long-suffering to destruction, and God is going to repeat the pattern with which we have become familiar. God had commissioned a prophet to tell Jeroboam he was to terminate Rehoboam's **authority** in Ephraim, had told Jeroboam's wife he intended to terminate the rule of Jeroboam's household there, and had commissioned a prophet to tell Baasha that his number was also up. Now God commissions the anointing of the first king in yet another line.

Either side of that anointing, however, are two more surprising anointings. First there is to be a new king in **Aram**, the area to the northeast approximately equivalent to modern Syria. This act of Elijah signifies that Yahweh is not merely a local god with power in Israel. Yahweh is God on the international scale. It is a conviction that will be central to the teaching of later prophets. The way history works out relates to what God is doing with Israel. The bad news in the present context is that Aram is to be a chief troubler of Israel for a century or two.

Further, Elijah is to anoint Elisha as his successor. This is also odd, because prophets do not get anointed. Anointing is a ceremony whereby the community sets apart a priest or a king and designates him as having been given authority by God. Only here and in Isaiah 61 is there reference to a prophet's being anointed. It rather looks as if God speaks metaphorically, because Elijah never actually anoints anyone. He does designate Elisha as his successor and thereby begins a chain of events whereby Hazael becomes king of Aram and Jehu becomes king of Ephraim, because Elisha does commission Hazael, and he commissions one of his own fellow prophets to anoint Jehu.

# 1 KINGS 20:1–21:7
### In the World and Also of the World

[1]Now Ben-hadad, king of Aram, had gathered his entire army; thirty-two kings were with him, along with horses and chariotry. He went up and besieged Samaria, and made war against it. [2]He sent aides to the city to Ahab the king of Israel [3]and said to him, "Ben-hadad has said this: 'Your silver and gold are mine; your lovely wives and children are mine.'" [4]The king of Israel replied, "In accordance with your word, my lord king, I and all that I have are yours. . . ." [13]But there: a certain prophet approached Ahab king of Israel and said, "Yahweh has said this: 'You see all this great force? Now. I am giving it into your hand today, and you will acknowledge that I am Yahweh. . . .'" [15]So he mobilized the young men of the provincial officers (they were two hundred and thirty-two) and after them mobilized the entire company, all the Israelites (seven thousand) [16]and they went out at midday. Ben-hadad was getting drunk in the tents, he and the thirty-two kings supporting him. . . . [20b]The Arameans fled and the Israelites pursued them. Ben-hadad king of Aram escaped on a horse, as did the cavalry. . . . [22] But the prophet approached the king of Israel and said to him, "Go, strengthen yourself, discover and see what you are to do, because at the turn of the year the king of Aram is going to come up against you."

*[Verses 23–43 relate how Ahab wins another victory against Aram despite huge odds, but a prophet condemns him for making a peace treaty with Ben-hadad.]*

<sup>21:1</sup>Some time afterward, Naboth the Jezreelite had a vineyard in Jezreel next to the palace of Ahab, king of Samaria. <sup>2</sup>Ahab spoke to Naboth: "Give me your vineyard so that it can be my vegetable garden, because it is right next to my house. In its place I will give you a better vineyard; [or] if it is good in your eyes, I will give you the price in silver." <sup>3</sup>But Naboth said to Ahab, "Yahweh forbid that I give you my ancestors' possession." <sup>4</sup>Ahab came home resentful and irate because of the word that Naboth had spoken to him. . . . He lay on his bed and turned his face away, and did not eat anything. . . . <sup>7</sup> His wife Jezebel said to him, "You are to exercise kingship over Israel now. Get up, eat something. Be cheerful. I myself will give you the vineyard of Naboth the Jezreelite."

I am getting ready for a task force that is meeting next week to discuss the use of the Bible in the Anglican Communion worldwide. The meeting will be complicated because we include members of the Episcopal Church in the United States as well as people who have left the Episcopal Church and in effect formed an alternative Anglican Church in the United States. The latter includes several parishes near where I live, and that development has resulted in monumentally expensive court cases to decide whether church buildings belong to the Episcopal Church or whether parishes that leave can take their buildings with them. Now, it's easy enough to accept that splits are happening in the church; that has been so from the beginning of the church's history, but there seems to be something odd about Christians taking one another to court in connection with them (as Paul notes in 1 Corinthians 6). How do we go about living in the world but living as people of God?

Poor Ahab is clueless about the question. In fact he seems clueless, period. He is a tragic figure, like Captain Ahab in *Moby Dick* who is named after him. He is king because his father was king; that was the only qualification he needed. The trouble is that his monarchy is not nominal like modern European monarchies. He exercises real power and has to make real decisions. Because he is a king in Israel, he is expected to make such decisions in light of the reality of God's relationship with Israel, but he also has to make them in light of the fact that he and his people live in the visible, material world alongside and interwoven with other kings and peoples. He is supposed to live in the world but not to be of the world, but the challenge is too big.

It was too big when it came to war. We know from chapter 19 that Ben-hadad's days are numbered, and when Ben-hadad shows up at the beginning of chapter 20, we half expect the story to tell us how God's declaration about him finds fulfillment, how he loses his throne and his life. If that is how things were supposed to work out, Ahab prevents them from doing so. We also know that Ahab's days are numbered, and we might also (or alternatively) have expected that Ben-hadad's attack on Samaria was a means whereby God chastised Ephraim for the apostasy in which Ahab led the people. The surprising good news for Ahab is that this is not so. Ben-hadad comes from **Aram** with a body of kings representing his empire (in our terms, they would be something like the mayors of their cities), and insists that Ahab surrender to it. Ahab doesn't mind surrendering his silver and gold and his best wives and children (!), but then Ben-hadad demands everything else. Ahab laments this to his people, and they urge him to stand firm. He does so rather splendidly with a challenge, pointing out that boasting about victory when you are fastening your sword onto your belt is one thing, but boasting about victory when you are unfastening your sword (that is, when the battle is won) is another. A prophet brings Ahab God's promise to surrender Ben-hadad's army to him and gives him God's victory plan, which Ahab implements.

The prophet returns and urges Ahab not to relax but to be ready for another attack. This time Ben-hadad makes the mistake of slandering **Yahweh**: "They beat us because we fought in the mountains, on their god's territory." As usual, the Israelites lacked the sophisticated military hardware of their opponents, but in the mountains this did not matter so much. Ben-hadad sees this as a fact of theological significance. Yahweh will not be able to win like that in the plain. So that is where he takes on the Ephraimites next time. A **man of God** assures Ahab that Yahweh will obviously have to show him where he is mistaken. The Israelites win an astounding victory, but then Ahab behaves in a magnanimous way of which we would approve but of which

God does not approve. Generous in victory, he declines to execute Ben-hadad and rather makes a **covenant** with him. This rings bells. The Judahite king Asa once made an alliance or covenant with a Ben-hadad (see chapter 15). It's probably a different Ben-hadad; the name is more a title than a personal name. But the issues are the same. What is Ephraim doing, as a people who allegedly belongs to Yahweh the God of Israel, in making a covenant with a king of Aram? "Because you set free the man I intended to be '**devoted**,' your life will become a substitute for his life, your people for his people." Ahab is behaving in a civilized and politically acute way, but that means living in the world's way, being in the world and also of the world. Thus rebuked, he goes home resentful and irate. He was only doing his best to behave in the wisest possible way.

He soon has more reason for feeling resentful and irate. By Western standards, Israel has a revolutionary view about land. Land belongs to God. God did, after all, create it. Human beings can't own land. They can't buy it, and they can't sell it. As the owner of the land, God is quite willing to let people use it. Indeed, God is keen on doing so; God created humanity to serve the land. So God allocates the land to people in order that they can serve it. God does so on the macro scale, allocating their territory to different countries. In Israel's case, God then does so on a smaller scale, in requiring that Israel allocate the land to the twelve clans by lot—that is a way of letting God make the decisions. It is then left to the individual clans to allocate the land to the groups and families within it. One can see that this arrangement might work OK when people are scattered over the country without there being a central government, but once there is a central government and once there are cities, things become more complicated. When the government needs land, it needs to be able to claim eminent domain (in U.S.-speak), to make compulsory purchase (in Brit-speak), while giving people proper compensation for the loss of their land for the good of the nation as a whole. Ahab makes that assumption. The trouble is that Naboth is old school. The vineyard that it would be convenient for the king to acquire has been Naboth's family holding for generations, and another equally good vineyard somewhere else would not be the same.

Two worldviews are clashing. Once again Ahab wants to live in the world on the basis of the assumptions that regularly obtain in the world. How can he run an efficient administration if he can't make strategic decisions about the land that adjoins the palace? He is clueless about how to deal with the way Naboth behaves, but fortunately he has a wife who knows what to do.

# 1 KINGS 21:8–29

## The Capital of Corruption

[8][Jezebel] wrote documents in Ahab's name, sealed them with his seal, and sent the documents to the elders and the citizens who lived in the city with Naboth. [9]She wrote in the documents: "Call for a fast and seat Naboth in front of the people, [10]and seat two worthless men opposite him. They are to testify against him: 'You have reviled God and the king.' Then take him out and stone him to death." [11]The men of the city, the elders and the citizens who lived in his city, did as Jezebel sent to them. . . . [14]They sent to Jezebel: "Naboth has been stoned to death." [15]When Jezebel heard that Naboth had been stoned to death, Jezebel said to Ahab, "Get up, take possession of the vineyard of Naboth the Jezreelite which he refused to give you for silver, because Naboth is not alive. He's dead. . . ." [17]But Yahweh's word came to Elijah the Tishbite, [18]"Arise, go down to meet Ahab king of Israel who is in Samaria. There, he is in Naboth's vineyard, where he has gone down to take possession of it. [19]Speak to him: 'Yahweh has said this: "Have you murdered and then taken possession?"' Speak to him: 'Yahweh has said this: "In the place where dogs lapped up Naboth's blood, dogs will lap up your blood, yours too."'" [20]Ahab said to Elijah, "Have you found me, my enemy?" He said, "I have found you, because you sold yourself to do what is wrong in Yahweh's eyes. [21]Now I: I am going to bring trouble on you. I am going to consume you up and cut off for Ahab those who urinate against a wall (bond and freed) in Israel. [22]I will make your household like the household of Jeroboam son of Nebat and the household of Baasha son of Ahijah, for the provocation you have offered. You made Israel sin.' [23]Yahweh also spoke about Jezebel: 'The dogs will eat Jezebel on the rampart of Jezreel. [24]The person who belongs to Ahab who dies in the city the dogs will eat;

the person who dies in the open country the birds in the heavens will eat. . . .'" ²⁷When Ahab heard these words, he tore his clothes and put sackcloth on his body, and fasted. He slept in sackcloth and went about quietly. ²⁸Yahweh's word came to Elijah the Tishbite: ²⁹"Have you seen that Ahab has bowed down before me? Because he has bowed down before me, I will not bring the trouble in his days. In the days of his son I will bring the trouble on his household."

Sitting on the subway on the way home last night, I overheard a conversation between two young men about the candidates for our upcoming gubernatorial elections. (Isn't that a great word, *gubernatorial*? We don't have it in British English, presumably because we don't have governors. The word *gubernatorial* rolls around your mouth, somehow.) One of them was lamenting the fact that the only reason people were in politics was to make money for themselves and that they spend much of their time swindling us ordinary people by means of taxes in order to spend the funds on prestige projects that are of little value to ordinary people. It reminded me of one or two news items I have noticed that have proclaimed this city or that city the corruption capital of the United States. The corruption often involves politics and the rigging of elections, but the main point is money.

It's not clear whether Ahab has moved his capital to Jezreel, and the story does describe him as "the king of Israel who is in Samaria," but evidently he has a palace in Jezreel, in the wide fertile vale in the center of **Ephraim**. Whether it is the official capital or not, Jezreel now becomes the nation's corruption capital. The rather childish way Ahab reacts to Naboth's refusal to sell his vineyard suggests he is a somewhat pathetic figure whose cluelessness contrasts with his wife's capacity to get things done. Maybe it is no coincidence that Elijah has not shown the slightest fear of Ahab but that he fled for his life when Jezebel declared the intention to treat him the way he himself had treated the **Master**'s prophets. Indeed, it can be easy for a man to know how to deal with a strong man but not easy to know how to deal with a strong woman. Further, as a **Phoenician** Jezebel takes for granted some assumptions about the relationship between religion and politics that contrast with the ones that the Israelites were supposed to hold and ones that are very common in other cultures. Like many people in Britain and the United States, she assumed there was a close relationship between her religious commitment and her national or political identity. The idea of distinguishing commitment to Caesar and commitment to God would seem odd. The Master committed the government of the nation to the king; the king served the Master, or (in Ahab's case) served **Yahweh**—whether you called God "the Master" or "Yahweh" mightn't make much difference to her. Either way, in insisting on holding onto his land when the king needed it, Naboth was resisting the religious and political basis on which the nation worked. At the same time, Jezebel evidently recognized the tension between her religious and political assumptions and the ones that her husband's society would recognize, and that is why she has to find a way of putting Naboth in his place that will work for them.

The elders would be the heads of the families in the city; the citizens would include the other adult males in these families, though not the servants, employees, and resident aliens. Such people might be more likely to be committed to Yahweh's way of looking at things than Jezebel was, and the story may not imply she actually took them into her confidence about the witnesses being liars. But the surface meaning of the story is that she could indeed trust them to collude with her and that she simply needed them to collude in holding a show trial. If so, she appeals to the nominal commitment of the community but knows that none of the leadership in the city truly affirms this commitment. She just has to hire a couple of people to lie on her behalf (two such people because of the requirement in Deuteronomy 17:6). That's not difficult in any city that wants to be the corruption capital of the nation. Part of the fiendish cleverness of Jezebel's action may be that the king can legitimately take over the property of a man who is executed for blasphemy, so that is the wrong she needs to accuse him of. His action means he no longer counts as part of Israel, and his land becomes forfeit. An incidental consequence will be that his family lose their land and are thrown on the streets.

The trouble is that Ephraim is not an ordinary nation. It is part of Israel as the people of God, part of Yahweh's people, a people that is special to God. God does not send prophets to corruption capitals in Britain or the United States because they do not have a special place in God's purpose (though of course God expects the church to operate prophetically). God did send one to Ahab.

One feature of the judgment God announces is that there is a kind of poetic justice about it. Ahab's blood will be shed where Naboth's blood was shed. The point about judgment is to restore the situation when things have got out of kilter, to restore balance, and this judgment will do so in a way that people can see so that they are reassured that God makes things work out. A second feature is that there is a consistency about God's judgment. It is not arbitrary. There is a pattern about the leadership of Jeroboam, Baasha, and Ahab, and there will be a pattern about their judgment. That point is underscored by the wording that recurs from earlier declarations of judgment—in the way the males are described and in the references to scavenger dogs eating up the remains of people on whom God's judgment has come.

Once again Ahab shows himself to be spineless, though on this occasion it works to his advantage. Jezebel is a woman who has made up her mind. She knows whom she serves. Ahab can be pushed this way and that, and Elijah pushes him. Elijah does not bid him to repent and gives no hint that he has any way of escaping the judgment that Elijah declares to be imminent. But the story presupposes something fundamental about the way prophecy works. When God declares that something is about to happen, it doesn't mean it has to happen; everything depends on the way people respond to what God says. In some sense Elijah's words bring Ahab to his senses, and this gives God the excuse to be merciful, which is always God's preference. God can continue to be long-suffering.

Ahab's repentance does not undo the attitudes and practices that Ahab and his predecessors have tolerated and encouraged in Ephraim. These will continue, and judgment will eventually come on Ahab's household (we will read about this in 2 Kings 9). The implication is not that the son will be punished for the father's sins irrespective of the son's stance. If the son repents, then the prophecy can be rescinded again. But the acts of parents tend to shape their children, and it is in this sense that the parents' sins are visited on their children.

## 1 KINGS 22:1-23

### Who Will Entice Ahab?

¹They stayed for three years with no war between Aram and Israel. ²In the third year Jehoshaphat the king of Judah went down to the king of Israel. ³The king of Israel had said to his staff, "You know that Ramoth-gilead belongs to us but we are holding back from taking it from the hand of the king of Aram?" ⁴He said to Jehoshaphat, "Will you come with me to do battle at Ramoth-gilead? . . ." ⁵Jehoshaphat said to the king of Israel, "Do inquire for the word of Yahweh today." ⁶So the king of Israel gathered the prophets, some four hundred individuals, and said to them, "Shall I go up to Ramoth-gilead to do battle, or desist?" They said, "Go up, and Yahweh will give it into the king's hand." ⁷But Jehoshaphat said, "Is there not any other prophet of Yahweh here so that we can inquire of him?" ⁸The king of Israel said to Jehoshaphat, "There is one other man to inquire of Yahweh from, but I repudiate him because he does not prophesy good for me but trouble—Micaiah son of Imlah." Jehoshaphat said, "Don't say that, your majesty." ⁹So the king of Israel called to an officer and said, "Hurry Micaiah son of Imlah here." ¹⁰The king of Israel and Jehoshaphat king of Judah were sitting, each on his throne, clothed in their robes, in the open space at the entrance of the gateway at Samaria, and all the prophets were prophesying before them. ¹¹Zedekiah son of Chenaanah had made himself iron horns, and he said, "Yahweh has said this: 'With these you will gore Aram until you finish them off.'" ¹²All the prophets were prophesying in this way, saying, "Go up to Ramoth-gilead and succeed. Yahweh will give it into the king's hand," ¹³while the aide who went to summon Micaiah spoke to him: "Now. As one mouth, the prophets' words are good for the king. Your word should be like the word of one of them. Speak something good." ¹⁴Micaiah said, "As Yahweh lives, what Yahweh says to me, that is what I will speak." ¹⁵When he came to the king, the king said to him, "Mic-

aiah, shall we go up to Ramoth-gilead to do battle, or desist?"
He said to him, "Go up and succeed. Yahweh will give it into
the king's hand." [16]The king said to him, "How many times am
I going to get you to swear that you will not speak to me anything but the truth, in Yahweh's name?" [17]So he said, "I have
seen all Israel dispersing into the mountains like sheep that
have no shepherd. Yahweh said, 'These people have no master. They should go back home each of them in safety.'" [18]The
king of Israel said to Jehoshaphat, "Didn't I say to you, 'He will
not prophesy good for me, but only trouble?'" [19][Micaiah] said,
"Therefore listen to Yahweh's word. I have seen Yahweh sitting
on his throne, with all the army in the heavens standing by him
on his right and on his left. [20]Yahweh said, 'Who will entice
Ahab so that he will go up and fall at Ramoth-gilead?' One said,
'In this way' and another said 'in this way.' [21]Then a spirit came
forward and stood before Yahweh and said, 'I am the one who
will entice him.' Yahweh said to him, 'How?' [22]He said, 'I will go
and be a deceptive spirit in the mouth of all his prophets.' [Yah-
weh] said, 'You shall entice. Yes, you will be able to. Go and do
it.' [23]So now, there: Yahweh put a deceptive spirit in the mouth
of all these prophets, when Yahweh decreed trouble for you."

I've recently started rewatching the television drama series *The
West Wing* from the beginning, and last night I saw a couple
of episodes about the Democrat-run White House offering a
job to a lawyer who is a totally convinced Republican who had
just run rings around a member of the White House staff in a
debate. The president insisted on hiring her because you want
the best people on your staff, and you especially want on your
staff really able people who disagree with you. Initially, the rest
of his staff think he is crazy, but they come to see the point.

Ahab is caught by the same dilemma. In this story, Elijah has
momentarily disappeared. Micaiah's bravery and the fact that
he is evidently well-known at the **Ephraimite** court show once
again how Elijah was too gloomy when he said that he was the
only prophet left who had a real commitment to **Yahweh** and
was consequently willing to stand up to the king. Actually, for
a while Ahab also seems to have disappeared; only when Micaiah reports what Yahweh has said will Ahab be named. All this
may indicate that the story was once told on its own, separate

from the collection of stories about Elijah and Ahab, and it thus opens a window on the kind of process of telling and preserving stories that lies behind a book such as 1 Kings. Once it is interwoven with the other stories, the effect of naming Jehoshaphat and not Ahab is to imply that Ahab is not really very important, as if the storyteller can't even remember his name. That nicely reverses the way the newspapers would see it, because Ahab is a much more important political figure than Jehoshaphat, but evidently Ahab needs Judahite help if he is to realize his political and military ambitions. Gilead is an area east of the Jordan River, in the modern state of Jordan. Some of the Israelite clans had asked to settle there, but it is geographically separate from the area west of the Jordan, and one can see that the **Arameans** could take the view that it belonged more logically to them.

While less important politically, Jehoshaphat is more aware of the way to go about war. First, you ask God whether this particular war is one to undertake. (Many Western Christians think it a strange idea that God could be involved in any war, but that assumption comes from our modern culture rather than from the Bible.) Actually Ahab also knows the rules for war; indeed, any traditional society assumes you will be wise to consult God about such an action. So Ahab consults the prophets.

Evidently Jezebel has far from eliminated prophets from Ephraim. These are not prophets who acknowledge the **Master** but prophets who acknowledge Yahweh. They behave like other prophets of whom we read in the Old Testament. "Prophesying" implies something like speaking in tongues, in the manner of the prophets who met Saul and were a sign that God really was commissioning him as king (see 1 Samuel 10). The sign that Zedekiah gives is the kind of sign that Jeremiah or Ezekiel will give. His name indicates that he is a worshiper of Yahweh just as Micaiah's name does (in both names, the last syllable is a form of the name "Yahweh"). Yet this prophet's activities show how it is quite possible to think you are serving God and to manifest spiritual gifts but be deluded and no better than prophets who know they serve the Master.

Conversely, a king like Ahab needed at least to go through the motions of consulting God, which means you gather around you advisers who will tell you in God's name what you want to hear. Maybe the most impressive thing about Jehoshaphat is his recognizing this dynamic. He wants to hear from the dissident voices.

In principle, Micaiah's picture of the decision-making process in heaven fits one that appears elsewhere in Scripture. God sits in the heavenly White House surrounded by the presidential cabinet and the various presidential aides, and together they decide on action to take on earth and on who is to take the action.

How dissident Micaiah's voice is! Like the idea of God's having an opinion about what wars one should fight, Micaiah's understanding of God's way of working in the world scandalizes Western Christian ideas, though again it matches the way Scripture speaks elsewhere. As God can bring judgment on people who have rejected the truth by making it even more impossible for them to understand the truth (see Mark 4:12 as well as passages such as Isaiah 6:9–10), so God can bring judgment by sending a message that isn't true. God uses people who are not really committed to bringing God's word as a means of bringing judgment on someone who doesn't really want to hear God's word. Initially Micaiah behaves as if he belongs to the same company. It is the first way he tests whether Ahab really wants to hear God's word. God continues to seek to get through to him by mercifully undermining the process of bringing judgment by explaining that dynamic to Ahab. It puts Ahab in the same position as he was at the end of the previous chapter. He can once more put aside impressive clothes in favor of **sackcloth**; he can fast and "go about quietly"; and he can give up his war plans. You could say that the juxtaposition of these two stories is to lay alternatives before a leader. Do you want to be the Ahab of chapter 21 or the Ahab of chapter 22?

## 1 KINGS 22:24–2 KINGS 1:1

### You Can Disguise, but You Can't Hide

²⁴Zedekiah the son of Chenaanah came forward, struck Micaiah on the cheek, and said, "How was it that Yahweh's spirit passed from me to speak with you?" ²⁵Micaiah said, "Well, you are

going to see, on that day when you come to an innermost room to hide." ²⁶The king of Israel said, "Take Micaiah and return him to Amon, the city governor, and Joash, the king's son, ²⁷and say 'The king has said this: "Put this man in prison. They are to give him slave food and slave water until I come [home] in safety."'" ²⁸Micaiah said, "If you really come back in safety, Yahweh has not spoken by me." (He said, "Listen, all you peoples.")

²⁹So the king of Israel and Jehoshaphat king of Judah went up to Ramoth-gilead. ³⁰The king of Israel said to Jehoshaphat, "[I am] putting on disguise and going into battle, but you dress in your robes." So the king of Israel disguised himself and went into battle. ³¹Now the king of Aram had ordered his thirty-two chariot commanders, "Do not do battle with anyone small or great except the king of Israel alone." ³²When the chariot commanders saw Jehoshaphat, they said, "Yes, he is the king of Israel," and turned to do battle with him. Jehoshaphat cried out, ³³and when the chariot commanders saw that he was not the king of Israel, they turned back from following him. ³⁴But a man drew his bow innocently, and hit the king of Israel between the links and the armor. [The king] said to his charioteer, "Turn round, get me out from the army, because I'm wounded." ³⁵The battle mounted that day while the king was kept standing up in his chariot facing Aram. He died in the evening. The blood from the wound poured down into the base of the chariot. ³⁶A shout passed through the camp as the sun set, "Each man to his city, each man to his land." ³⁷So the king died and came to Samaria, and they buried the king in Samaria. ³⁸They washed the chariot by the pool of Samaria, and the dogs licked up his blood as the prostitutes washed, in accordance with the word Yahweh had spoken.

*[1 Kings 22:39–2 Kings 1:1 summarizes Ahab's reign, then back-tracks to recount how Jehoshaphat came to be king of Judah and to summarize his reign in mostly positive terms, and then finally recounts how Ahab's son Ahaziah succeeded him.]*

A friend of mine recently became attracted to a woman I also know, and he arranged to have lunch with her last week, taking with him his mental list of questions he felt he needed to ask of a potential wife. Being smitten by her looks and her smartness, he had not been inclined to take any notice of my observation that she was monumentally critical by nature. I don't mean she would be critical of someone she loved; it is more that she is critical of most other people, and I myself find this wearing. When they met for lunch, however, she was somewhat sick (she had strep throat or something) and didn't look as attractive as she usually does. This didn't stop her from being as critical (and as smart) as she usually is, but it did stop my friend from being overcome by her looks and her intelligence, and it enabled him to realize that this wasn't actually a relationship it would be wise for him to try to develop. It was just the coincidence of her being sick that enabled him to come to this realization, though (wisely) he wasn't prepared to say that God brought about the strep throat for his benefit. (And for all I know, she found him and his list of questions objectionable and/or was simply not interested in him at all; I have only his side of the story.)

The Old Testament includes many stories of the role played by coincidence in making good things happen for people and in making bad things happen in fulfillment of God's purpose. The stories of Ruth and Esther include a number of examples. Perhaps it's no coincidence that those stories concern the actions of ordinary people, as does this story of the anonymous archer who accidentally hits Ahab. You don't have to be someone very important to do something that is really important. It doesn't happen because you were trying to "make a difference." You were just going about your job. Maybe the man doesn't even know that it is his arrow that hits the king. He shoots "innocently." It's an odd word to use. Innocence usually suggests integrity or soundness. It almost implies he wasn't trying to kill anyone at all. Certainly he wasn't trying to kill Ahab or trying to be the means of God's will finding fulfillment. Yet that is what he became.

Whereas God's declaration of judgment on Ahab in the previous chapter had spoken of his dying an early death, his turning to God and God's declaration of mercy might then have seemed to imply that he would live a long life and die in bed (though it did not make that promise explicit). Yet it rather looks as if that turning to God was shallow and short-lived. God's commitment to mercy is now overwhelmed, as God's earlier declaration of judgment was overwhelmed. God's relationship

105

with people is always a dynamic one. God doesn't have a plan that is foreordained to evolve. God's purpose is worked out in dialogue with people's responses, and it is worked out through acts like the random action of the anonymous archer who shot Ahab by accident. Presumably Jehoshaphat doesn't realize that Ahab is setting him up as a decoy for the **Aramean** archers, or perhaps Jehoshaphat (who has been portrayed as a man who reveres God) knows he has nothing to fear.

God had sent Elijah with that warning about the dogs licking up Ahab's blood, and this has happened, which shows that God's sovereignty is involved in events, but the Old Testament doesn't picture God foreordaining or planning the details of events such as the archer's shooting in a particular direction. Rather, intentional human acts and coincidences "accidentally" contribute to the fulfillment of God's word.

Like Elijah, Micaiah nearly paid with his life for delivering God's word. Ahab naively assumes that silencing the man who declares God's word will stop the word's being fulfilled. He was wrong. He also naively assumed that disguising himself from human enemies would stop the word's being fulfilled. Again he was wrong. The man's arrow fulfilled both God's word through Elijah and God's word through Micaiah.

## 2 KINGS 1:2–18

### The Lord of the Flies

[2]Ahaziah fell through the lattice in his upper floor in Samaria, and he was sick. He sent aides and said to them, "Go and inquire of the Master Zebub, the god of Ekron, whether I will live on after this injury." [3]But Yahweh's aide—he spoke to Elijah the Tishbite, "Set off, go up to meet the aides of the king of Samaria and speak to them: 'Is it for lack of a God in Israel that you are going to inquire of the Master Zebub, the god of Ekron? [4]So, therefore, Yahweh has said this: "The bed you have climbed into, you will not get down from, because you will actually die."'" Elijah went, [5]and the aides returned to [Ahaziah]. He said to them, "Why have you returned?" [6]They said to him, "There was a man came up to meet us. He said to us, 'Go, return to the king who sent you and speak to him:

"Yahweh has said this: 'Is it for lack of a God in Israel that you are sending to inquire of the Master Zebub, the god of Ekron? Therefore the bed you have climbed into you will not come down from, because you will actually die.'"" [7]He spoke to them: "What was the manner of the man who came up to meet you and spoke these words to you?" [8]They said to him, "A man with lots of hair and a leather wrap fastened round his waist." He said, "It was Elijah the Tishbite." [9]He sent to him a captain of fifty and his fifty men, and he went up to him. There: he was sitting at the top of a mountain. He spoke to him: "Man of God, the king himself has spoken: come down." [10]Elijah replied to the captain of fifty, "If I am a man of God, may fire come down from the heavens and consume you and your fifty men." Fire came down from the heavens and consumed him and his fifty men. [11][The king] again sent to him another captain of fifty and his fifty men. . . . [12b]Supernatural fire came down from the heavens and consumed him and his fifty men. [13]He again sent a third captain of fifty and his fifty men. The third captain of fifty went up, and came and fell down on his knees before Elijah and asked him for grace. He spoke to him: "Man of God, may my life and the life of these fifty servants of yours be valuable in your eyes! [14]Yes, fire has fallen from the heavens and consumed the first two captains of fifty and their fifty men. But now, may my life be valuable in your eyes." [15]Yahweh's aide spoke to Elijah, "Go down with him. Don't be afraid of him." So he got up and went down with him to the king. [16]He spoke to him: "Yahweh has said this: 'Because you sent aides to inquire of the Master Zebub, the god of Ekron (is it for lack of a God in Israel to inquire of his word?), therefore the bed you have climbed into, you will not get down from, because you will actually die.'" [17]And he died in accordance with Yahweh's word which Elijah spoke. Jehoram [his brother] became king instead of him, because he had no son. [18]The rest of the acts of Ahaziah which he did: these are indeed written down in the annals of the kings of Israel.

There are more positive and less positive understandings of human nature. The word *zebub* means *fly*, so the title "**Master** Zebub" or "Lord Zebub" would mean "Lord Fly" or "Lord of the Fly." Now *Lord of the Flies* was a mid-twentieth-century novel by William Golding. The novel starts in the manner of the television series *Lost*, with an air crash on a remote island, survived only by some preteen boys. They seek to find a way of living together, but their story embodies a rather gloomy understanding of how that attempt might be expected to work out; there is much conflict among the boys. The Gospels also use a similar-sounding title, Beelzebul, to refer to Satan; in Hebrew, "Master Zebul" would mean something like "Exalted Master." It is a plausible title for a **Canaanite** god.

Sometimes the Old Testament expresses its disapproval of foreign gods by twisting their names a bit, and Master Zebub, "Lord of the Fly," might be an example. In other words, Ahaziah actually sent for advice and help to a god he called the Exalted Master, but the deliberate Israelite misspelling of his name dismisses him as the Fly Master. Yet Fly Master might be a real name, which could then point to the reason why Ahaziah sent for advice to him. Merely falling through a window from an upper floor would not need to be life-threatening, but if an injury that resulted from such a fall went septic, you would be in deep trouble. The Lord of the Flies would then be a god who might be able to deal with the kind of diseases that flies carry, diseases similar to septicemia. Ahaziah's recourse to this god (and to one who lives in a **Philistine** city like Ekron, for goodness' sake) would be parallel to the recourse to Canaanite gods that were supposed to be able to make the harvest go well, recourse that the Old Testament condemns elsewhere. Whether this god is the Fly Master or the Exalted Master, Elijah points out that such recourse implies that there isn't a God in Israel that you could go to when you got ill. It implies that **Yahweh** is of no earthly use. It's a quite radically apostate statement by the leader of a people who are supposed to be committed to Yahweh. The stakes in this story are high.

That fact doesn't stop us disliking the way the story then unfolds, with the hapless military losing their lives for following the king's orders. Here it's not that Elijah directly kills them, as he killed the Master's prophets in 1 Kings 18. Fire from the sky kills them. The implication is that God colludes with Elijah's conviction that the military deserve to die. Like Ahaziah himself, the soldiers are not merely asserting themselves against another human being but asserting themselves against God. The point is implicit in their addressing Elijah as **man of God**. If they recognize that he represents God, they should behave accordingly. His being a man of God, someone who represents God, is shown by the fact that he is able to call on supernatural power.

We might be inclined to think that it's not a fact; maybe this is "just a story." The formulaic way it's told might suggest that this is so—there is a first military detachment, then a second one, then a third one who react to Elijah rather differently. But if you object to the narrative content, it's just as objectionable as "just a story" as it is if it's history. It still raises the question of why God was willing to have the story in his book and what we are supposed to learn from it. Jesus once refused his disciples' suggestion that they call down fire on people who rejected him (Luke 9:52–56), but elsewhere he talks a lot about people ending up in fire (e.g., Matthew 25:41). Like other Old Testament stories, this one is less frightening than the way Jesus tells people like these soldiers that they will burn in hell. It assures us that the real God will win out and that the real God's truth will triumph. It warns us to take the real God seriously and warns us that we can't hide behind the fact that we were given orders by some earthly master.

English translations of the Bible usually distinguish between "angels" of God and "messengers" of the king, but the Hebrew word for **aide** is the same for both, and this story points to the implication of this fact. There is an earthly king with his aide or aides and a heavenly King with his aide or aides. It is tempting for the earthly king and his aides (and the king's other subjects) to think that the earthly king is the one who has decisive power and authority. It is not so. The heavenly King and his aides (supernatural and earthly) count for more.

## 2 KINGS 2:1–3:3

### The Cloak and the Power of Elijah

[1]When Yahweh took up Elijah to the heavens in a whirlwind, Elijah had gone with Elisha from Gilgal. [2]Elijah said to Elisha, "You should stay here, because Yahweh has sent me on to Bethel." Elisha said, "As Yahweh lives and as you yourself live, I

will definitely not leave you." So they went down to Bethel. ³The disciples of the prophets at Bethel came out to Elisha and said to him, "Do you recognize that Yahweh is going to take your lord from you today?" He said, "Yes, I myself recognize it. Be silent." ⁴Then Elijah said to him, "Elisha, you should stay here, because Yahweh has sent me on to Jericho." He said, "As Yahweh lives and as you yourself live, I will definitely not leave you." So they came to Jericho. . . . ⁶Then Elijah said to him, "You should stay here, because Yahweh has sent me to the Jordan." He said, "As Yahweh lives and as you yourself live, I will definitely not leave you." So the two of them went. . . . ⁸Elijah got his cape, rolled it up, and hit the water. It divided in both directions, and the two of them crossed on dry ground. ⁹As they crossed, Elijah said to Elisha, "Ask whatever I should do for you before I am taken from you." Elisha said, "Could a double share in your spirit come onto me." ¹⁰He said, "You have asked something difficult. If you see me taken from you, so it will happen for you. If not, it will not happen." ¹¹They were continuing to walk and speak, and there—fiery chariotry and fiery horses. They separated the two of them, and Elijah went up in a whirlwind to the heavens. . . . ¹⁴[Elisha] got Elijah's cape, which had fallen from him, hit the water, and said, "Where is Yahweh, the God of Elijah? Yes, him?" When he hit the water, it divided in both directions and Elisha crossed. ¹⁵The disciples of the prophets at Jericho at a distance from him saw him and said, "Elijah's spirit has settled on Elisha!" They came to meet him and bowed low to the ground before him.

*[Verses 16–18 relate how the disciples of the prophets search for Elijah but cannot find him.]*

¹⁹The city's people said to Elisha, "Now. The position of the city is good, as my lord sees, but the water is bad and the region makes people childless." ²⁰He said, "Get me a new bowl and put salt in it." They got it for him, ²¹and he went out to the water spring and threw the salt there. He said, "Yahweh has said this: 'I am healing this water. No more will death and childlessness come from there.'" ²²The water has been healthy until this day in accordance with the word of Elisha, which he spoke.

²³He went up from there to Bethel. As he was going up the road, small boys came out of the city and mocked him. They said, "Go up, baldy, go up baldy!" ²⁴He turned round and saw

them and put them down in Yahweh's name, and two bears came out of the forest and mauled forty-two of the boys. [25]He went from there to Mount Carmel and from there came back to Samaria.

[Second Kings 3:1–3 recaps how Jehoram becomes king of Ephraim.]

I once had to change a flat tire by the Dead Sea. I jacked the car up and in the process of changing the tire or loosening or tightening the wheel nuts, I lay on the sandy but hard ground. It was summer and hot, and when I got up a whole layer of skin peeled off my back (without it hurting or doing lasting damage). It's weird down there, a thousand feet below sea level. People who go to Israel are often advised to take a copy of their local newspaper with them so that they can be photographed floating in the Dead Sea reading the newspaper and then get their photo in its next issue. It really can be done. The Jordan Rivers empties into the Dead Sea, but it's a dead end; its water leaves the Dead Sea only by evaporation. The minerals in the water, which are good for us in small quantities, stay there, so the water is undrinkable and so dense it supports you so that you can get that photo taken.

That's the background to the first of a number of stories about Elisha doing little miracles, some relating to the lives of the **disciples of the prophets**. Most of them strike Western readers as either trivial (like the purifying of the water) or objectionable (like the cursing of the little boys). So they are worth our paying attention to because they push us into different ways of thinking from the ones that come naturally to us. That will be so whether or not we are inclined to think that they actually happened. For myself, I am not sure what to think about that question. On one hand, I am inclined to think that there's no smoke without fire. I find it hard to believe that there would be lots of stories of this kind about Elijah and Elisha if they never did anything that raised people's eyebrows. On the other hand, we have noticed the formulaic nature of some of the stories; the threefold nature of the account of Elijah's last visitation round the prophetic communities is another example. Further, there is a folkloric or fairy-tale aspect to some of them. So maybe the scriptural writers have picked up folkloric or fairy-tale motifs in order to convey something of the significance of Elijah, and even more of Elisha. If so, that's a way of conveying how important these prophets truly were.

In Hebrew the "Dead Sea" is the "Salt Sea," and one can imagine that the entire water supply in the Jericho area nearby was affected by the mineral content of the water table. But the reason that Jericho exists and is the flourishing city it is (even today) is the miraculous fact that the area also boasts a pure fresh-water supply. In a Western context we can take our water supply for granted, but most human communities have not been able to do so, and whether you have a good water supply really is a matter of life and death. (It's not clear whether the Hebrew word I have translated "childlessness" means women had difficulty conceiving or had miscarriages, or even that the land was infertile.) As a vaccination with a small dose of something such as tuberculosis can immunize you against that disease, so salt removes the saltiness of the Jericho spring (not because regular physics works that way; it's an extraordinary transformation). As well as being a sign of God's caring for the everyday life needs of its people, Elisha's purifying the water is a sign of his being a prophet in the line of Moses.

More explicitly, Elisha is a prophet in the line of Elijah. While God had told Elijah to anoint Elisha, he never does so, perhaps because he recognizes that God had spoken metaphorically, but metaphorically he does now anoint him when he asks what Elisha wants him to do for him. (It is such a searching question, recalling the question God asked Solomon in 1 Kings 3.) Admittedly, it is almost as if Elijah is trying to avoid designating Elisha as his successor, as if he is trying to put him off or to get rid of him; but if so, Elisha passes this test. Usually prophets don't have the chance to volunteer (Isaiah is the other great exception); it is a commission that is thrust upon you. The double share of someone's legacy is the share allocated to the firstborn son, in recognition of the fact that he has responsibility for the family's welfare and future, and for the fulfilling of its responsibility to vulnerable people outside it such as widows and orphans and immigrants. In effect Elisha is asking to have the resources that will make it possible for him to be Elijah's successor. Elijah knows he cannot decide that he will have them (notwithstanding that commission to anoint him); it is God's business. The story thus points to another aspect of the relationship between divine decision making and human volunteering in connection with someone's becoming a prophet. Elijah's parting of the waters shows him to be someone who stands in the line of Moses; Elisha's then being able to do so shows that he comes next in this line. (It is another unnecessary miracle. You can wade the Jordan River. Ruth and Naomi did so. But it makes a point.)

Elijah's disappearance also parallels that of Moses in Deuteronomy 34, though Moses did die; it thus even more closely resembles Enoch's disappearance in Genesis 5. In Jewish tradition Elijah thus joins these three as people who might be able to give us revelations from God; there are a number of "revelatory" books associated with their names, though these were actually written many centuries after their day. That will also be one reason why it is possible for Moses and Elijah to appear to Jesus (see Mark 9). Neither of them had died and been buried in the regular way, and both could be thought of as having gone to share in the life of heaven with other heavenly beings like the **aides** sent by means of those fiery chariots to fetch Elijah. (So there's no great link with the idea of resurrection.)

The story of the boys and the bears further underscores Elisha's importance as God's servant. The reference to his baldness likely refers to a tonsure like that of a monk. While it suggests a striking contrast to the assumption elsewhere that people devoted to God's service would grow their hair long, it fits the culturally widespread assumption that whether you wear your hair very long or very short, you may well be making a statement. So the boys are jeering at someone whom anyone could recognize as a servant of God, and in bidding him to "go up" they are telling him to carry on past their city, to go away. Once again, while Jesus would no doubt forbid his disciples to act like Elisha as he forbade them to act like Elijah, his words show that it is only temporarily that people get away with belittling Jesus. In the end they will pay with their lives.

# 2 KINGS 3:4–27

## The Ultimate Sacrifice

⁴Now Mesha, king of Moab, was a sheep breeder. He used to pay the king of Israel a hundred thousand lambs and the wool of a hundred thousand rams. ⁵When Ahab died, the king of Moab rebelled against the king of Israel. ⁶At that time King Jehoram left Samaria and mobilized all Israel, ⁷and went on to send to Jehoshaphat king of Judah to say, "Given that the king of Moab has rebelled against me, will you go with me to Moab to do battle?" He said, "I will go up. . . . ⁸By which route shall we go up?" [Jehoram] said, "The route through the Edom wilderness." ⁹So the king of Israel, the king of Judah, and the king of Edom went, and marched around on a seven-day route. But there was no water for the army or the animals following them. ¹⁰The king of Israel said, "Oh no! Yahweh has summoned these three kings in order to give them into the hand of Moab!" ¹¹But Jehoshaphat said, "Isn't there a prophet of Yahweh here from whom we can inquire of Yahweh?" One of the king of Israel's staff replied, "Elisha the son of Shaphat, who poured water on Elijah's hands, is here." ¹²Jehoshaphat said, "Yahweh's word is with him." So the king of Israel and Jehoshaphat and the king of Edom went down to him. ¹³Elisha said to the king of Israel, "What do you and I have in common? Go to your father's prophets and your mother's prophets." The king of Israel said to him, "No, because Yahweh has summoned these three kings to give them into the hand of Moab." ¹⁴[Elisha] said, "As Yahweh Armies lives, before whom I stand [in attendance], were I not respectful of Jehoshaphat king of Judah, I would not look at you or see you. ¹⁵But now, get me a musician." When the musician played, Yahweh's hand came on him, ¹⁶and he said, "Yahweh has said this: 'This wash is going to make pools and pools.' ¹⁷Because Yahweh has said this: 'You will not see wind, you will not see rain, but that wash—it will fill with water. Both you and your cattle and your animals will drink.' ¹⁸This is a small thing in Yahweh's eyes. He will give Moab into your hand. . . ." ²⁰So in the morning at the time for making the offering—there, water was coming from the direction of Edom. The area filled with water.

²¹When all the Moabites heard that the kings had come up to do battle with them, all those who could fasten a belt and

upwards [in age] let themselves be summoned, and they stood at the border. [22]When they got up early in the morning, the sun was shining over the water, and from a distance the Moabites saw the water red like blood [23]and said, "This is blood! The kings have actually taken up the sword against each other. Each man has struck down his neighbor. Now, to the plunder, Moab!" [24]So they came to the Israelite camp, but the Israelites rose up and struck down the Moabites. . . . [26]The king of Moab saw that the battle was too tough for him . . . [27]and got his eldest son who was to reign as king in place of him, and sacrificed him as a burnt offering on the wall. A great wrath came on Israel, and they departed from there and went back to the land.

The writer of a letter in today's newspaper, in the aftermath of the U.S. president's firing of his top commander in Afghanistan, asks whether "we must continue to sacrifice our brave men and women" there. By the time you read this, we will probably know whether the United States and its allies can think in terms of having succeeded in Afghanistan; then the "sacrifice" may seem to have been worthwhile. The image of sacrifice is a telling one in this connection. In commenting on Genesis 22 in *Genesis for Everyone* I noted how Abraham's near-sacrifice of Isaac provided the poet Wilfred Owen with an image that compared and contrasted with the actual sacrifice of our brave men (not so many women then) in the First World War, and it did the same in the context of Vietnam for Leonard Cohen.

Sacrificing your sons and daughters is both the most unintelligible and the most intelligible of acts. It is unimaginable because they are the most precious thing in the world to you. That is the case because of your natural human feelings for them and because they represent the future of your family and your people. If they are gone, who will look after the farm (and look after you) as you grow older, and after you are gone? Yet precisely their irreplaceable import in your heart and their irreplaceable value makes them the most significant sacrifice you could make. Paradoxically, the sacrifice that imperils your future is the sacrifice that you hope may safeguard your future. So **Canaanites** and Israelites and Moabites, like modern Western people, were willing to make this sacrifice. (The rules in the **Torah** told

Israelites not to do so, and that story about Abraham and Isaac would remind them that God had earlier looked in the eye the possibility of asking this sacrifice but had then not required it, but material in the Prophets shows they did not take too much notice of that, and archaeological discoveries confirm it.)

It was a desperate act, and you would undertake it only in a great crisis. A great crisis has come to Moab. **Ephraim** continues to be a regional power, and Moab (the other side of the Dead Sea from Judah) has to pay taxes to Ephraim in return for the "privilege" of living under its umbrella. Its king is a sheep breeder in the sense that he rules a country whose economy focuses on sheep. Maybe he paid his taxes simply in the form of the wool, or in the case of the lambs in the form of the animals themselves; it is not clear what Ephraim would do with all that wool, which would come to one or two animals' wool per person per year. Maybe Ephraim would use the wool in trading deals with other peoples. First Kings 12 has already provided a vivid illustration of the way a king's death and a new king's accession is a dangerous moment for a regime, and it is not surprising that Mesha makes this the moment to declare independence from Ephraim. Equally, the new king knows he has to assert his authority in decisive fashion, though Jehoram's attempt to do so comes unstuck (like Rehoboam's in 1 Kings 12).

The combined forces of Ephraim and Judah join up with those of Edom, south of Moab and southeast of the Dead Sea; evidently Ephraim is also in a position to lean on Edom. They march down the west side of the Dead Sea and round the south end of it. For most of the way the country is extremely inhospitable, as is implied in the story of Elisha and the water spring in 2 Kings 2, and it rather looks as if the kings have not thought through the logistics of their expedition. The Ephraimite and the Judahite king then model two ways of responding to such a situation—blame God for your mistakes without talking to God, or ask God what is going on and what to do. Like the boy who advised Saul in 1 Samuel 9 and the girl who will advise Naaman in 2 Kings 5, one of Jehoram's staff has more insight about spiritual resources than his boss. Elisha is then as unfazed by his king as he will be by Naaman, but he is persuaded to seek a word from **Yahweh**. Again like Saul, he is helped in this connection

116

by some music. Music often has the capacity to open people up to transcendent realities in a way that silent thinking or prayer or reflection cannot. In the Bible, if you want to seek God, you do so with the help of noise and music, not silence.

So Elisha brings God's word to the kings. It promises the water they need, which comes in abundance. It also promises a conclusive victory, and initially the miraculous supply of water also promises to be the means of bringing about a marvelous victory. This is then the moment when Mesha offers his sacrifice. A desperate situation requires desperate measures, and as the king he is the one who has to take them. And they work.

How so? What is this wrath that comes on Israel? Is it Yahweh's wrath? Is it the wrath of Chemosh, the Moabite god? Is it simply wrath—is that a way of describing the way victory is turned into catastrophe? Does the sacrifice work by galvanizing the Moabites? Does it work by paralyzing the Israelites? It seems that the storytellers do not know and do not pretend to explain what they do not know. While spiritual or theological insight sometimes makes it possible to know things, it does not always do so. There are strange things that happen in life that we cannot explain, and we have to live with them on the basis of the clues God has given us about the big picture that we can understand. It is encouraging that the Scriptures do not pretend to know everything; it is then easier to trust them when they think they do know things.

Extraordinarily, we have a commemorative inscription on a stone slab that was erected by Mesha himself, and it may give his account of this event without referring to the sacrifice of his son (though it may refer to some other conflict between Ephraim and Moab). The inscription, called the "Moabite Stone" or the "Mesha Stele" is now in the Louvre in Paris. Mesha, too, refers to Israelite domination over Moab and to a new king's determination to extend that domination. He thanks Chemosh for delivering him "whereas Israel [that is, Ephraim] has perished forever." His hyperbole matches that in other parts of the Old Testament, which sometimes declares that Israel has annihilated a people and then refers to them subsequently in a way that shows we are not supposed to take such language too literally.

# 2 KINGS 4:1–44

## A Tale of Two Women

¹Now a certain woman among the wives of the disciples of the prophets cried out to Elisha, "Your servant, my husband, is dead, and you yourself know that your servant was someone who revered Yahweh, and a creditor is coming to take my two children for himself as servants." ²Elisha said to her, "What am I to do for you? Tell me what you have in the house." She said, "Your servant has nothing at all in the house except a jug of oil." ³He said, "Go and ask for containers for yourself from outside, from all your neighbors, empty containers. Don't make it a few. ⁴Come in, shut the door behind you and your children, and pour [oil] into all these containers. Remove [each] full one." ⁵She went from him and shut the door behind her and her children. People were bringing [containers] to her and she was pouring. ⁶When the containers were full, she said to her son, "Bring me another container," but he said to her, "There isn't another container"; and the oil stopped. ⁷She came and told the man of God. He said, "Go and sell the oil and pay your debt, and you and your children can live on what is left."

⁸One day Elisha traveled to Shunem. An important woman was there, and she pressed him to eat, and whenever he traveled, he would stop over there to eat. ⁹So she said to her husband, "Now. I recognize that it is a holy man of God who travels to us all the time. ¹⁰Let's make him a little walled room on the roof and put a bed for him there and a table and a chair and a lamp. When he comes to us he can stop over there." ¹¹One day he came there and stopped over in the room on the roof and lay down there, ¹²and said to Gehazi, his boy, "Call this Shunammite woman. . . ." ¹⁶He said, "At this season next year you are going to be holding a son." She said, "Don't, my lord, man of God, don't deceive your servant." ¹⁷But the woman conceived and had a son at this season the next year as Elisha declared to her.

¹⁸The child grew up, but one day he went out to his father, to the reapers, ¹⁹and said to his father, "My head, my head!" He said to a boy, "Carry him to his mother." ²⁰He carried him and took him to his mother, and he sat on her lap until noon, and died. . . . ²⁵She set out and came to the man of God on Mount Carmel. . . . ²⁸She said, "Did I ask for a son from my lord? Didn't

I say, 'Don't encourage me'?". . . ³²Elisha came to the house and there—the boy was dead, laid on his bed. ³³He went in and shut the door behind the two of them and pleaded with Yahweh. ³⁴He climbed up and lay on the child, put his mouth on his mouth, his eyes on his eyes, his hands on his hands. As he crouched over him, the child's flesh warmed up. ³⁵He returned and went into the house here and there, then climbed up and crouched over him, and the boy sneezed seven times. Then the boy opened his eyes. ³⁶[Elisha] called Gehazi and said, "Call the Shunammite woman." He called her and she came to him. He said, "Pick up your son."

*[Verses 37–44 close off the story and tell two more stories of wonders performed by Elisha.]*

Among my friends are a number of young couples who have been hoping to have children, and it has never happened. They then go in for medical examinations of various kinds and for treatment of various kinds. One couple had eggs implanted, but they never "stuck," and I think the couple have now become reconciled to never having children. In the case of another couple, a doctor decided that the wife needed a certain form of treatment and encouraged her to think that this might solve the problem. I imagine it was hard then to live with that encouragement. You don't know whether to believe the doctor (and maybe if you don't believe, it won't happen?). You don't want the encouragement to be something that eventually leads to a deflation worse than the gloom you already felt. Then last year this particular woman got pregnant, and you wonder whether this time will lead only to miscarriage (I wondered that; I didn't dare ask them whether they wondered that). But two weeks ago she had her baby!

Maybe the Shunammite woman experienced a more profound discouragement than my first friend when she had the implants and they didn't work, or than my second friend might have experienced if she had never conceived or had miscarried. It looks as if this woman from Shunem had come to terms with not being able to have children, and she had directed her energy in other directions, like giving hospitality to a wandering prophet. Like many Old Testament stories, this story shows how women can be people of initiative and action—they are not confined to doing what their husbands say. Shunem is a village in the fertile plain in the center of **Ephraim**, not so far from Jezreel and thus below Mount Carmel, where Elisha has his base. As usual, the story assumes that the ground floor of a house comprises the regular family quarters and that the roof is the place for privacy or for doing something special. It is Elisha's appreciation of the woman's care for him that leads to his encouraging his servant to ask what he can do for her. She tells him she has everything she needs, and it is Gehazi who points out that she has no son and that her husband is old. The implication is not merely that they will be unable to have children but that she will be left on her own sooner rather than later. Who will then look after her?

There is no "Thus says the Lord" and no praying in Elisha's response. Elisha is a **man of God**; that is what the woman calls him. The implication is that he has supernatural power. Now it's quite possible to believe that someone has supernatural power, or just to recognize that God has the power to heal or give new life, but not to be able to imagine that this power will be exercised on one's personal behalf. It's the kind of thing that happens to other people, not to me, we think. And most of the time we are right. Most childless couples do not have the experience that comes to this couple. Yet somehow the fact that some couples do have this experience can be an encouragement to the majority who don't.

The fact that the woman has a hard time believing what Elisha says places no obstacle to its coming true; what God does isn't necessarily dependent on our faith. But the fulfillment of Elisha's promise is only half this story. Maybe it is sunstroke that overcomes the boy, out in the fields in the heat of harvest time. Again his mother is the one who exercises initiative, ignoring her husband's objections to her hastening to Elisha's base on Mount Carmel. "What if he's not there?" He's there all right, and he's surprised not by what has happened to the boy but by the fact that "**Yahweh** has hidden it from [him] and not told [him]." Just because you are a man of God with supernatural insight and supernatural power doesn't mean you can see and do everything. Elisha attempts to send Gehazi off to see what can be done for the boy, but the woman will not be fobbed off by that action, so Elisha follows. The process whereby the boy is resuscitated again presupposes that Elisha's very person contains mysterious power. Life can flow from him to the boy. Stories about Jesus using spit and mud in healing a blind man and needing to try more than once in one case (Mark 8; John 9) will parallel these stories about Elisha. The last story in the chapter concerns Elisha's miraculously feeding a hundred people with a relatively small number of loaves; it, too, will thereby eventually show how Jesus exercises a ministry like Elisha's. One can't produce generalizations from the stories about the way healing works; one simply stands astonished and hopeful before what God sometimes does.

The story about the widow of one of the **disciples of the prophets** illustrates some overlapping dynamics. Jesus points out that there were many widows in Israel in Elijah's day (Luke 4:25), and the situation hasn't changed in Jesus' own day. There are no social security or widow's benefits; it is your extended family and your neighbors who are supposed to help you through when you are in difficulties, but the presupposition of the story may be that the whole community is in difficulty. You aren't necessarily protected from such trouble by the fact that your husband was a person who was truly devoted to God and involved in ministry. Evidently the woman (or her husband, before he died) had taken out a loan in the hope that the situation would improve; maybe they would get a decent harvest and be able to pay the loan back. It hasn't happened. The collateral on the loan would then be that the children's labor would pay back the loan. This didn't mean they would be slaves, and if the system worked in accordance with the **Torah** they would be free again after a while, but the arrangement wouldn't be much fun for mother or children.

Because we don't have miraculous experiences like those of these two women, it's tempting for us to assume these are "just stories," and there is no way of establishing whether or not this is so. Perhaps it makes little difference. If they relate things that happened, such things are unlikely to happen for us. Whatever is the case, they are present in Scripture to invite us to wonder at God's capacity to make extraordinary things happen and also to be open to being God's agents in reaching out in some way to women who can't have children or lose their children or lose their husbands.

## 2 KINGS 5:1–6:7

### A Skin Disorder Removed and Imposed

5:1Now Naaman, commander of the army of the king of Aram, was someone important to his lord, and highly regarded, because through him Yahweh had given deliverance to Aram, but the man was a powerful warrior with a skin disorder. 2The Arameans had gone out raiding and had captured from Israel a little girl who waited on Naaman's wife. 3She said to her mistress, "If only my master were in the presence of the prophet in Samaria. Then he would remove his disorder from him." 4[Naaman] went and told his master, "The girl from Israel has spoken such and such," 5and the king of Aram said, "Get yourself off and go, and I will send a letter to the king of Israel." So he went, took with him ten talents of silver, six thousand shekels of gold, and ten suits of clothes, 6and brought the letter to the king of Israel: "Now, when this letter comes to you: right, I have sent my servant Naaman to you so you may remove his skin disorder from him." 7When the king of Israel read the letter, he tore his clothes and said, "Am I God, to kill or make alive, that this man is sending to me to remove a skin disorder from someone? Because surely you can recognize and see that he is seeking a quarrel with me." 8When Elisha the man of God heard that the king of Israel had torn his clothes, he sent to the king saying, "Why have you torn your clothes? He should come to me, so he may recognize that there is a prophet in Israel."

9Naaman came with his horses and chariotry and stopped at the door of Elisha's house. 10Elisha sent an aide to say, "Go and wash seven times in the Jordan, and your skin will come back for you and be clean." 11Naaman was furious and went off. He said, "Well. I said to myself, 'He will definitely come out and stand and call in the name of Yahweh his God and wave his hand at the place and remove the disorder. 12Aren't Amanah and Pharpar, the rivers in Damascus, better than all the water in Israel? Couldn't I wash in them and be clean?'" So he turned and went off in a rage. 13But his staff came forward and spoke to him. They said, "Father, had the prophet spoken to you of a big thing, wouldn't you do it? How much more when he said to you, 'Wash and be clean'?" [14]So he went down and immersed himself in the Jordan seven times in accordance with the word of the man of God, and his skin came back like a little boy's, and it was clean. [15]He returned to the man of God, he and all his retinue, came and stood in front of him, and said, "Right. I acknowledge that there is no God in all the earth except in Israel. So now do accept a gift from your servant." [16]He said, "As Yahweh lives, before whom I stand [in attendance], I will not." [Naaman] pressed him to, but he refused. [17]Naaman said, "May there not then be given to your servant two mules' load of earth, because your servant will no longer make a burnt offering or a sacrifice to any other god but Yahweh? [18] With regard to this matter, may Yahweh pardon your servant: when my master goes into Rimmon's house to bow down there, and he leans on my arm so that I have to bow down there in Rimmon's house—when I bow down in Rimmon's house, may Yahweh pardon your servant in this matter." [19a]He said to him, "Go and be well."

[Second Kings 5:19b–6:7 relate how Gehazi tells Naaman that Elisha has changed his mind about the gift and Elisha declares that his disorder will come on Gehazi. They then tell of another of Elisha's "trivial" miracles.]

Yesterday was the fourth Sunday in the month, and as usual on that Sunday we didn't have a "proper" sermon; the rector sat on a chair and invited the congregation to tell us what they heard God saying to us out of the Scripture readings (it's only a little church, so this is practicable as it would not be in a big church.) The philosophy of that practice is the awareness that ordinary people are likely to show as much spiritual insight as rectors or theology professors (I try to keep quiet during the time of sharing, though I did not succeed yesterday). One or two of the people who often make contributions to the discussion are also people who from time to time circulate encouraging and thought-provoking e-mails round the congregation.

The Naaman story illustrates how ordinary people sometimes see things that leaders can't see. Translations traditionally refer to Naaman's problem as leprosy, but that word has changed its meaning over the centuries and is now misleading. The Hebrew word doesn't denote a deformity that makes someone's limbs wither but rather a skin ailment. While it did not mean people had to avoid contact with others, as this story shows, they did have to be wary about it. While you had this skin disorder, you could not go to the sanctuary to offer a sacrifice, and anyone who had close contact with you might "catch" the taboo that attached to you; so a person who wanted to go to the sanctuary would need to be wary of coming too close to you (hence Luke 17 speaks of some people with this skin ailment keeping their distance from Jesus). A plausible theory about why a skin ailment could be viewed thus is that it made your body look as if it were degenerating in the way it does when we die (compare the story about Miriam's ailment in Numbers 12). So the ailment was redolent of death; and death was incompatible with being with God. You couldn't go into God's presence when you looked like death.

It wasn't possible to do anything about this skin disorder except hope that it would go away. Except that this poor young girl who has been captured in war knows someone who can do something about it. She could have been pardoned for thinking to herself "this **Aramean** general deserves this disorder and more for what he has done to us Israelites, and to me in particular," but instead she speaks up and tells her mistress about the prophet who could remove it.

The king of Aram shows some insight in being willing to believe the girl, though the price he assumes he must pay suggests he has had some bad experiences with the Aramean health insurance system (but actually the problem is described as something like a disorder rather than as an illness; the story consistently talks about "removing" the disorder and about "cleanness" rather than about healing it, so that this is not a healing story). The **Ephraimite** king has less excuse for his clueless response. One can perhaps understand Naaman's attitude to Elisha, who doesn't even bother to come to the door to see the great general but just sends one of his staff with some stupid-looking instructions. After all, Naaman knows how the exercise of spiritual gifts is supposed to work, and it's not by bathing in a muddy stream. It is again the ordinary guys, the members of his staff, who have the spiritual insight. They realize that one thing you can know about spiritual gifts is that you can never predict how they will work. There are no rules. God doesn't work by rules.

While there may not be rules, there may be a rationale, though you may be able to see it only afterward. It often puzzles us (or even agonizes us) why God heals some people and not others. Here, Naaman gets the cleansing when there are lots of people with his disorder in Israel who just have to live with it. Naaman gets the cleansing because God is demonstrating that there is a prophet in Israel—that God is speaking and acting there. There is something significant about the Jordan River even though it is no more impressive than the rivers in Damascus; it is in the land where the God of Israel is especially at work.

Naaman does get it and thus comes to share the wisdom of ordinary people like the unnamed little girl and his own unnamed staff. While the Old Testament story focuses mostly on God's working with Israel, it does from time to time remind its readers that God's working with Israel has all the nations as its broader concern, and a story like this is an example. Naaman comes to recognize that there is no God in all the earth except in Israel. Yet he can hardly stay in Canaan like a resident alien such as Ruth the Moabite or Uriah the Hittite. He has a job to go back to. He reminds us of the Middle-Eastern sages who come to see Jesus and worship him yet then have to go back to their homeland. How can Naaman possibly do so? He has been to the holy land, the land where **Yahweh** is especially active, so he takes back enough Israelite soil for him to be able to stand on each day when he prays and offers sacrifice. It will be as if he is back in that holy land, and when he has to look as if he is worshiping the god of the Arameans, in his heart he will be worshiping Yahweh. There are Muslims today who do this rather than cut themselves off from their community and risk their lives.

In Luke 4, Jesus hints at a different significance in Elisha's cleansing of Naaman rather than an Israelite with his disorder: it is a kind of judgment on Israel itself. If this is one warning note in the story, another is the tailpiece about Gehazi. You could say he is just being practical. He seems to be Elisha's senior aide, and maybe he has the job of making the household finances work. But his action confuses the message that emerges from the action of the **man of God** and the God who stands behind him, and he pays a terrible price.

## 2 KINGS 6:8–23

### Horses and Chariots of Fire around Elisha

[8]When the king of Aram was waging war on Israel, he took counsel with his staff, saying, "My camp will be at such-and-such a place," [9]but the man of God sent to the king of Israel saying, "Take care not to pass this place, because the Arameans are going down there." [10]So the king of Israel sent to the place of which the man of God had told him and warned it, and took care there, more than once or twice. [11]The mind of the king of Aram was agitated about this matter. He summoned his staff and said to them, "You must tell me who of us is on the king of Israel's side!" [12]One of his staff said, "No, my lord king, because it is Elisha the prophet in Israel who tells the king of Israel the things you speak in your bedroom." [13]He said, "Go and see where he is. I will send and get him."

They told him, "There he is, in Dothan." [14]He sent horses and chariotry there, and a strong force. They came by night and encircled the city. [15]The man of God's attendant got up early and went out, and there: the force was surrounding the city, with horses and chariotry. His boy said to him, "Oh no, my lord, what shall we do?" [16]He said, "Don't be afraid, because there are more with us than with them." [17]Elisha pleaded, "Yahweh, will you open his eyes so he sees." Yahweh opened the boy's eyes and he saw: and there, the mountains were full of fiery horses and chariotry surrounding Elisha. [18][The Arameans] came down against him, and Elisha pleaded with Yahweh, "Will you strike down this nation with dazzling." He struck them down with dazzling in accordance with Elisha's word. [19]Elisha said to them, "This is not the way, and this is not the city. Follow me and I will take you to the man you are looking for," and he took them to Samaria. [20]When they came to Samaria, Elisha said, "Yahweh, open these people's eyes so they can see." Yahweh opened their eyes and they saw: there, they were inside

126

Samaria. ²¹When he saw them, the king of Israel said, "Shall I strike them down, strike them down, father?" ²²He said, "You will not strike them down. Are you going to strike them down like people you took captive with your sword and your bow? Put food and water in front of them so they can eat and drink and go to their lord." ²³He prepared a great banquet for them, and they ate and drank. Then he sent them off and they went to their lord, and the Aramean raiders no longer invaded Israel.

Over recent years the way I pray has been revolutionized by the awareness from the Prophets that when we pray we are taking part in debates in God's cabinet in heaven. Stories like the one about Micaiah in 1 Kings 22 illustrate how God doesn't just sit alone in heaven deciding things, any more than God takes all the necessary actions in the world without using other agents. God chairs a cabinet and makes decisions in light of its debates. Prophets don't just listen; they take part, and that is what we do in prayer. That's why prayer is important; as in any meeting, if some people don't take part, then that influences the course of the debate and the decisions that are made. Even just naming people in prayer, as I do quite a bit, reminds the decision-making body not to forget them. Heaven is a much more complicated place than we often think, and what happens on earth relates to what happens in heaven.

Related to this fact is the way Elisha can sometimes know about the **Arameans**' military plans, perhaps because his access to the cabinet meetings means he hears the heavenly representatives of nations such as Aram reporting on events and plans. This facility issues in the frustration of the Aramean king, to our amusement but not to his. The entities that take part in the cabinet debates are not just the decision makers but the forces that take the action, as 1 Kings 22 also suggests (not that their actions are always in keeping with the will of the chair of the cabinet, to judge from some Old Testament passages and from our own experience). There is no separation between the judicial or legislative branch and the executive branch. Elisha knows this is so and needs his assistant to understand it if he is not to get into a panic. What possible chance does a prophet and his staff have against the Aramean army? Answer: loads of chance when you realize the real dynamics of what happens on earth. There is a whole other realm of reality and activity that the assistant needs to take into account. What you see (with ordinary eyes) is not the only clue to what you get.

So Elisha's access to the cabinet and to its president means he can ask for action on earth and see things happen. It does not always work. In the story of the Shunammite woman, he was himself puzzled at the fact that God had not told him about the boy's death. Sometimes prophets ask for things (argue for things in the cabinet) and lose the debate; at least Jeremiah testifies to that experience. You don't always get your way in the debate (that is, you don't always get your prayers answered), but sometimes you do. On this occasion Elisha does, and it enables him to impose another frustrating experience on the Arameans in a way that is amusing for us but not for them.

It's also a great example of how to be a peacemaker. Sometimes Elisha brings judgment down on people, though it's more often on Israel than on foreigners. Like Elijah (and Jesus), he is more interested in bringing judgment on the people of God than on other peoples. We are wise to resent the way the prophets bring such judgment; they are a threat to us. In keeping with his showing mercy to the Aramean Naaman, he shows mercy to the Aramean army. Let's not just be soft, he says in effect. Let's get God to demonstrate some power over them—not to "blind" them (a word modern translations use) but to "dazzle" them, just temporarily. Let's show them they have bitten off more than they can chew. Then let's show magnanimity in victory and throw them a party. Then let's send them home safe and sound. Imagine the story they told when they got home! It's not surprising that they gave up hostilities for a while, though the next story will indicate they needed to repeat this course of learning.

You may think that the model for how prayer works and emerges from a story like this and from the prophets' account of their experience is rather anthropomorphic. You may think the same about their model for an understanding of the interrelationship of the activity of heavenly and of earthly forces. That's fine; devise another model. But make sure it accounts for the realities the story presupposes. What we see on earth is not all there is to reality, and prayer is not designed to change us but to change what happens. Until we can devise another model that represents those realities, we would be wise not to abandon Elisha's model as if it is not very sophisticated.

## 2 KINGS 6:24–7:20

### Shoot the Messenger

²⁴After this, Ben-hadad king of Aram mobilized his entire army and went up and besieged Samaria. ²⁵There was a great famine in Samaria. So: they were laying siege to it until a donkey's head was worth eighty silver [shekels] and a quarter of a liter of pigeon dung was worth five silver [shekels]. ²⁶The king of Israel was passing by on the wall when a woman cried out to him. . . : ²⁸ᵇ"This woman said to me, 'Give up your son and we will eat him today, and we will eat my son tomorrow,' ²⁹and we cooked my son and ate him. The next day I said to her, 'Give up your son and we will eat him,' but she hid her son." ³⁰When the king heard the woman's words, he tore his clothes, and as he passed by on the wall, the people looked: there, sackcloth on his flesh underneath. ³¹He said, "This and more may God do to do me if the head of Elisha son of Shaphat stays on him today." ³²Elisha was sitting at home and the elders were sitting with him. [The king] had sent a man ahead of him. . . . ³³ᵇHe said, "Now. This trouble is from Yahweh. Why should I wait for Yahweh anymore?" ⁷:¹Elisha said, "Listen to Yahweh's word. Yahweh has said this: 'This time tomorrow: a measure of flour [will go] for a shekel, two measures of barley for a shekel, at the gate of Samaria." ²The officer, on whose arm the king depended, replied to the man of God, "If Yahweh is going to make windows in the heavens, could this thing happen?" [Elisha] said, "Now. You are going to see it with your eyes, but you won't eat of it."

³There were four men with skin disorder at the city gate. They said to one another, "Why are we sitting here until we die? ⁴If we say, 'Let's go into the city,' there's famine in the city and we'll die there, and if we sit here, we'll die. Come on, let's surrender to the Aramean camp. If they let us live, we'll live. If they put us to death, we'll die." ⁵So they set off at dusk to go to the Aramean camp, but came to the edge of the Aramean camp,

and there—no one was there. ⁶The Lord had made the army hear the sound of chariotry, the sound of horses, the sound of a huge army. They had said to one another, "Now. The king of Israel has hired against us the kings of the Hittites and the kings of Egypt," ⁷and they had set off and fled at dusk. They had left their tents and horses and donkeys, the camp as it was, and fled for their lives. ⁸So these men with skin disorder came to the edge of the camp and went into a tent and ate and drank and carried silver and gold and clothes from there and went and buried it. . . . ⁹But they said to one another, "We are not doing right. This day is a day of good news. We are keeping quiet. We will wait until morning light, then [our] waywardness will find us out. Come on, let's go and tell the king's household. . . ."

¹⁶So the people went out and plundered the Aramean camp, and a measure of flour [went] for a shekel and two measures of barley for a shekel, in accordance with Yahweh's word. ¹⁷In charge of the gate the king had appointed the officer on whose arm he depended, and the people trampled on him in the gate, and he died, as the man of God had spoken.

*[Verses 17b–20 summarize this closing note to the story.]*

I muse from time to time on why it is that many Christians today fret about war more than Christians in previous ages. It's not simply because they are following Jesus—at least, most previous generations of Christians did not think this way, and many Jews, agnostics, and atheists share that modern attitude. Is it a reaction to the nature of modern weaponry, which does such terrible things to people? Is it that modern communication makes it impossible for us to evade awareness of what happens on the battlefield? Is it that combatants come home from war horribly wounded in body and spirit rather than dying on the field, so that the cost of war continues to be visible in their subsequent lives? According to some estimates, 20 percent of combatants in Iraq and Afghanistan will develop symptoms of post-traumatic stress disorder, such as a kind of emotional numbness. You don't have any feelings, positive or negative—neither joy or love nor anger or hostility.

This story about the siege of Samaria makes me think that the effect of war is not so different from its effect in the twenty-first century. Women are eating their babies. If that doesn't require emotional detachment, I don't know what does. It's not the only passage in the Old Testament that refers to their doing so. The siege of a city was a central feature of warfare in the ancient world. It was a simple affair. You sat outside a city (perhaps your enemy's capital, as in this story), and you cut off its supply lines. The food that would have become the city's food becomes yours while you sit it out until starvation makes the city surrender or weakness make its people a pushover. Nobody would normally eat donkey's head stew, but desperate situations generate desperate results. (I assume that the pigeon dung was cooking fuel, but it might be a term for some kind of unappetizing seeds or husks.)

In the meantime, people experience moral breakdown. I imagine we are not to think of the women killing their babies simply in order to eat them, though maybe I am being squeamish. But in the circumstances of siege, babies are more vulnerable than adults, partly because their mothers' nursing systems would close down through lack of nourishment, and the babies would simply die. In such circumstances, cannibalism sometimes follows. But how desperate a situation is it that women can eat the bodies of their babies? This story presupposes that it is the king's job to settle disputes among people in the community and that they have the right to ask him to rescue them from unfairness and oppression and to put things right by replacing injustice with fairness and freedom. The woman is concerned with whether the king will fulfill his responsibility to decide a case of alleged deceit or fraud. She has lost any sense of the enormity of their action in eating their babies.

In turn, her protest causes the king to reveal his own hidden sense of hopelessness before God and his resentment in relation to Elisha. Is he resentful because it was Elisha who required the king to release the **Arameans** so that now they are in a position to cause such suffering to **Ephraim** again? Is he blaming Elisha as God's agent in bringing judgment on Ephraim? Is the siege the fulfillment of Elisha's word? Is he failing to use the power inherent in him as a **man of God**? Is he failing to intercede with God for the relief of the siege? What hope can the king have for the future? Lashing out at the prophet is a way of lashing out at the God who is bringing such terrible trouble on the city. It is also thereby a refusal to take any responsibility, as if God's action has anything to do with the way the king has been leading his people. There is some contrast between the way the king sends a hostile aide to Elijah and the way the elders, the senior members of the community, are sitting with Elisha, apparently in some way seeking to discover what God is going to do rather than just giving in to hopelessness like the king and his aide.

Whereas God previously closed the Arameans' eyes but opened the eyes of Elisha's attendant, now God opens the Arameans' eyes so that they see what the attendant came to see, though ironically they assume that the chariots and horses belong to other earthly armies rather than to heavenly armies. Unlike Naaman but like the men in Luke 17, the men with skin disorder are staying in isolation from their families. It's not quite clear why they are doing so; there's nothing in the Old Testament that requires it, and they themselves assume they can go back into the city if they wish, but in the circumstances there is no point in their doing so; there is no food there. Perhaps they are in temporary quarantine like Miriam. Perhaps the community has assumed that their affliction has come about because of their sin, like Miriam. Perhaps putting them in quarantine is one of the ways the community is avoiding anything that might displease God in order to open up the possibility of God's coming to act on its behalf. It is then neat that the people in quarantine are the people who discover what God has done. Conversely the man who can't believe that God is going to act on the city's behalf loses the chance to share in its results.

## 2 KINGS 8:1-29

### It Was Just a Coincidence

[1]Elisha spoke to the woman whose son he brought to life, saying, "Set off and go, you and your household, and sojourn somewhere or other, because Yahweh has summoned a famine and it is indeed going to come on the country for seven years." [2]The woman set off and acted in accordance with the word of the man of God. She went, she and her household, and sojourned in Philistine country for seven years. [3]At the end of the seven

years the woman came back from Philistine country and went to appeal to the king about her house and farmland. [4]The king was speaking with Gehazi, the man of God's boy, saying, "Do tell me all the great things that Elisha has done." [5]He was telling the king how he had brought the dead to life, and there—the woman whose son he had brought to life was appealing to the king about her house and her farmland. Gehazi said, "My lord king, this is the woman and this is her son whom Elisha brought to life." [6]The king asked the woman, and she told him, and the king assigned an official to her, saying, "Give back all that belongs to her and all the income from her farmland from the day she left the country until now."

[7]Elisha came to Damascus, when Ben-hadad the king of Aram was ill. He was told, "The man of God has come here." [8]The king said to Hazael, "Take a gift with you and go and meet the man of God and inquire of Yahweh from him, 'Will I recover from this illness?'" [9]Hazael went to meet him and took a gift with him, all the good things of Damascus, forty camel loads. He came and stood in front of him and said, "Your son, Ben-hadad king of Aram, sent me to you, saying, "Will I recover from this illness?" [10]Elisha said to him, "Go, say to him: 'You will definitely recover.' But Yahweh has shown me that he will definitely die." [11]He kept his face frozen until [Hazael] was embarrassed, and the man of God wept. [12]Hazael said, "Why is my lord weeping?" He said, "Because I know the evil you will do to the Israelites. Their fortresses you will set on fire. Their young men you will slay with the sword. Their little ones you will tear to pieces. Their pregnant women you will rip open. [13]Hazael said, "What is your servant, a dog, that he should do this mighty deed?" Elisha said, "Yahweh has shown me you as king over Aram." [14]He left Elisha and came to his lord, and he said to him, "What did Elisha say to you?" He said, "He said to me, 'You will definitely recover.'" [15]But next day he took a cloth, dipped it in water, and spread it over his face, and he died. So Hazael reigned instead of him.

*[Verses 16–29 summarize the reigns of Joram/Jehoram and Ahaziah in Judah, during the reigns of Jehoram/Joram in Ephraim. Both nations thus had a king whose name could be spelled in two ways. (For clarity, I will refer to the Judahite king as Joram, and the Ephraimite king as Jehoram.)]*

I had a visit yesterday from a student on another campus of our seminary who wanted to talk about postgraduate study. The visit arose out of the fact that she had been on the seminary's list of Anglican/Episcopal students, a list I had obtained because I wanted to invite them to a meeting. In fact, I hadn't realized that this list covered students on all our campuses, and I received puzzled notes from people in places such as Seattle wondering why I was inviting them to dinner in Pasadena and whether I was paying their airfare. If I had realized the nature of the list, I would never have invited this woman, who lives two hours drive away. But I did, and she came, and that led into other conversations that might help her realize her ambitions. It was all just a coincidence.

Coincidence plays a big part in the Shunammite woman's story. It was through coincidence that she knew Elisha, as he happened to travel her way, though it was not through coincidence that she suggested to her husband that they support him, and it was not through coincidence that she was able to have a baby and then able to ask Elisha to intervene when the child died (2 Kings 4). It was that earlier consequence that ultimately resulted in her getting the heads-up to take refuge elsewhere during a famine.

The story is allusive about the background. Maybe the famine is "just one of those things," like some famines in Genesis (a prophet could still speak of it as something God brings about); but perhaps it is an act of chastisement on **Ephraim** for its faithlessness, as by implication has been the case with the earlier famines mentioned in connection with Elijah and Elisha. The woman then gets a heads-up because she is one of the few people who are responsive to Elisha. It rather looks as if her husband is dead, and she is the effective head of the family (her husband was already old when their son was born). She is thus in a similar position to Naomi in the story in Ruth. Taking refuge in another country is what Elimelek and Naomi had done; we are familiar with the way this works out in our own world when poverty and lack of work drive people to move from parts of the Americas, Asia, Eastern Europe, and Africa to the United States and Western Europe. Both women end up exercising responsibility for the family's destiny and for its land. The story provides another illustration of the natural way a woman can exercise that responsibility. In the formal sense she would do so only if her husband were dead, but a number of Old Testament stories show that there was no assumption that a woman cannot exercise responsibility for the family, its land, and its destiny. For the Shunammite the move evidently imperiled the family's land more seriously than happened in Naomi's case, maybe simply because old assumptions were breaking down in the way the story of Ahab and Naboth's vineyard shows.

Some of the uncertainties about the story issue from the fact that all this is background to a new coincidence. The Shunammite and her family arrive back in the country, and she needs to appeal to the king for the restoration of their land, which has evidently and naturally been taken over by someone else. As was the case in the previous story, the king's responsibility includes a commitment to seeing that the society functions in a proper and fair way in accordance with the principles that God has laid down for it, and people have the right to appeal to the king when their neighbors are not operating that way and when matters cannot be resolved between them. She shows up to make her appeal at just the time Elisha's assistant is talking to the king about what he did for her. When Israelites read this story, did they ask what had happened to the skin disorder that Elisha had called down on Gehazi, which was to attach to him and his descendants forever (2 Kings 5)? Did they infer that this did not stop Gehazi from living an ordinary life? Or did they infer that he had repented and found restoration?

In turn the background of the second story lies earlier, in the account of God's instructing Elijah to undertake three anointings (1 Kings 19). Elijah never undertook literal anointings, though he did pass on his mantle to Elisha, and Elisha now perhaps effectively commissions Hazael; he will shortly commission the literal anointing of Jehu. Hazael is evidently an official in the royal court at Damascus. It's not clear why Elisha was in Damascus, but his reputation has preceded him, and Ben-hadad sends Hazael to consult him. Like other international figures in the Old Testament story, such as his compatriot Naaman, he recognizes that the power of **Yahweh** and the power and insight of Yahweh's prophet are not confined to Israel, and he thus provides a counterexample to the story with which 2 Kings began, of an Ephraimite sending off to a foreign god when he is sick. Yahweh's power and insight extend to wherever Yahweh wishes.

Does Elisha simply tell Hazael to lie to his master? The story in 1 Kings 22 has already illustrated God's willingness to send words of deceit to someone, as an act of judgment. But maybe Elisha's message contains a more subtle but chilling ambiguity and reflects the mysterious interplay between divine will and awareness, on one hand, and human probabilities and initiatives and responsibilities, on the other, as well as a mysterious tension between the divine willingness to chastise and the divine grief in doing so. No, the king's illness is not fatal, so at one level the answer to his question is that he will recover. But no, he will not recover, because something else will intervene. Has Hazael no ambitions to be king? The subsequent success of his forty-year reign perhaps makes this unlikely. Does God intend Hazael to kill Ben-hadad? The story does not quite say so, though it makes clear that God and Elisha know he intends to kill him, and they do not exactly forbid him to do so. Perhaps their concern lies somewhere else, with the trouble that is going to come to Ephraim as a result of Hazael's reign, over which Elisha weeps; that is the reason for telling the story. Does he recognize that it will be God's means of chastising Ephraim for its faithlessness? Or is his weeping designed to summon Hazael back from his intentions as assassin and king?

## 2 KINGS 9:1–37

### The Man Who Drives Like a Madman

¹Now Elisha the prophet had summoned one of the disciples of the prophets and said to him, "Hitch up your clothes, take this flask of oil with you, and go to Ramoth-gilead. ²When you arrive there, look for Jehu son of Jehoshaphat son of Nimshi there. When you arrive, get him away from the midst of his fellows and take him to an inner room. ³Take the flask of oil and pour it on his head and say, "Yahweh has said this: 'I anoint

you king over Israel.' Then open the door and flee. Don't delay."
[4]So the boy went (the prophet's boy) to Ramoth-gilead. [5]When
he arrived, there: the army commanders were sitting together.
He said, "I have a word for you, commander." Jehu said, "For
which one of us?" He said, "For you, commander." [6][Jehu] got
up and went into the house, and [the boy] poured the oil on his
head and said to him, "Yahweh, the God of Israel, has said this:
'I anoint you king over Yahweh's people, over Israel. [7]You are to
strike down the household of Ahab, your lord, and I will take
redress from Jezebel for the blood of my servants the prophets
and the blood of all Yahweh's servants. . . .'"

[16]Jehu got into his chariot and went to Jezreel, because
Jehoram was there in bed [ill]. Ahaziah the king of Judah had
come down to see Jehoram. [17]The lookout was standing on the
tower in Jezreel, and he saw Jehu's group coming. He said, "I
see a group. . . . [20b]The driving is like the driving of Jehu son
of Nimshi, because he drives wildly." [21]Jehoram said, "Hitch
it up!" and they hitched up his chariot, and Jehoram king of
Israel went out, with Ahaziah king of Judah, each in his chariot.
They went out to meet Jehu, and encountered him on the land
of Naboth the Jezreelite. [22]When Jehoram saw Jehu he said,
"Are things well, Jehu?" He said, "What can be well during
the immoralities of your mother Jezebel and her many forms
of divination?" [23]Jehoram turned round and fled, and said to
Ahaziah, "Treason, Ahaziah!" [24]as Jehu took his bow in his
hand and hit Jehoram between the shoulders. The arrow went
out through his heart and he fell down in his chariot. . . .

[30]Jehu came to Jezreel. When Jezebel heard, she put mascara
on her eyes and did her hair and watched through the window.
[31]When Jehu came through the gate, she said, "Are things
well, Zimri, murderer of your lord?" [32]He lifted his face to
the window and said, "Who is with me? Who?" Two or three
officials looked toward him. [33]He said, "Throw her down!"
They threw her down, and some of her blood spattered on the
wall and the horses, and they trampled on her. [34]He went in and
ate and drank, and said, "Do attend to this accursed woman
and bury her, because she is the daughter of a king." [35]So they
went to bury her, but they could not find anything of her, only
the skull and the feet and the palms of the hands. [36]They came
back and told him, and he said, "It is Yahweh's word that he
spoke by means of his servant Elijah the Tishbite: 'On the land

of Jezreel the dogs will eat Jezebel's flesh. ³⁷Jezebel's carcass will be like dung on the face of the fields on the land of Jezreel, so that people will not be able to say, "This is Jezebel."'"

My parents so loved movie star Bette Davis that they named my sister after her. They married in 1938, the year Bette Davis won an Oscar for her central role in the film *Jezebel*. As "Jezebel" she is Julie Marsden, a powerful, proud, sexy, loving Southern belle on the eve of the Civil War in New Orleans. (I am not going to think about what all this implies about my mother or my father.) It's by no means the only way in which history has turned Jezebel into a sexual fantasy figure. Popular culture did it again a decade or so later in the Frankie Laine song *Jezebel*, and more recent hit songs have taken up the same motif. Jezebel is the tempter, the seducer, the deceiver.

That is not the Old Testament's take on Jezebel. As queen she was a woman who knew how to use her power to support her man, and she was a serious devotee of the **Master** who also knew how to use her power in that connection. She had used her position to see that Ahab could take over the land that logically belonged to the palace and to see that the proper religion of her **Phoenician** homeland was properly recognized in **Ephraim**. Decades have passed, and she is now the queen mother. The widow of the previous king who was thus the mother of the present king was often an important figure in the Middle East, and Jezebel has grown from being a powerful and assertive young queen to being a powerful and assertive senior figure at court. Jehu knows that the right term for her encouraging worship of the Master in Ephraim is "immoralities." The point about that expression is not that there is a sexual element to her activities. It is that the practices of Phoenician religion may be OK in Phoenicia (or may not be; it rather depends on what the practices are), but they are not OK in Israel. They involve an unfaithfulness to **Yahweh** that is equivalent to a husband's or a wife's unfaithfulness.

Elijah had killed four hundred prophets, though the story didn't actually say what God thought of his action. God had told him to anoint Jehu, but he had not done so, and neither had Elisha. Elisha does, however, commission one of the **disciples**

**of the prophets** to undertake the act. Perhaps it is for discretion's sake that Elisha does not go himself. Perhaps it is also for discretion's sake that the young prophet acts in private, though this follows the pattern of an event such as Samuel's anointing of Saul. The chapter later makes clear the reason Jehu is on the other side of the Jordan at Ramoth-Gilead, an important border town between Ephraim and **Aram**. The army was there to defend it against the Arameans, but the king had been injured and had returned to Jezreel to recuperate. It's not explicit that Jehu is commander-in-chief in the king's absence, but if he is technically just one of the senior officers, the prophet's word immediately turns him into much more.

The unnamed young prophet says a lot more than Elisha commissions, though what he says restates words of God from earlier, and it is unlikely that we are to infer that he went beyond his commission. There are two elements in the judgment that God imposes. Jehu is to end the rule of Ahab's line. The fact that Ahaziah is also a descendant of Omri might give Jehu justification for throwing in the death of the Judahite king when he fails to make good his escape. God's message specifically refers to Ahab, the father of the current king, Jehoram, whose reign Jehu will actually terminate. Nor does it refer to Ahab's own father, Omri, whose line Jehu will also actually terminate. Omri does not count so much for 1 and 2 Kings. It was Ahab who had been responsible for real religious degeneration in Ephraim. It is every trace of him that needs eliminating. When the king asks Jehu whether things are well, more literally he asks, "Is there **peace**?" One can imagine his being concerned about what is happening in Ramoth-gilead, hoping that it is in this connection that Jehu has raced to Jezreel. But there can be no more peace or well-being for Ahab's household.

The other element in the judgment is that every trace of Jezebel is also to be eliminated. In the prophet's words, the basis for her judgment is not the worship of false gods that Ahab had encouraged as a result of her arrival, but the slaughter among the devotees of Yahweh that she had herself encouraged. With poetic justice her son's death comes about on the very plot of land that she had enabled the king to acquire by engineering the death of its proper owner. In Jehu's words to Jehoram, reference

139

to Jezebel's religious commitment finds its further place in that allusion to her "immoralities."

In a sense Jehu meets his match in Jezebel. Like her son, she asks Jehu if things are well ("Is there peace?"), but she does so with more overt irony or calculation. She knows that the game is up and that Jehu's answer to Jehoram applies to her, too. She goes on to address him as Zimri, which is actually the name of Jehu's precursor and role model as an army officer who had killed his king and assumed the throne. Zimri had reigned for only a week and had then lost his life and been replaced by Jezebel's own father-in-law, Omri. In effect Jezebel was hinting that people who live by the sword die by the sword, though in Jehu's case she was wrong. Jehu's coup will result in the establishment of his own line in Ephraim, and it will rule for nearly a century, the last significant dynasty before Ephraim's fall to the **Assyrians**.

Contrary to the impression given by the way Jezebel came to be turned into a sexual fantasy figure, in making herself look good as Jehu approaches, the elderly queen mother is not hoping to seduce him but is insisting on meeting her death with the dignity appropriate to her position as "the daughter of a king." But if Jehu has any true intention of facilitating that desire, he leaves it too late and is frustrated, and the result of his delay is that God's own word is fulfilled.

## 2 KINGS 10:1–35

### The Great Sacrifice for Baal

[1]Now Ahab had seventy descendants in Samaria. Jehu wrote letters and sent them to Samaria, to the officials in Jezreel, the elders, and Ahab's guardians, saying, "Now, when this letter reaches you . . . , [3]see who is the best and most upright of your lord's descendants, put him on his father's throne, and fight for your lord's household." [4]But they were very, very fearful, and said . . . , [5b]"We are your servants. Anything you say, we ourselves will do. We will not make anyone king. Do what is good in your eyes." [6]So he wrote them a second letter: "If you are on my side and you are going to listen to my voice, take the heads of the men (your lord's descendants) and come to me this time

tomorrow in Jezreel." The king's descendants, seventy of them, were with the important people in the city, who were bringing them up. ⁷When the letter came to them, they took the king's descendants and slaughtered the seventy of them. They put their heads in baskets and sent them to him in Jezreel. ⁸An aide came and told him, "They have brought the heads of the king's descendants." He said, "Put them in two heaps at the city gate until morning." ⁹In the morning he went out and stood and said to all the people, "You are in the right. Yes, I myself conspired against my lord and slew him, but who struck down all these? ¹⁰Recognize how there will fall to earth nothing of Yahweh's word, which Yahweh spoke concerning the household of Ahab, since Yahweh has done what he spoke by means of his servant Elijah." ¹¹Jehu struck down all that remained of the household of Ahab in Jezreel, and all his important people, his friends, and his priests, until he allowed no survivor to remain to him. . . . ¹⁷He came to Samaria and struck down all the people who remained to Ahab in Samaria until he had eliminated them, in accordance with Yahweh's word that he spoke to Elijah.

¹⁸Jehu then gathered all the people and said to them, "Whereas Ahab served the Master a little, Jehu will serve him much. ¹⁹So now, all the Master's prophets, all his servants, and all his priests—summon them to me. Not one is to be missing, because I have a great sacrifice for the Master. No one who is missing will live. . . ." ²⁵But when he had finished making the burnt offering, Jehu said to the outrunners and the officers, "Come, strike them down. No one is to get out." The outrunners and the officials struck them down with the edge of the sword and left them and went to the city of the Master's house. ²⁶They brought out the columns of the Master's house and burnt them. ²⁷They demolished the Master's columns and demolished the Master's house and turned it into latrines, as it is until this day. ²⁸Jehu eliminated the Master from Israel; ²⁹only, the offenses of Jeroboam the son of Nebat with which he caused Israel to offend—Jehu did not turn away from them (the gold calves at Bethel and at Dan). ³⁰But Yahweh said to Jehu, "Because you have acted well, doing what was upright in my eyes (in accordance with all that was in my mind you have acted toward the household of Ahab), your sons to the fourth [generation] will sit on the throne of Israel."

*[Verses 31–35 close off and sum up the account of Jehu's reign.]*

Each August 30 in my home city of Birmingham, England, the Roman Catholic Church celebrates the martyrdom of a woman called Margaret Ward. In the reign of Elizabeth I, when it was against English law to practice the Roman Catholic faith, a Roman Catholic priest called William Watson was in prison in London. Margaret Ward helped him escape but was found out, tortured, and eventually hanged in 1588 on that day (most other dioceses mark the occasion on a different date, for reasons I don't know). There were of course analogous executions of Protestants during the decades when the practice of Protestant faith was against the law. A century later in Massachusetts, nineteen women and five men were hanged after being found guilty of witchcraft. Throughout Christian history it has been regular practice for Christians to execute one another on the basis of their having contravened proper Christian faith in a serious way.

Elijah and Jehu would have been more sympathetic with such actions than are many Christians nowadays. Surely no one is surprised that Jehu is a man who can be as violent as Elijah in that bloodbath in Samaria; you do not get to be an army commander by being squeamish, and the way Jehu drove also suggests the kind of aggressive energy he had. Initially the story does not comment on what God thinks of his action, but we don't have to take divine omniscience into account in inferring that God could surely figure out that any coup instigated by Jehu will be a bloody affair, and eventually the chapter explicitly expresses God's approval of what Jehu did to Ahab's household.

Actually, there are few bloodless coups, for reasons that may be defensible on more than one ground. The history of Israel has already taken for granted that a new ruler may be wise to dispose of anyone identified with the old regime; we can see such a dynamic lying behind the story of David. But beyond this, the story of Jehu, like the story of Elijah, sees God's judgment being worked out in these events. Obviously the actions of Ahab, Jehoram, and Jezebel cannot be tolerated, but they also cannot merely be stopped. The point about the action against them is not to take personal vengeance and maybe not even to deter anyone else from committing the same wrongs, but to eliminate an evil and declare judgment on it.

Jehu's initial action after the assassinations in Jezreel, the key city in the central valley, is to send a message to Samaria in the mountains, the nation's capital. In effect he challenges the king's court to decide which side they are on. If they are loyal to Jehoram and the line of his father, Ahab, they will want to crown someone from this line as Jehoram's successor. We need not take the number "seventy" too literally; among others, Gideon was also described as having seventy "sons" (in both cases they might be sons but might also include grandsons). It does indicate that there are plenty of people to choose from among the descendants of Ahab for whom their guardians have some responsibility (this is the sense in which they are "Ahab's guardians"). Jehu's challenge is a little like Goliath's: "Choose your champion, and we will fight it out."

The story proceeds with macabre humor. First, the guardians, elders, and officials in Samaria have about as much courage as the Israelites facing Goliath, and the only person with Davidic guts in this story is Jehu himself. Then Jehu writes them a second letter with a delicious ambiguity residing in the Hebrew word for "heads"; it also resides in that English word. "Bring the heads to me," he says. Is he referring to the men who are the heads of the community or to the heads that sit on these people's shoulders at the moment? The leadership in Samaria jump for the meaning that means the death of Ahab's descendants, which suits Jehu just as various people's deaths had once suited David.

Jehu's macabre humor continues as he calls for a great festival in honor of the **Master**, at which a great sacrifice is to be offered. He makes sure that no people but the worshipers of the Master are present and that all those who are the worshipers of the Master are there; and he turns them into the sacrifice.

The Old Testament is ambivalent about capital punishment; it is much more inclined to threaten it than to implement the threat. It takes the same attitude to the action of a person such as Jehu. He acts by divine commission and with divine approval, though also with the implication that the action is not uncongenial to the man himself. Further, a century later God tells the prophet Hosea to name his second son Jezreel because he "will soon attend to the household of Jehu for the bloodshed at Jezreel, and put an end to the monarchy of the household of Israel" (Hosea 1:4). Jehu's story provides an example of a motif that recurs in the Old Testament. God becomes deeply involved in events that encourage people to do things to realize their own ambitions and bring death and destruction to other people when God knows that death and destruction are indeed the appropriate punishment for these people. But the Old Testament does not imply that the agents of death and destruction cease to be responsible for their wrongdoing and are not subject to punishment for it. The motif reappears in the New Testament; such dynamics are integral to Jesus' execution.

The scary aspect to the story is that we cannot assume that the mere fact of God's using us (or other people) as the means of acting in the world says anything about the moral rightness of our actions (or of other people's actions). Jehu emphasizes that the actions he takes are the means of God's word being fulfilled, but that does not mean he is off the hook morally.

# 2 KINGS 11:1–21

## Two Unusual Covenants

¹When Athaliah, the mother of Ahaziah, saw that her son was dead, she arose and wiped out all the royal offspring, ²but Jehosheba, daughter of King Joram, sister of Ahaziah, took Ahaziah's son Joash and stole him away from among the king's sons who were being killed, him and his nanny, in a bedroom. So they hid him from Athaliah and he was not killed. ³He was with her in Yahweh's house hiding for six years, while Athaliah was reigning over the country. ⁴In the seventh year, Jehoiada sent and got the centurions over the Carites and over the outrunners and brought them to him into Yahweh's house. He sealed a covenant with them and made them swear an oath in Yahweh's house, and showed them the king's son. ⁵He ordered them, "This is the thing that you are to do. A third of you come on the Sabbath and keep guard over the king's house. ⁶A third are at the Sur Gate. A third are at the gate behind the outrunners. You are to keep guard over the house. . . . ⁸You are to surround the king on all sides, each man with his weapons

in his hand. Anyone who approaches the ranks is to be put to death. Be with the king when he comes out and when he goes in. . . ." ¹²Then he brought the king's son out and put the diadem and the declaration on him, proclaimed him king, and anointed him. They clapped, and said, "Long live the king." ¹³Athaliah heard the sound of the outrunners [and] the people, and came to the people at Yahweh's house. ¹⁴She saw: there, the king was standing by the column in accordance with the custom, the officials with their trumpets were by the king, and all the people of the country were rejoicing and blowing trumpets. Athaliah tore her clothes and called, "Treason, treason!" ¹⁵But Jehoiada the priest ordered the centurions who were appointed over the army and said to them, "Take her out. . . ." ¹⁷Jehoiada sealed a covenant between Yahweh, the king, and the people, to be Yahweh's people, and between the king and the people. ¹⁸All the people of the country went to the Master's house and tore it down. . . . ²⁰All the people of the country rejoiced, while the city was quiet. Athaliah they had put to death with the sword at the king's house. ²¹Jehoash was seven years old when he became king.

The idea of **covenant** has been very important in the history of the United States and in the development of American democracy as a way of understanding relationships in the human community. Etymologically, the word *covenant* includes the idea of people "coming together" to agree on something; a covenant is an agreement, but the agreement concerns not merely some facts but the way the people live together. When settlers at New Plymouth formulated the Mayflower Compact in 1620, they entered into a covenant with one another for their community's "better ordering and preservation" under God. Ideally, living in a covenant relationship implies that the nation is a group of people who accept responsibility to and for one another under God. Not long after the Mayflower Compact, Thomas Hobbes and John Locke were also developing in Europe a secular form of covenant-based political thinking that also came to influence American thinking. So there came into being constitutions that were covenantal without being religious.

The covenant thinking that was so important in the history of the American colonies sometimes saw itself as following the example of Jehoiada's covenant making. The links and the differences are worth noting.

The essence of covenant thinking is the making of a commitment when there is no external authority that can impose it on you and no law that can apply sanctions to you if you break its terms. In the absence of these possibilities, you make a considered and serious commitment and solemnly swear your acceptance of this obligation. Not to keep the commitment would mean letting yourself down, falling short of your own standards, failing to be yourself. In this story the first covenant is a solemn obligation Jehoiada extracts from the groups of palace guards when he takes them into his confidence about the coup he is about to attempt.

Jehoiada's subsequent broader covenant was distinctive in involving God, king, and people, and by implication it involved all three parties in all possible combinations. It is a covenant between God and king; it thus presupposes something that the development of American covenantal democracy turned its back on. Judah has been living with the aftermath of the influence of Omri's household on it. Paradoxically, despite Jehu's assassination of Ahaziah, Omri's household lives on in Judah in a way it does not in **Ephraim**. In Ephraim, Jehu also saw that the entirety of the household was eliminated. In Judah, events had worked in the reverse way.

Understanding the background requires some recap. Ahaziah's father and predecessor as king of Judah was Joram, and he had married a woman from the Ephraimite royal family called Athaliah. Connecting some dots suggests she may have been Ahab and Jezebel's daughter, but whether that is so or not, she was Jezebel's soul sister. She shared Jezebel's religious commitments, her decisiveness and energy, her capacity to get her husband to do what she thought right, and her ruthlessness. While attitudes to **Yahweh** never got out of hand in Judah to the extent that they did in Ephraim, Athaliah took them to a new low point. Her husband died in middle age, and their son Ahaziah succeeded him, with Athaliah as the powerful queen mother. Jehu's assassination of her son led her to set about disposing of the rest of the (male) royal family in the time-honored

146

way. That makes it possible for her to reign as queen herself, the only queen to reign in Jerusalem in First Temple times.

Alas from her angle, her purging was less thorough than she thought. One of her husband's daughters by another wife has ensured that one of Athaliah's baby grandsons survives. This woman evidently colludes to ensure his survival with Jehoiada, "the priest"—what would later be called the high priest. There was evidently some tension between two groups in Jerusalem. There were people who identified with Athaliah and were sympathetic to worship of the **Master**, who could be expected to resist the coup and try to kill the young prince when he is produced. There are also people who have stuck by commitment to Yahweh. They include Jehosheba and Jehoiada. They also include the Carites and outrunners, groups of palace guards.

They wait until he is seven years old and then stage their own coup. Although Joash will evidently be only a puppet king until he grows up, the covenant needs to involve him. God's covenant with David's line invests promises in him; it also imposes expectations on him. He needs to be committed to being "a man after God's heart" in the sense of being someone committed to Yahweh. The diadem and the "declaration" that are put on him express both sides of that commitment; in the **Torah** the "declaration" is the document detailing the terms of the covenant with the people as a whole that is put in the covenant **chest**.

The covenant also involves the relationship between king and people. Psalm 72 describes the nature of this mutual expectation. The king has a responsibility for seeing that the life of the community is exercised on the basis of the haves sharing with the have-nots rather than taking advantage of them. The people have a responsibility for recognizing the king's authority.

Beyond that, the covenant involves a relationship between the people and God. The existence of a monarchy does not leave the people without responsibility for their relationship with God. The king no more gets between them and God than the priests do. "The people of the country" seem to be the ordinary people whom the priest successfully expects to take the right side in the conflict.

# 2 KINGS 12:1–21

## Life's Just Not Fair

¹Jehoash became king in the seventh year of Jehu, and he was king for forty years in Jerusalem. His mother's name was Zibiah from Beersheba. ²Jehoash did what was upright in Yahweh's eyes all his days, as Jehoiada the priest taught him. ³Only, they did not remove the high places; the people were still sacrificing and burning incense at the high places.

⁴Jehoash said to the priests, "All the silver from the holy offerings that is brought into Yahweh's house . . . ⁵the priests are to receive for themselves, each from his assessor, and they themselves are to repair the damage to the house, anywhere damage is found." ⁶But by the twenty-third year of King Jehoash the priests had not repaired the damage to the house. ⁷So King Jehoash, the priest Jehoiada, and the [other] priests and said to them, "Why are you not repairing the damage to the house? So now do not receive the silver from your assessors but give it for the damage to the house." ⁸The priests agreed not to receive money from the people and not to repair the damage to the house. ⁹The priest Jehoiada took a chest and bored a hole in its lid. He put it by the altar, on the right as a person comes into Yahweh's house. The priests who were guards of the threshold put there all the silver that was brought to Yahweh's house. ¹⁰When they saw that the amount of silver in the chest was great, the royal scribe would come up with the high priest and they would secure and count the silver found in Yahweh's house. ¹¹They would put the silver that had been quantified into the hands of the workmen appointed to Yahweh's house. They would give it out to the carpenters and builders who were working in Yahweh's house, ¹²and to the masons and stonecutters, and to get wood and dressed stone to repair the damage to Yahweh's house, and for anything that went out in connection with Yahweh's house. . . . ¹⁵They did not keep a reckoning of the men into whose hand they gave the silver to give the workers, because they were acting honestly. . . .

¹⁷At that time Hazael the king of Aram came up and did battle against Gath and captured it. When Hazael set his face to go up to Jerusalem, ¹⁸Jehoash king of Judah got all the holy things that Jehoshaphat, Jehoram, and Ahaziah his ancestors as kings of Judah had consecrated, and his own holy things, and all the

gold that could be found in the treasuries of Yahweh's house and the king's house, and sent them to Hazael, king of Aram, and he went away from Jerusalem. [19]The rest of Joash's acts, all that he did: they are indeed written down in the annals of the kings of Judah. [20]His staff arose and formed a conspiracy, and struck down Joash at Beth-millo, which leads down to Silla. [21]Jozabad son of Shimeath and Jehozabad son of Shomer, of his staff—they struck him down. After he died, he was buried with his ancestors in the city of David, and his son Amaziah reigned in his place.

The man who would have been my boss in my present job, David Hubbard, first interviewed me over lunch in a hotel in London in 1981. He was one of the most creative, innovative leaders in theological education in the United States and took the seminary from being a significant but conventional and average-sized seminary to being a complex one and the biggest seminary in the world. Oddly, like me he had a disabled wife, and like me he was an Old Testament professor. Four years before I eventually joined the seminary faculty, he retired, and two years later he dropped dead, at an age still younger than I am now and an age when you might have thought he still had a decade or two ahead of him, either to sit on the beach at Santa Barbara with his wife or to do lots more significant things in the world of theological education or of Old Testament study.

It's a common enough story. It's Jehoash's story (except that David Hubbard was not the victim of a faculty plot). First and Second Kings are often concerned to show how kings and people get their just deserts in life: as God once said to the priest Eli, "The person who honors me I will honor, but the person who despises me will be disdained" (1 Samuel 2:30). And much of the time the two books can provide evidence that this is so. Yet part of their genius is that they don't pretend that the principle always works out, and in the latter part of the books the story of Jehoash is one of several illustrations of its failing to do so. When 2 Chronicles comes to retell these stories, it characteristically makes a point of trying to explain the apparent exceptions. It's hard to hold together both the generalization ("Things usually do work out fairly") and the reality of exceptions ("Often they don't"), and it's tempting either to pretend that there are no exceptions (so when things go wrong for people, it must be because they have sinned) or to abandon the generalization and wonder why life actually works out in a totally random way (so we have "the problem of suffering"). First and Second Kings invite us to the less comfortable position of believing both in the generalization and in the reality of the exceptions.

Jehoash was just a boy when put on the throne by Jehoiada and his associates, and this makes it natural to mention the way Jehoiada would have continued to act as the young king's mentor as he grew up. (His name can also be spelled Joash, but there is also an Ephraimite king of that name with both spellings, so I will keep *Jehoash* for the Judahite king and *Joash* for the Ephraimite king.) Neither Jehoahaz nor Jehoash saw any need to do anything about the **high places**. Further, the story also lifts a corner on the veil concealing some tricky questions about the temple and the priesthood and about the relationship of monarchy and temple without resolving them all. Had the temple fallen into disrepair over some years? Had Jehoiada been neglecting other aspects of his responsibilities? Or is its need of restoration linked to the worship of the Master that had been encouraged by Athaliah? Instead of answering those questions, the story focuses on commending the king for the way he took responsibility for taking the necessary action.

His assumption is that the offerings people bring should be able to finance the work that is needed. While sometimes they might bring offerings in kind that would actually be sacrificed, when they were coming from a distance it would often be simpler to bring cash equivalents, or they might turn their offerings into cash at the temple—hence the references in the Gospels to the need for moneychangers in the temple. The assessors are then the people who do the relevant calculations and thus facilitate the process whereby the cash comes into the priests' coffers (though cash is a misleading word, since money has not yet come into use in Judah, so the story refers to "silver"). Thus the priests can use the money they receive from the assessors to pay workmen for the repairs.

The trouble is they fail to get the work done. The story does not say how long they were prevaricating, nor does it say they were diverting the money into their own bank accounts. Once again its focus lies on Jehoash's action, which further reverses the relationship between palace and temple and between Jehoash and his mentor—who would now be getting old. His new arrangement takes the collection of the cash and its disbursement out of the hands of the priests and under the control of someone from the palace. Maybe the implication is that it's wise for pastors to focus on pastoring and let people who understand administration focus on administration. Only the transfer of the cash to a chest involves the priests—specifically, the priests who guard the threshold. These are the priests who make sure that people who would defile the temple don't come in; for instance, they would tell people with a skin disorder (of the kind we have encountered in one or two of these stories) whether they should stay outside the sanctuary for a while.

So what a fine, wise guy Jehoash is! Then things fall apart. First, Hazael (**Yahweh**'s anointed!—see 1 Kings 19; 2 Kings 8) takes action to extend his sphere of influence, perhaps especially for trade reasons, in a way that threatens Judah and Jerusalem. That leads Jehoash to buy him off in a way that reverses the kind of commitment to the temple on which the chapter has focused, though the story does not actually say that he acted wrongly in doing so. And eventually he loses his life to a conspiracy among his own staff, which historically might be related to the way relations between palace and temple have become trickier over the years (that's the implication of the Chronicles version of his story).

## 2 KINGS 13:1–14:29

### The God Who Can't Resist the Temptation to Be Merciful

¹In the twenty-third year of Jehoash, son of Ahaziah, king of Judah, Jehoahaz son of Jehu became king over Israel in Samaria, for seventeen years. ²He did what was displeasing in Yahweh's eyes and followed the offense of Jeroboam son of Nebat that he caused Israel to commit. He did not turn from it. ³So Yahweh's anger flared against Israel, and he gave them

into the hand of Hazael king of Aram and of Ben-hadad son of Hazael continuously. [4]Jehoahaz entreated Yahweh's favor, and Yahweh listened to him, because he saw Israel's affliction, because the king of Aram afflicted them. [5]Yahweh gave Israel a deliverer, and they came out from under the hand of Aram, and the Israelites lived in their tents as they had previously. [6]Only they did not turn from the offenses of Jeroboam's household that it caused Israel to commit. They walked in them, and further, the Asherah stood in Samaria. . . . [8]The rest of the acts of Jehoahaz and all that he did, and his power: these are indeed written down in the annals of the kings of Israel. [9]Jehoahaz slept with his ancestors and was buried in Samaria. His son Joash became king instead of him. [10]In the thirty-seventh year of Jehoash king of Judah, Joash son of Jehoahaz became king of Israel in Samaria, for sixteen years. [11]He did what was displeasing in Yahweh's eyes. He did not turn from all the offenses of Jeroboam son of Nebat that he caused Israel to commit. He walked in them. . . .

[14]Now Elisha was sick with the sickness of which he died, and Joash the king of Israel went down to him. He wept over him and said, "Father, father, the chariotry of Israel and its cavalry!" [15]Elisha said to him, "Get a bow and arrows." He got himself a bow and arrows. [16][Elisha] said to the king of Israel, "Ride your hand on the bow." He rode his hand on the bow. Elisha put his hands on the king's hands [17]and said, "Open the windows eastwards." He opened them, and Elisha said, "Shoot!" He shot, and [Elisha] said, "Yahweh's deliverance arrow! A deliverance arrow against Aram! You will strike Aram at Aphek so as to finish it off!" [18]Then he said, "Get the arrows," and he got them. He said to the king of Israel, "Strike the ground." He struck the ground three times, then stopped. [19]The man of God was angry with him and said, "Striking the ground five or six times! Then you would have struck Aram so as to finish it off, but now you will strike Aram [only] three times."

[20]Elisha died and was buried. Now raiders from Moab invaded the country at the turn of the year, [21]and once people were burying someone and there—they saw the raiders. So they threw the man into Elisha's tomb, and when the man touched Elisha's bones, he came to life and stood on his feet!

[22]While Hazael king of Aram afflicted Israel all the days of Jehoahaz, [23]Yahweh was gracious to them and had compassion

on them. He turned his face to them for the sake of his covenant with Abraham, Isaac, and Jacob. He was not willing to annihilate them, and he has not thrown them out from before his face even until now.... ²⁵Joash son of Jehoahaz took back from the hand of Ben-hadad son of Hazael the cities that he had taken from his father Jehoahaz in war. Three times Joash struck him down and recovered Israelite cities.

*[Chapter 14 summarizes the reigns of Amaziah in Judah and Jeroboam son of Joash in Ephraim.]*

Yesterday in church, the person who was doing the first Scripture reading, from the Prophets, said as she came up to the lectern, "I don't really want to read this passage." After she had read it, our rector said he had been struggling with it all through the week. He was going to preach on the reading from the Gospels, but he invited the congregation to share their thoughts on and reactions to this first passage. It came from Amos 7 and included a colorful warning about God's angry judgment on the priest who had told Amos to shut the hell up and not prophesy. How do we handle such passages? Of course, someone pointed out (actually it was me) that Jesus is at least as colorful and straight in his warnings. So how do we relate to such a God and to such a Jesus?

These stories in 1 and 2 Kings raise the same question, as they keep describing the way God gets angry with Israel and takes action against the people because of their waywardness. Second Kings 13 encourages us to lift our heads and see that God's abandonment never turns out to be complete or final. There is a consistency about the life of **Ephraim**. You could say that the nation was conceived in sin, the sin of Jeroboam son of Nebat (1 Kings 12). Kings such as Jehoahaz and Joash are still walking Jeroboam's way, and they are paying the penalty in the form of the invasions of Hazael—the **Aramean** king whose anointing God had commissioned precisely for this purpose. But Jehoahaz pleads with God to have mercy, and God responds by sending them a deliverer (we don't know who this was) as happened in the book of Judges. The Israelites are free to go home ("tents" is an archaic expression for their homes; only a few pastoralists might be literally living in tents).

There is no reference to God's action being a response to Jehoahaz's repenting and giving up the service of the **Masters** and the **Asherah**. The reason God has mercy is that "he saw Israel's affliction, because the king of Aram afflicted them." The affliction God saw was the affliction that God had commissioned, but God could not resist Jehoahaz's plea to bring it to an end. Literally Jehoahaz "softened **Yahweh**'s face." Yahweh was focusing on being hard-faced toward Ephraim; Jehoahaz managed to get Yahweh to focus on what the people were going through and thus to stop being hard-faced. Maybe, we might infer Yahweh was thinking, maybe showing them mercy will win their repentance, win them to turn away from the Masters and come back to me properly. It didn't happen.

The closing part of the chapter spells out further what is going on in God's heart and draws on some key Old Testament ideas about God. God's action is an expression of God's grace. It's the first reference to God's grace since Solomon's prayer at the dedication of the temple (1 Kings 8–9), but grace has underlain the entire story. God's action is also an expression of God's compassion. It's the first reference to God's compassion in 1 and 2 Kings, but we know about compassion because it was the motherly feeling for her baby displayed by one of the women in 1 Kings 3. Third, God's action issues from God's **covenant** commitment, specifically to Israel's ancestors. The trouble with that commitment was that no concrete conditions attached to it, so God can't get out of being faithful to that covenant and its promises simply because Israel doesn't keep its side of the bargain. The covenant wasn't a bargain.

All this meant that God wasn't willing (you could say God wasn't able) to annihilate them or throw them out, "even until now." When is this "now"? Prophets such as Elijah and Elisha and kings such as Jehoahaz and Joash lived in the ninth century; Hazael died about 806 BC. But for the author of these books, the "now" is much later. The **Assyrians** put Ephraim out of business, nearly a century later, in 722, but the period covered by these books covers the best part of another two centuries. There was no nation of Ephraim to see. This statement thus makes an astonishing and bold statement of faith. When the only Ephraimites you can see are some people who

154

took refuge in Judah when their nation fell and some people who now have Assyrian immigrants living among them, many of whom have forgotten what it means to be Ephraim—God has not forgotten. They are still before his face. Let some more centuries pass, and the area of Ephraim will be part of Israel again. It was where Jesus came from. I remind myself of these dynamics of Ephraim's experience when I am disheartened by the near-demise of the church in Europe.

The closing stories about Elisha leave modern people scratching their heads and feeling uncomfortable, though people in traditional societies find them more intelligible. The stories don't fit the way modern people look at the world. We might view their assumptions as worryingly close to magic, and/or we might simply say we don't believe them. So as usual we need to ask why God might be willing to have such stories in his book. One implication of the first story emerges from Joash's greeting to Elisha on his deathbed: "Father! Father! The chariotry of Israel and its cavalry!" (They are words Elisha himself used when Elijah was taken off by God: see 2 Kings 2). It's tempting to think that the servant through whom God works is key to your security and success. Elisha wants Joash to see otherwise and to take responsibility under God for taking hold of God's power, but Joash only half-succeeds in doing so. The second story suggests an opposite point. Elisha doesn't stop doing things just because he is dead. There is still life in him.

## 2 KINGS 15:1-16:20

### How Not to Render to Caesar

*[Chapter 15 summarizes the reign of Azariah (Uzziah) and Jotham in Judah and of Zechariah, Shallum, Menahem, Pekahiah, and Pekah in Ephraim. Among other things, the tumultuous history of the Ephraimite monarchy in this period means the fulfillment of God's warning to Jehu about the destiny of his line.]*

16:1In the seventeenth year of Pekah son of Remaliah, Ahaz son of Jotham became king of Judah. 2Ahaz was twenty years old when he became king, and he reigned sixteen years in Jerusalem. He did not do what was upright in the eyes of

Yahweh his God like David his ancestor. [3]He walked in the way of the kings of Israel. Further, he passed his son through the fire in accordance with the abhorrent practices of the nations that Yahweh dispossessed before the Israelites, [4]and sacrificed and burned incense at the high places, on the hills, and under every flourishing tree. [5]Then Rezin king of Aram and Pekah the son of Remaliah king of Israel came up to Jerusalem to do battle. They besieged Ahaz but could not prevail. [6]At that time Rezin king of Aram regained Elat for Aram. He cleared out the Judahites from Elot, and Edomites came to Elat and have lived there until this day.

[7]Ahaz sent aides to Tiglath-pileser king of Assyria saying, "I am your servant and your son. Come up and deliver me from the hand of the king of Aram and from the hand of the king of Israel, who are arising against me." [8]Ahaz got the gold and silver that could be found in Yahweh's house and in the treasuries of the king's house and sent them to the king of Assyria as a gift, [9]and the king of Assyria listened to him. The king of Assyria went up to Damascus, captured it, exiled it to Kir, and put Rezin to death. [10]King Ahaz went to meet Tiglath-pileser the king of Assyria at Damascus, and he saw the altar at Damascus. King Ahaz sent Uriah the priest a picture of the altar and a plan of it, for its entire construction, [11]and Uriah the priest built the altar. In accordance with all that King Ahaz had sent from Damascus, so Uriah the priest did, before King Ahaz came from Damascus. [12]When the king came from Damascus, and when the king saw the altar, the king moved toward the altar and went up on it [13]and offered his burnt offering and his grain offering, poured his libation, and spattered the blood of his fellowship offerings on the altar. [14]The bronze altar that was before Yahweh—he moved it from the front of the house (between the [new] altar and Yahweh's house) and put it by the side of the [new] altar, to the north. [15a]King Ahaz ordered Uriah the priest, "Offer the morning burnt offering and the evening grain offering, the king's burnt offering and his grain offering, the burnt offering of all the people of the country, their grain offering, and their libations, on the great [new] altar. All the blood of the burnt offering and all the blood of the sacrifice you are to spatter on it."

*[Verses 15b–20 close off Ahaz's reign.]*

A recent graduate of our seminary was telling me on Friday that the seminary faculty is divided between people who avoid saying things that students would disagree with and people who don't mind saying such things. The logic (she thinks) is that the problem with saying things that students will disagree with is that it may issue in negative student evaluations, and negative student evaluations may mean you don't get tenure. So the second category of professor tends to include the people who already have tenure. Now, if the graduate is right, the professors' logic is full of holes; students have diverse views, so whatever you say, you will be disagreeing with some of them. I make a point of doing so, and it's not the reason I get negative evaluations (unless the students are hiding their real reasons for those). Further, in tenure meetings I have never heard such considerations taken into account. Yet it is of course the case that the things we say and do are influenced by our assumptions about the views of people with power over us (for instance, our students—or our congregations, if we are pastors).

That's Ahaz's problem, or one of his problems. He is unfortunate enough to live in the time when Israel's political horizon broadens exponentially. Throughout the Old Testament story so far, the only big power Israel has had to worry about is Egypt, but in recent centuries their problems have been their immediate neighbors, such as Moab, Edom, and Ammon to the east and **Philistia**, **Phoenicia**, and **Aram** to the west, northwest, and northeast. Now the **Assyrians** have carved out an empire in Mesopotamia in the northern part of modern Iraq and have extended their sphere of influence and assertion of control to the west for the sake of the trade potential that lies in that direction ("It's the economy, stupid"). Geography means that their ambitions more directly affect Aram and **Ephraim**, not least because of their place on the trade routes, though they will have affected Judah, too. Ahaz's appeal to the Assyrian king on the basis of being his servant and son presupposes that Judah accepts Assyria's overlordship; it is on this basis that it can appeal to Assyria.

Chapter 15 relates how the reign of Menahem sees Tiglath-pileser first showing up in Ephraim, in about 740 (in chapter

15 he is called Pul). His own records mention the tribute payment he received from Menahem, raised by taxes on the ordinary people. The story suggests this was a price Menahem paid for Assyrian support—maybe against internal enemies, maybe against those other local foes. Tiglath then invaded Ephraim a decade later in the time of King Pekah, occupied much of northern Ephraim, including Galilee (which was key to control of the trade routes), and transported many of its inhabitants. We also learn from Isaiah how these developments started affecting Judah in Pekah's reign. Ephraim and Aram have become allies instead of enemies because of a desire to resist Assyria, and they lean on Judah to join them in doing so. Judah's response is to appeal directly to Assyria for support against Ephraim and Aram.

These events suggest another take on the complexity of the challenge that is involved in being the people of God while also living in the real world. Here one political embodiment of the people of God (Ephraim) is allying with another nation (Aram) to resist the superpower, and it is then joining with that ally in threatening the other embodiment of the people of God (Judah) and invading its country. That other embodiment of the people of God is then appealing to the superpower for support against its own brother, and even bears responsibility for the fact that the superpower undertakes its first invasion of Ephraim.

Further, that inevitably involves its king in various concessions to the superpower. Admittedly Ahaz can hardly blame everything on that pressure. Second Kings portrays him as engaging in the same kind of traditional worship as features in Ephraim itself as well as adding the **Canaanite** practice of sacrificing a child as a way of demonstrating the kind of commitment to God to which God might reasonably be expected to respond positively. The story may also imply that the king's involvement in offering the first sacrifices on his new **altar** raises further questions. It is a king such as Jeroboam who personally climbs the altar to offer sacrifice; when David and Solomon "offer sacrifices," the story may assume that it was the priests who undertook the actual sacrificial ritual on the king's behalf. It is unlikely that all Ahaz's deviant action could be blamed on Assyrian pressure.

Ahaz did have to make it financially worthwhile for the
Assyrians to bother to come and protect Judah against Ephraim
and Aram. He also demonstrates his subservience in introduc-
ing into the temple an altar like the one he found in Damascus,
the Aramean capital, now under direct Assyrian rule. The Old
Testament does not suggest that every time you make an altar
you have to follow God's prescription, any more than we do
when we build a church. But it is a different matter deliberately
to design an altar to fit what the superpower will approve so
that it becomes as much a way of acknowledging Caesar as a
way of acknowledging God. Second Kings expresses its implicit
critique in a different way to Isaiah, but it complements it. Isaiah's point to Ahaz is that the challenge and security of Judah
lie in relying on **Yahweh**, but to Ahaz that wouldn't seem a very
practical way of living in the world.

The close of the account of the new altar provides a useful summary of the temple's worship round as practiced at one
stage in Israel's history. Offerings at daybreak give thanks for
the night's rest and dedicate the day to God. Offerings at sun-
set give thanks for the day and seek God's protection for the
night. As well as the burnt offerings and the libations of wine
(the whole of which go up to God) there are the grain offerings
and the "sacrifices"—that is the fellowship sacrifices, which the
people and God share, as some is burnt and some is eaten as a
festive meal by the people in God's presence. At one level the
worship is quite orthodox, but it has been made subservient to
the demands of the political situation.

# 2 KINGS 17:1–41

### The Fall of the Northern Kingdom

[1]In the twelfth year of Ahaz king of Judah, Hoshea son of Elah
became king over Israel in Samaria, for nine years. [2]He did
what was displeasing in Yahweh's eyes, only not like the kings
of Israel who were before him. [3]Shalmaneser the king of Assyria
went up against him, and Hoshea became his servant and sent
him an offering. [4]But the king of Assyria discovered treachery
in Hoshea. . . . [5]The king of Assyria went up against the entire
country. He went up to Samaria and besieged it for three years.

⁶In the third year of Hoshea, the king of Assyria took Samaria. He transported Israel to Assyria and settled them at Halah and Habor, the river Gozan and the cities of Media. ⁷It happened because the Israelites had offended against Yahweh their God who had brought them up from Egypt, from under the hand of Pharaoh the king of Egypt. They had revered other gods ⁸and lived by the laws of the nations that Yahweh had dispossessed from before the Israelites. . . . ¹³Yahweh had testified against Israel (and Judah) by means of every prophet, every seer, saying, "Turn from your wrong ways, keep my commands and laws according to all the teaching that I commanded your ancestors and sent to you by means of my servants the prophets." ¹⁴But they did not listen. They stiffened their neck, like their ancestors who did not trust in Yahweh their God. ¹⁵They rejected his laws, his covenant that he sealed with their ancestors, and his declarations with which he charged them. They went after emptiness and became empty, [went] after the nations around them, when Yahweh had commanded them not to act like them. . . . ¹⁹Judah, too, did not keep the commands of Yahweh their God but walked by the laws of Israel, which it had practiced. . . . ²³ᵇSo Israel went into exile from its soil to Assyria, until this day.

²⁴The king of Assyria brought people from Babylon, Cuthah, Avva, Hamath, and Sepharvaim and settled them in the cities of Samaria in place of the Israelites. They took possession of Samaria and settled in its cities. ²⁵When they first settled there they did not revere Yahweh, and Yahweh sent lions among them and they became killers among them. . . . ²⁷So the king of Assyria commanded, "Send there one of the priests you exiled from there. They are to go and settle there and teach them the requirement of the God of the land. . . . ²⁹But the different nations would make its own god, each of them, and set them up in the house at the high places that the people of Samaria had made. . . . ³³They would revere Yahweh but serve their own gods according to the requirement of the nations from which they had been exiled. ³⁴To this day they are acting in accordance with the former requirements. They are not revering Yahweh and not acting in accordance with the laws and requirements laid on them and the teaching and command Yahweh gave the descendants of Jacob, who was given the name Israel. . . . ⁴¹ᵇTheir children and grandchildren are acting as their ancestors did, to this day.

I suspect that people think I am an upright kind of guy, and they are not exactly wrong, but I have stories in my past of which I am ashamed and about which they don't know, and I am not about to tell you these either. They still cause me shame, but that sense of shame isn't demoralizing; I have come to terms with my actions and sought forgiveness for them. The positive significance of the shame is that it continues to inhibit me from acting in the same way again. I also know stories about messes that other people have gotten into that are similar to mine, sometimes with results that have been more devastating, and those stories are significant for me too. They reinforce the motivation to avoid getting into those messes again.

Those dynamics operate on the corporate level in this account of the devastating fall of **Ephraim**, which terminated its existence as a nation. We again have to remind ourselves that these stories are not merely contemporary newspaper reports or journal entries. They are more like a memoir in which someone reflects with the benefit of some distancing on the significance of their experience. Or rather, they are like the kind of memoir in which someone reflects on the life and experience of a family member (and someone with whom the writer has had a rather stormy relationship). First and Second Kings constitutes **Judah**'s later reflection on its brother Ephraim's life, reflection that is concerned not so much to understand Ephraim's story for its own sake but to discover what Judah needs to learn for its own life.

One possible context for a first edition of this memoir is the century that immediately followed. Whereas Samaria fell in 722, Judah continued in existence as a nation until 587. For the next century or so, Ephraim's story stands as a warning to it. It must learn from its brother's fate. It needs to read Ephraim's story in light of where it ended and of the religious and theological evaluation this chapter offers.

It didn't do so: "Judah, too, did not keep the commands of **Yahweh** their God but walked by the laws of Israel, which it had practiced." The next context for an edition of this memoir is the decades that follow Judah's consequent fall in 587, the period at which 1 and 2 Kings will eventually end.

A further context in which we can imagine the story being read, and maybe a context for another edition, is the life of Judah later in that same century. At the hand of **Assyria** and **Babylon**, Ephraim and Judah went through analogous experiences. Religiously they resisted the authority of Yahweh and politically they resisted the sovereignty of the superpower, and both acts of resistance had the same consequence. God raised up Assyria and then Babylon as the means of chastising the two nations, and one way they did so was by transporting part of their population. In both cases a superficial read of the story could suggest they transported the entire population, but in both cases that looks like an oversimplification. But the Assyrians likely did transport more of Ephraim than the Babylonians did of Judah, and they also brought people from elsewhere to settle in their place (as the Babylonians did not). It was a more permanent moving around of the peoples in their empire. The Old Testament never records an account of Ephraimites coming back. They became the "ten lost tribes of Israel."

In some sense the population of Ephraim thus became mixed. There were people in Ephraim who escaped the transportation (the Old Testament talks about some moving to Judah, and for some of them that might have been temporary; further, the way these things usually work would suggest that others took temporary refuge in places like Moab and Ammon). Second Kings describes a different kind of mixing: the new population combined adherence to Yahweh with adherence to the gods they brought with them from their homelands.

That mixing is then the background to relations between Judah and Samaria as described in Ezra and Nehemiah, by whose time **Persia** has taken over as superpower. By now "Samaria" is the name of the area that was once Ephraim. Both Judah and Samaria are provinces of the Persian empire. The leadership in Samaria wants to share in the religious life of Judah and Jerusalem, but the Judahite leadership is afraid that their alleged religious interest is too enmeshed with a political interest in controlling affairs in Judah.

This memoir provides them with some religious rationale for their resistance. In their relationships with Samaria, they need to remember the origins of the community there and the mixed nature of its religious commitment. In their own life, too, the Judahite people are still influenced by the traditional religion of the peoples who live around them. It wouldn't take much for any mixedness of the religion of people in Samaria to affect people in Judah. They also need to learn from this memoir. "The past is never dead. It's not even past," wrote William Faulkner in his novel/drama *Requiem for a Nun*([New York: Random House, 1951], act 1, scene 3).

There are two bases for the memoir's critique of Ephraim and Judah in this chapter and for its implicit warning to the later community. It talks much about laws, requirements, commands, and teaching, and here it will have in mind the kind of expectations expressed in the **Torah**, and probably particularly in Deuteronomy. There are lots of links between Deuteronomy and the books that follow it (Joshua, Judges, Samuel, Kings); Deuteronomy outlines how Israel was supposed to live in the promised land, and the story that follows details how they failed to do so. The second basis is the teaching of the prophets. First and Second Kings have referred to prophets such as Elijah and Micaiah, but during the last years of Ephraim's life Amos and Hosea have been working in Samaria, warning about the catastrophe that hangs over the nation, but it has taken no more notice of the prophets than it did of the Torah. Once more, the later generation for which these books are written needs to learn that lesson and start taking the Torah and the Prophets seriously.

## 2 KINGS 18:1–37

### The Bird in a Cage

[1]In the third year of Hoshea son of Elah king of Israel, Hezekiah son of Ahaz began to reign as king of Judah. [2]He was twenty-five years old when he became king, and he reigned twenty-nine years in Jerusalem. His mother's name was Abi daughter of Zechariah. [3]He did what was upright in Yahweh's eyes in accordance with all that David his ancestor had done. [4]He was the one who removed the high places, broke up the columns, cut down the Asherah, and crushed the bronze snake that Moses had made, because until that time the Israelites had

been making offerings to it (it was called "The Bronze"). ⁵It was on Yahweh the God of Israel that he relied. After him there was no one like him among all the kings of Judah, or that were before him. ⁶He stuck to Yahweh. He did not turn from following him but kept the commands that Yahweh had issued Moses. ⁷Yahweh was with him. Wherever he went out, he was successful. But he rebelled against the king of Assyria and did not serve him, ⁸and he himself struck down the Philistines as far as Gaza and its borders, from the lookouts' tower to the fortified city. . . .

¹³In the fourteenth year of King Hezekiah, Sennacherib king of Assyria came up against all the fortified cities of Judah and took them. ¹⁴Hezekiah king of Judah sent to the king of Assyria at Lachish saying, "I have offended. Turn from me. What you put upon me, I will bear." The king of Assyria required of Hezekiah king of Judah three hundred talents of silver and three hundred and thirty talents of gold. ¹⁵Hezekiah gave him all the silver that could be found in Yahweh's house and in the treasuries of the king's house. . . .

¹⁷The king of Assyria had sent the Tartan, the Rab-saris, and the Rab-shakeh from Lachish to King Hezekiah in Jerusalem with a large force. . . . ¹⁸ᵇEliakim son of Hilkiah who was over the household, Shebna the scribe, and Joah son of Asaph the recorder went out to them. ¹⁹The Rab-shakeh said to them, "You should say to Hezekiah, 'The Great King, the king of Assyria, has said this: "What is this reliance on which you rely? ²⁰You say [to yourself] 'Just the words of someone's lips are strategy and strength for battle.' Now, on whom do you rely that you have rebelled against me? ²¹Right. You are now relying for yourself on the support of this broken reed, on Egypt. When someone leans on it, it goes into his palm and pierces it. That's what Pharaoh the king of Egypt is to all the people who rely on him. ²²But if you say to me, 'We rely on Yahweh our God,' isn't he the one whose high places and altars Hezekiah has removed. . . ? ²⁵Is it now without Yahweh that I have come up to this place to destroy it? It was Yahweh who said to me, 'Go up to this country and destroy it. . . .' ³²ᵇAnd don't listen to Hezekiah when he deceives you, saying, 'Yahweh will rescue us.' Did the gods of the nations, any of them, rescue his country from the hand of the king of Assyria. . . ?"'" ³⁷So they came . . . to Hezekiah with their clothes torn and told him the Rab-shakeh's words.

When my sons were babies, we would play trust exercises with them, though I'm not sure whether we or they realized this was what we were doing. They would leap from some height, such as a wall, knowing that father or mother would catch them. As little children (if we have reason to think our parents are trustworthy), we probably find this easy. Growing up, we discover that not everyone is trustworthy, and we may hesitate to jump. As a psychiatrist, my wife used to get people to do formal trust exercises, which would involve getting a patient to fall backwards into the arms of someone else. In doing that, there is a moment when you reach the point of no return. If you let yourself go beyond that point, you are not going to be able to stop your fall. You have made a commitment and are absolutely dependent on the person who says he or she is going to catch you. You have to trust that you can rely on this person

That is Judah's position, and Hezekiah's position as its leader. At first you get the impression that Hezekiah is unequivocally a great guy, but then the portrait becomes a bit mistier. Maybe it's appropriate that he is described as someone whose great uprightness compares with David's, because David was actually a somewhat ambiguous person. The people who read the Bible are divided into those who find it helpful to have stories of great heroes who can be an inspiration and flawed heroes who can be an encouragement, and the Bible meets both needs in the way it describes its heroes. So Hezekiah is more radical in his commitment to **Yahweh** than any other Judahite king so far. He is the first king to close down the **high places** as well as to destroy the pillars (associated with **Canaanite**-style worship) and the **Asherah**. You can read about the origin of the bronze snake in Numbers 21; it had started off as a sacramental means of God's healing people, but it had become something more like an idol for people.

As well as being wise in religious matters, Hezekiah was also initially successful in military and political affairs. His campaigns against the **Philistines** were likely part of his preparation for standing up to **Assyria**, but his rebellion against Assyria was a disaster. It provoked the Assyrian king into attacking Judah in 701 BC. Sennacherib recorded his own account of the invasion in an inscription in his capital, Nineveh. He speaks of besieging and taking forty-six of Hezekiah's fortified cities (which ironically he gave over to the Philistines) and taking huge amounts of plunder. Hezekiah he shut up in Jerusalem "like a caged bird." In 2 Kings 18, I take verses 13–16 as a summary of the event; what follows then gives us the details. But while it's easy in principle to relate this story to Assyrian records, it's hard to disentangle "pure history" from a story designed to bring home a message about trust in God.

It's not clear whether Hezekiah had no business rebelling against Assyria, as his successors had no business rebelling against **Babylon**. What is clear is that the rebellion triggered the great spiritual, religious, and political issue Hezekiah had to face as well as the quality that makes him a hero: "It was on Yahweh the God of Israel that he relied." In this chapter I have translated the word as "rely" though elsewhere it is translated as "trust." In the books of Kings, the verb "trust" or "rely" came for the first time only in the previous chapter; **Ephraim** did not trust in God. It comes for the second time in the opening commendation of Hezekiah just quoted, and it runs through the confrontation between the Assyrians and the Judahites that dominates this chapter.

Sennacherib is besieging Lachish, Judah's biggest city after Jerusalem. Lachish is down from the mountain chain where Jerusalem stands, down in the western foothills, nearer the trade routes and those Philistine cities, and guarding the route up into the mountains. As his inscription implies, he succeeded in taking the city (indeed, he erected a commemoration of this particular achievement in his palace at Nineveh). While he is doing so, he sends off some of his lieutenants to give Hezekiah notice that the pincer is tightening. Jerusalem is the only remaining obstacle to the complete subjugation of Judah. It would be wise to surrender now. Sennacherib knows that Jerusalem will be his biggest challenge, located as it is in the mountains in a good defensive position. He will save himself a lot of trouble if he can get Hezekiah to surrender, and Hezekiah will get off more lightly than if he makes Sennacherib use up resources on what might be a long siege.

In the lieutenants' argument, the word "trust" or "rely" plays a key role. The question "What are you relying on?" is a telling one. Isaiah 30–31 makes clear that Judah was relying on Egypt as an ally when it rebelled against Assyria. Isaiah points out theological considerations that make this a stupid policy; the Assyrians point to political considerations. The Judahites are behaving as if they think that the words of the Egyptians can be relied on and thus can be the key to military victory. It's not so. Without realizing it, the Assyrians speak a prophetic word to the Judahites.

Suppose the Judahites are doing what we know they are supposed to do and are relying on God. The Assyrians' argument is then rather clever. What about the fact that Hezekiah has destroyed so many of God's sanctuaries in Judah (that is, the high places)? Does that mean he can still rely on God? Their next argument is even cleverer. It was God who sent the Assyrians on this expedition. They are God's agents. It is as if the lieutenants have read Isaiah, because Isaiah says exactly this. Assyria is the club that God wields in order to bring chastisement on Judah (Isaiah 10).

So far they have not made a single error, but then they make a calamitous mistake. Even if God wanted to rescue Judah from Sennacherib, would he be able to do so? Have the gods of any other nations rescued them from Assyria? It is a calamitous mistake because it reveals that Sennacherib uses God-talk only as a way of trying to manipulate people. He doesn't actually believe that God is active in the world in a way that could affect him. At least, he doesn't believe this about Yahweh the God of Israel.

The Judahite leaders return to their king in horror at Sennacherib's blasphemy, but in reality the blasphemy is good news. Surely Yahweh cannot resist the temptation to put Sennacherib in his place.

## 2 KINGS 19:1–37

### What to Do with Tricky Mail

[1]When King Hezekiah heard this, he tore his clothes and covered himself in sackcloth. He went into Yahweh's house [2]and sent Eliakim, who was over the household, Shebna the scribe, and the senior priests, wearing sackcloth, to the prophet Isaiah

son of Amoz. [3]They said to him, "Hezekiah has said this: 'This is a day of distress and rebuke and disgrace, because [it is as if] children have come to the point of birth but there is no strength to give birth. [4]Perhaps Yahweh your God will listen to all the words of the Rab-shakeh, whom his lord the king of Assyria has sent to insult the living God, and will rebuke him for the words that Yahweh your God heard, and you will lift up a plea for the remains that can be found.'" [5]So King Hezekiah's staff came to Isaiah, [6]and Isaiah said to them, "Yahweh has said this: 'Don't be afraid of the words you have heard with which the king of Assyria's boys have blasphemed me. [7]Now. I am putting a spirit in him, and he will hear a report and go back to his country, and I will make him fall by the sword in his country.'" [8]The Rab-shakeh went back and found the king of Assyria doing battle against Libnah (because [the Rab-shakeh] had heard that he had moved on from Lachish). [9]Then he heard about Tirhakah the king of Sudan: "Now: he has come out to do battle with you." So he again sent aides to Hezekiah, saying, [10]"You are to say this to Hezekiah, king of Judah: 'Your God on whom you are relying should not deceive you, saying, "Jerusalem will not be given into the hand of the king of Assyria." [11]Now. You have heard what the kings of Assyria have done to all the countries, devoting them, and are you going to be rescued. . . ?'"

[14]Hezekiah took the letter from the hand of the aides and read it out, and went up to Yahweh's house. Hezekiah spread it out before Yahweh. [15]Hezekiah pleaded before Yahweh and said, "Yahweh, God of Israel, who sits [enthroned] over the cherubs: You are God, you alone, for all the kingdoms of the earth. You made the heavens and the earth. [16]Yahweh, bend your ear and listen. Yahweh, open your eyes and look. Listen to the words of Sennacherib that he has sent to insult the living God. [17]Yahweh, the kings of Assyria really have put to the sword the nations and their countries. . . . [19]But now, Yahweh our God, do deliver us from his hand, so that all the kingdoms of the earth may acknowledge that you, Yahweh, are God, you alone." [20]Then Isaiah son of Amoz sent to Hezekiah, saying, "Yahweh the God of Israel has said this: 'I have listened to the plea you have made to me concerning Sennacherib, the king of Assyria.'"

*[Verses 21–37 detail God's word of judgment concerning the king of Assyria and its fulfillment.]*

I used to be the principal of a seminary in England; being a principal is a cross between being a president and a provost in the United States. From Monday to Friday my assistant would open the mail, but on Saturday I would do so and thus be the first person to see the tricky letters. Among them there might be one telling me that the bishops are reducing the number of people we can admit next year. Or the university with which we are affiliated might be changing the regulations that govern degrees in a way that will be complicated to implement in the seminary. Or a local rector might be complaining about something a student has done in his parish. (Or even a weird seminary in California might be wanting to offer me a job.) I used then to be glad that I could do what Hezekiah does in this story. I don't think I ever literally stood in the middle of my office and held up to God one of those tricky letters and said, "Look at this!" But in my imagination that's what I was doing.

The beginning of 2 Kings 19 relates how Hezekiah did this metaphorically. The first time **Assyrian** forces made the trek up the mountains from Lachish, their leaders had stood across from the walls of the city as they besieged it and declared how impossible it was that God should preserve Jerusalem. In one sense there is nothing new here to cause Hezekiah to tear his clothes and put on **sackcloth**. The city has been under siege for a while, though the determination expressed by the lieutenants evidently threatens to push Hezekiah over the edge. What remains of Judah resembles the leftovers from a meal, Hezekiah reflects; Sennacherib has taken control of and/or destroyed most of the country. In a Western context, if a woman is about to give birth but for some reason cannot do so, the obstetrician briskly does a C-section. In a traditional society, the woman and the child die. This is the fate that threatens Jerusalem, as Hezekiah sees it.

It is not this alone that devastates Hezekiah but rather the Assyrian king's slighting of God. When someone blasphemes God and you are in the vicinity, it is almost as if you need to be wary of getting caught in the crossfire or in the fallout of the explosion that may follow. You will be wise to make sure and to make clear that you dissociate yourself from the blasphemy.

In addition to going into the temple to stand before God, Hezekiah sends his staff to discover Isaiah's reaction to what has happened. It's actually a bit odd that 2 Kings doesn't make more mention of prophets such as Isaiah, Micah, Hosea, and Amos (a different person from Isaiah's father, Amoz) who were active in this period, or mention later prophets such as Jeremiah, but maybe it's because they have books of their own. One reason for including these stories about Isaiah is that they are also stories about Hezekiah, one of the great heroes of 2 Kings, but Isaiah is integral to them. Here, the prophet's initial message to Hezekiah's staff outlines the message he gives at much greater length in the last part of the chapter.

It's a nice touch that he refers to the Assyrian king's lieutenants as his "boys"; it's probably capable of being a more technical term than comes across in English, but nevertheless it underlines their insignificance. God has nothing to fear of them, and therefore Judah has nothing to fear of them. The point is implied in another way by the way Isaiah introduces his message, using the phrase "**Yahweh** has said this" (in traditional translations, "Thus says the Lord"). A story such as this one reflects the background of that phrase. When the Assyrian king's top lieutenant delivered his ultimatum to Hezekiah's aides, he introduced it by saying, "The Great King, the king of Assyria, has said this. . . ." That's the standard way an aide would introduce his king's message. He is relaying something the king said to him before he set off to deliver it.

Prophets who take up that form of expression are also relating messages that a king had formulated before they set off to deliver them; and this King is a much more impressive one than the self-styled "Great King" of Assyria. God is in a position to get the so-called Great King simply to go home. God's declaration could be fulfilled by the king's hearing a true report of trouble back home or by his hearing a false rumor along those lines; the spirit could thus be a spirit of deception or of appropriate fear or of irrational fear. Often, you don't know what the fulfillment of a prophecy will look like until it happens. What actually happens is that he hears a true report of trouble arriving from the south and then later returns home and gets assassinated.

It is the results of that army advancing from the south that must have made it seem to Hezekiah as if the cavalry had arrived over the hill in the nick of time, as the king of Assyria is diverted from giving his attention to Jerusalem. While in principle it's easy to relate the events in 2 Kings 18–19 with Assyrian records, it's more complicated to fit them with Egyptian history. But in principle the background to the chapter's reference to Tirhakah is that a dynasty from Sudan did rule Egypt in some periods of its history, so that the actions of a Sudanese general are the actions of Egypt. There is a significant irony there. Both Isaiah and the Assyrian politicians have warned Hezekiah not to rely on Egypt; yet in the end it is actually Egypt that God uses to relieve Jerusalem of Assyrian pressure. Once again it shows how prophecy isn't designed to be a kind of literal forecast of how events will turn out. Usually the way prophecy is fulfilled is quite a surprise.

It's the Assyrian king's reaction to this event that generates the letter Hezekiah takes into the temple so as to wave it before God and say, "Have a look at this then!" It is a great model for prayer. So is the way Hezekiah actually addresses God, reaffirming truths about Yahweh's being the Lord of the whole world (including the Assyrian empire), urging God to look and listen and deliver, leaving to God exactly what to do, and closing with the reminder that delivering Judah from Assyria could contribute to the whole world's acknowledging Yahweh.

## 2 KINGS 20:1–21

### How to Gain and Lose God's Sympathy

[1]In those days Hezekiah became deathly ill. The prophet Isaiah son of Amoz came to him and said to him, "Yahweh has said this: 'Put your household in order, because you are going to die, not recover.'" [2]He turned his face to the wall and pleaded with Yahweh, [3]"Oh, Yahweh, do be mindful of how I have walked before you in truth and been whole in spirit and done what is pleasing in your eyes." Hezekiah wept and wept. [4]Isaiah had not left the middle court when Yahweh's word came to him: [5]"Go back and say to Hezekiah, the ruler of my people, 'Yahweh, the God of your ancestor David, has said: "I have listened to your

171

plea. I have seen your tears. Now. I am going to heal you. On the third day you will go up to Yahweh's house. ⁶I will add fifteen years to your life and I will rescue you and this city from the hand of the king of Assyria. I will protect this city for my sake and for my servant David's sake."'" ⁷Isaiah said, "Get a block of figs." They got it and put it on the inflammation, and he recovered.

⁸Hezekiah had said to Isaiah, "What is the sign that Yahweh will heal me and that I shall go up to Yahweh's house on the third day?" ⁹Isaiah said, "This will be the sign for you from Yahweh that Yahweh will do the thing that he has declared. Shall the shadow go ten steps or return ten steps?" ¹⁰Hezekiah said, "It is easy for the shadow to lengthen ten steps, not that it should return back ten steps." ¹¹So the prophet Isaiah called to Yahweh, and he made the shadow return back ten steps on the steps where it had gone down, on the steps of Ahaz.

¹²At that time Berodach-baladan son of Baladan the king of Babylon sent a letter and a gift to Hezekiah because he had heard that Hezekiah was ill. ¹³Hezekiah heard about them and showed them everything in his treasure house, the silver, the gold, the spices, and the fine oil, and his equipment house and everything that was to be found in his storehouses. There was nothing Hezekiah did not show them in his house and in all his realm. ¹⁴The prophet Isaiah came to King Hezekiah and said to him, "What did these men say? Where did they come from to you?" Hezekiah said, "From a far country, Babylon." ¹⁵[Isaiah] said, "What did they see in your house?" Hezekiah said, "They saw everything in my house. There was nothing I didn't show them in my storehouses." ¹⁶Isaiah said to Hezekiah, "Listen to Yahweh's word. ¹⁷Now. Days are going to come when everything in your house and everything your ancestors stored up until this day will be carried to Babylon. Not a thing will remain,' Yahweh has said. ¹⁸'Some of your sons who will come forth from you, whom you will father, will be taken and will be eunuchs in the palace of the king of Babylon.'" ¹⁹Hezekiah said to Isaiah, "The word Yahweh has spoken is good." He said, "Is it not so, if there is to be well-being and stability in my days?" ²⁰The rest of Hezekiah's acts and all his power, and how he made the pool and the conduit and brought the water into the city: these are indeed written down in the annals of the kings of Judah. ²¹Hezekiah slept with his fathers, and his son Manasseh reigned instead of him.

My wife Ann had multiple sclerosis for forty-two years until she died a year ago. We and other people prayed for her healing on lots of occasions in many ways, supported by a number of high-profile figures in the world of praying for healing. She never got healed. Yet it was not the case that God simply ignored all those prayers. God gave her a ministry that she exercised through her having to live with her increasing disability, and God made a man out of me through my having to live with it. Sometimes people say that prayer is designed to change us, not to change God, and that's a very dangerous half-truth. Prayer is designed to change God, but prayer is part of a relationship, and you can't predict ahead of time how the interactions in a relationship will work out.

Hezekiah proved that prayer can change God. It's typical that a prophet such as Isaiah tells you what is going to happen as if it's fixed, but the way stories then unfold indicate that it's not fixed at all. That can be bad news. When God wants to do something good for you but you don't respond with trust and commitment, that response may change God's mind (it may not—in this respect, too, relationships with God, like any relationships, are not predictable). The good news is that when God tells you that things are going to turn out badly for you, your response may change God's mind. Hezekiah's story shows that when bad things threaten us, it may not relate to what we deserve. Hezekiah has an illness that looks as if it will kill him, but the story doesn't say that it was a punishment for his sin. Indeed, the way his story has been told so far makes him something of a spiritual hero. Connecting some dots would suggest that he must be about forty, and that's actually not a bad age in a traditional society, so in a sense he couldn't complain if he gets an illness that kills him. It's just one of those things. But he can appeal to his life of commitment to **Yahweh** in appealing for Yahweh to heal him, and it looks as if this is something Yahweh takes into account in answering his prayer, though it is explicitly the tears that move God.

Of course, many committed people do not have that kind of experience (the story of his great-grandson, Josiah, will illustrate the point). Here, too, God's relationship with us is not predictable. This doesn't mean it's random; God may be taking into account things other than your needs and longings (as the story of Job shows). It does mean that it's always worth behaving like a child in relation to its father and refusing very easily to take no for an answer. The story is also notable for the way Isaiah (rather in the manner of Elisha) combines bringing a word from God with using traditional medicine. Like washing in the Jordan when you have a skin ailment, the "treatment" in question would hardly be effective in countering a potentially fatal illness, but God seems to like using physical means in a sacramental way.

Indeed, the reference to going to God's house suggests links with stories such as that of Naaman and of Hezekiah's own great-grandfather Uzziah, who was struck with a skin ailment as a punishment from God. If he had some skin ailment, Hezekiah would not be able to go to the temple, and the promise of speedy freedom to do so would be a significant one. That might explain his focus on this aspect of his healing in asking for a sign. The nature of the sign is unclear. There is no need to infer that God changed the actual movements of the planets, though of course God could do so. For the sign to work, some unusual changes in the process whereby the shadows of evening lengthened would be enough to provide Hezekiah with his sign.

Hezekiah's being a more ambiguous person than is implied by some of the statements about him, including his own self-description to God, perhaps underlines the significance of God's reference to being moved by his tears rather than by his self-defense. The ambiguity is underlined by the last story we are told about him. In his day **Assyria** is at the height of its power. Maybe no one would have guessed that it is actually soon to begin its decline, but when you are the superpower, nobody likes you, and everyone would like to see you fall or, even better, would like to replace you. It will transpire that **Babylon** is the power that will do so. The further reference to Hezekiah's illness suggests that the opening "at that time" does not mean that its king's sending an embassy to Judah follows on Hezekiah's recovery; it preceded it. But the embassy did not come just on a sympathy visit. It is a sign of Babylon's increasing assertiveness, though the particular context may be a recent Babylonian revolt against Assyrian power for which Babylon seeks Judah's support. Hezekiah's showing the embassy all his resources is a sign that he was willing to be drawn into such an alliance.

Isaiah knows something Hezekiah does not know. Maybe a shrewd politician could have guessed how the wind was blowing, but superpowers often show a capacity to reinvent themselves, and maybe Assyria could have done so. Isaiah's knowledge that it will not do so reflects prophetic insight rather than political savvy. "Listen to Yahweh's word," he says. Yes, Babylon is going to seize the reins of power in the Middle East and replace Assyria as the Mesopotamian power that controls Judah's destiny. It might seem, then, that Hezekiah is backing the right horse in allying with Babylon. But Yahweh enables Isaiah to look beyond the rise of Babylon. Once it is the superpower, its relationship with Judah will be very different from the one it seeks now. It is Babylon that will terminate the life of Judah as a nation as Assyria terminated the life of **Ephraim**, and it will take the Judahite leadership into **exile** as Assyria took many of the Ephraimites into exile. And if you are the superpower, it's safer to have eunuchs running your household; so that will be the fate of some of Hezekiah's descendants. It's not clear how cynical Hezekiah's response is. Maybe he is properly grateful that the calamity will not come for a while.

The closing note relates to his vital work in safeguarding Jerusalem's water supply in times of siege (see 2 Chronicles 32).

## 2 KINGS 21:1–26

### How to Be the Bad Guy

[1]Manasseh was twelve years old when he became king, and he reigned fifty-five years in Jerusalem. His mother's name was My-delight-is-in-her. [2]He did what was displeasing in Yahweh's eyes in accordance with the abhorrent practices of the nations that Yahweh dispossessed before the Israelites. [3]He rebuilt the high places that his father Hezekiah had destroyed, and set up altars for the Master and made an Asherah, as Ahab, king of Israel, had done. . . . [5]He built altars for all the heavenly army in the two courts in Yahweh's house. [6]He made his son pass through fire and practiced divination and the study of omens. . . . [9b]Manasseh led [Israel] astray to do greater wrong than the nations Yahweh

175

annihilated before the Israelites. [10]Yahweh spoke by means of his servants the prophets, [11]"Because Manasseh, king of Judah, has done these abhorrent things (he has done wrong greater than the Amorites did before him) and has also made Judah offend with his lumps [of wood], [12]therefore Yahweh the God of Israel has said this: 'Now. I am bringing trouble on Jerusalem and Judah such that everyone who hears it—both his ears will screech. [13]Over Jerusalem I will stretch Samaria's measuring line and the house of Ahab's scale. I will wipe Jerusalem clean as one wipes a dish clean and turns it on its face. [14]I will abandon the remains of my property and give them into the hand of their enemies. They will be plunder and loot for all their enemies, [15]because they have done what is displeasing in my eyes and have been provoking me from the day I brought them out of Egypt to this day.'" [16a]Indeed, Manasseh shed very much innocent blood until he filled Jerusalem end to end.

*[Verses 16b–22 relate how Manasseh's son Amon succeeded him and continued his policies.]*

[23]Amon's staff conspired against him and killed the king in his house, [24]but the people of the country struck down all those who had conspired against King Amon. . . . [26]He was buried in his tomb in the garden of Uzza, and his son Josiah became king instead of him.

I sometimes wish I knew what was going to happen in the future, though when I think about it, I am not so sure it's a good idea. When my wife was diagnosed with her multiple sclerosis, if I had known how it would progress over four decades, I don't know how I could have coped with the knowledge. Yet as the decades unfolded, I did cope. In recent days I have read one or two reports about early detection of Alzheimer's. Would I want to know that I am going to contract the disease, given that there is no treatment and I can't do anything about it? I don't think so! Yet we have a natural instinct to want to know how the future will turn out, and sometimes this knowledge can be useful because we can do something about it and evade the problem. So we spend vast amounts of resources on research in the physical sciences, economics, and so on, in the hope that this knowledge may increase our sense of control.

That instinct is the background to the recourse to divination and other ways of studying omens that was a recurrent feature of Israel's life. It will be an extra-pressing concern if you are the king (or the head of a family or a pastor or a seminary president) because you have to think not only about your own destiny but about that of the people for whom you are responsible. Many of the stories in 1 and 2 Kings have shown how it is sometimes possible for people to discover what is going to happen and then to take appropriate action: it is **Yahweh** who can make this possible, and it is people such as prophets who mediate the knowledge. But you can never be sure that Yahweh will tell you what you want to know, so it doesn't really put you in control. Second Kings portrays Manasseh as an extreme version of a man who wants to know (this is the focus of the way he encourages worship at the **high places** and worship of the **Master** and **Asherah**); it dismisses Manasseh's images as "lumps [of wood]" (or maybe of excrement).

A distinctive feature of his worship is his involvement in the worship of the heavenly army, the planets and stars. It is a widespread belief that the movements of the planets and stars can tell you about coming events; hence the popularity of astrology in Western culture. Manasseh also has recourse to various other forms of divination, which might involve looking at the internal organs of animals. Discovering the future could involve making contact with dead family members in the way Saul did (1 Samuel 28) on the basis of their now having access to knowledge that people still living their earthly lives did not have. Sacrificing a child would relate to making contact with the dead. All this stands in conflict with the way the **Torah** expected Israel to relate to God.

Despite this involvement, Manasseh reigns for fifty-five years, so there is some irony about his becoming the poster child for how not to behave like the king of Judah. Admittedly the fifty-five years will have included a period during which he was co-king with Hezekiah, perhaps in connection with Hezekiah's illness (see the comments on 1 Kings 15), but even when we have made allowance for that convention, it was a long reign, worthy of a poster child for faithfulness. Once again 1 and 2 Kings does not claim one hundred percent effectiveness for its generalizations about how commitment leads to blessing and waywardness leads to trouble.

His mother's name was Hephzibah, "My-delight-is-in-her." One can equally understand Hephzibah to mean "My delight is in it," a title God later gives to Jerusalem in Isaiah 62:4. The name she gave her son means "He makes [me] forget" (perhaps he made her forget the pain of childbirth or forget the pain of some loss, such as the death of an earlier child). These names abound in ironies. The grimmest is that the way he exercises his leadership means that Jerusalem quite ceases to be a place in which God delights. The mention of the **Amorites** is telling in this connection. Way back, God had told Abraham that his offspring could not enter the land that God was promising them until the waywardness of the Amorites was complete (Genesis 15:16). The waywardness of Judah is now complete, as the waywardness of the Amorites became complete. Indeed Judah has outdone the Amorites, which is quite an indictment, and Judah is about to lose the land, as the Amorites did. Judah has already been drastically reduced, but God will throw out even what remains. There is no hope in the idea of "remains," a "remnant," that is expressed here. (Of course, as usual God will not be able to be as tough-minded as that.)

There might be political and/or religious considerations lying behind the assassination of Amon by his staff, their elimination by "the people of the country," and the installation of his successor (for instance, there might be people who sided with **Assyria** and/or people who sided with Egypt and/or people who advocated Judah's independence), but the story is not interested in such factors. By implication it sees God's will being worked out again in the death of Amon and the installation of Josiah. There are events that are hard to interpret, but there are events that need no interpretation.

## 2 KINGS 22:1–23:24

### Last Chance to Take the Torah and the Prophets Seriously

¹Josiah was eight years old when he became king, and he reigned thirty-one years in Jerusalem. His mother's name

was Jedidah, daughter of Adaiah of Bozkath. ²He did what was upright in Yahweh's eyes. He walked in all the way of his ancestor David. He did not turn right or left. ³In the eighteenth year of King Josiah, the king sent Shaphan son of Azaliah son of Meshullam to Yahweh's house, saying, ⁴"Go up to Hilkiah the senior priest so that he may weigh the silver that has been brought to Yahweh's house, which the guards of the threshold have collected from the people. ⁴They are to give it into the hand of the workmen appointed to Yahweh's house. . . ." ⁸Hilkiah, the senior priest, said to Shaphan, the scribe, "I have found a Teaching Scroll in Yahweh's house." Hilkiah gave the scroll to Shaphan, and he read it out. . . . ¹¹When the king heard the words in the Teaching Scroll, he tore his clothes. ¹²The king ordered Hilkiah the priest, Ahikam son of Shaphan, Achbor son of Micaiah, Shaphan the scribe, and Asaiah the king's servant, ¹³"Go, inquire of Yahweh for me and for the people and for all Judah concerning the words of this scroll that has been found, because great is Yahweh's wrath that has flared against us because our ancestors did not listen to the words in this scroll by acting in accordance with all that is written concerning us." ¹⁴So Hilkiah the priest went, with Ahikam, Achbor, Shaphan, and Asaiah, to Huldah the prophetess, the wife of Shallum son of Tikvah son of Harhas, keeper of the vestments. She lived in Jerusalem in the Mishneh [Quarter]. They spoke to her, ¹⁵and she said to them, "Yahweh the God of Israel has said this: 'Say to the man who sent you to me: ¹⁶"Yahweh has said this: 'Now. I am going to bring trouble on this place and on its inhabitants, all the words of the scroll that the king of Judah read out. . . . ¹⁹[But] because your mind softened and you bowed down before Yahweh when you listened to what I had spoken against this place and its inhabitants (becoming a desolation and a belittling) and you tore your clothes and wept before me, I also for my part have listened' (Yahweh's declaration). ²⁰"Therefore, now. I will gather you to your ancestors and you will be gathered to your great tomb when things are well. Your eyes will not see all the trouble that I am going to bring on this place.'"'" They took the message back to the king.

²³:¹ The king sent and gathered to him all the elders of Judah and Jerusalem, ²and the king went up to Yahweh's house. Everyone in Judah and all the inhabitants of Jerusalem were with him, as were the priests and the prophets, the entire people, young

and old. He read in their hearing all the words in the covenant scroll that had been found in Yahweh's house. [3]The king stood by the column and sealed the covenant before Yahweh, to follow Yahweh and keep his commands, declarations, and laws with all his mind and soul, by establishing the words of this covenant that were written on this scroll. The entire people stood by the covenant. [4a]The king ordered Hilkiah, the senior priest, the priests of the second order, and the ones who guard the threshold to bring out from Yahweh's palace all the implements made for the Master and for Asherah and for the entire heavenly army, and burn them.

*[Verses 4b–24 detail Josiah's destruction of all improper forms of worship in Jerusalem, and in Bethel and elsewhere in Ephraim, and his proclaiming of a great Passover celebration.]*

Being the principal of a seminary occupied the middle ten years of my time as a professor. I had felt no desire to be in that position, but once it became clear that it was the right thing for a time, I realized that it gave me opportunity to push the seminary in directions I thought were important (though "pushing" is different from "taking" or "driving," in that it requires some cooperation or at least not too much resistance; I had to win the seminary's willingness to go in the direction I pointed rather than thinking I could force it to go where it did not wish to go). For instance, it's easy for a seminary's academic life and its life of worship and prayer to live in separate compartments. I wanted to encourage the development of more unity about them. As an ordinary professor I could act and argue and model to that end, but being the principal gave me more power to influence things.

Josiah finds himself in that position, as his grandfather Manasseh had been to negative ends. Indeed, Josiah's reformation chiefly involves undoing his grandfather's radical innovations. Manasseh had also been a kind of reformer. He reasserted the traditional religion of the land, the religion that maybe most Israelites had practiced over the centuries. As a reformer, Josiah had to be a great innovator. This involved abolishing the **high places**, which had been a part of Israelite religion throughout Israel's history in the country. Sometimes they were places where **Yahweh** was worshiped; sometimes they were places where Israel worshiped other gods. The same applies to the Jerusalem temple, but if you were a king who wanted to make sure Israel was worshiping Yahweh and doing it properly, you were in a position to make sure it happened in the Jerusalem temple. It would be virtually impossible to control what happened at sanctuaries all over the country. So Josiah closes them down. The story is most specific about the innovative nature of the Passover celebration he proclaims, which was unlike any other that had ever been celebrated in the country because it was focused on Jerusalem. When Israel was flourishing, it would be impractical to say that people could worship God only at a sanctuary from which many people lived hundreds of miles away. By Josiah's day Israel has been cut down to Judah, and Judah has been cut down to the size of a county or two, so requiring people to come to Jerusalem, at least for the festivals, becomes a more practical possibility.

The **Torah** scroll that both scared and inspired Josiah seems to have been some form of Deuteronomy; at least, when you compare what Josiah did with the content of the various parts of the Torah, you get most matches with Deuteronomy. The Torah is not just one piece of teaching given to Israel before the people reached **Canaan**; it brings together several versions of God's instructions to Israel as these were given via people such as priests and prophets over the centuries in different contexts. So we can learn a bit about the origin and background of these various versions of that teaching by comparing them with the ongoing story of Israel's history. The lynchpin for understanding that process has been the way Josiah's great reformation seems to be the moment when Deuteronomy becomes a living force in Israel's life. We do not know whether it had been gathering dust in a corner of the temple for a year or a decade or a century, but this is when it comes to life.

It wasn't simply the discovery of the scroll that stimulated the reform movement; the discovery happened as a result of work on the temple that Josiah had already initiated. Maybe politics and faith come happily together for Josiah as they came unhappily together for Manasseh. Whereas it would have been hard for Manasseh to resist **Assyrian** pressure, and it was tempting for him to match his religious policy to the political pressures, Assyria is now in decline, and one action by Josiah could imply doing the right thing by Yahweh and asserting Judah's independence. Nevertheless, commissioning the work on the temple does bring Josiah more than he bargained for (unless, of course, he had himself arranged for the scroll to be hidden behind the air-conditioning system). As well as copious instructions about loyalty to Yahweh and how that is to work out, Deuteronomy incorporates hair-raising warnings about what will happen to Israel as a consequence of doing the kind of things the community is doing in Josiah's day. In the first instance, it makes Josiah go and ask a prophet what action to take (this may seem a bit odd, because Deuteronomy incorporates pretty clear implications). The casual way the story refers to Huldah indicates that it takes for granted the activity of female as well as male prophets. Huldah has temple connections, and if she was involved in ministry in the temple, this would explain the fact that Hilkiah would go to her rather than someone better known to us such as Jeremiah.

The combination of reading Deuteronomy and consulting Huldah stimulates the making of a **covenant**; Deuteronomy is the great covenant book within the Torah. Strictly, the chapter records the remaking of the covenant, as the covenant with Israel's ancestors had been remade at Sinai and in the plains of Moab (the event recorded by Deuteronomy itself) and in the land of Canaan when Israel got there. A little like the unusual covenant in 2 Kings 11, it involves God, king, and people. Usually God takes the initiative in covenant making, but in a context like this Josiah knows they need to take some action. He knows he needs to make his commitment and also that the people need to make theirs. His privilege and responsibility as a leader is to embody a proper response to God in his own life and then use his influence on the people so that they make their response to God.

## 2 KINGS 23:25–24:16

### How to Undo a Reform

<sup>25</sup>There was no king before [Josiah] who turned to Yahweh with all his mind and soul and might in accordance with all Moses'

teaching, and after him none arose like him. ²⁶Yet Yahweh did not turn from the great angry blazing with which his anger blazed against Judah because of all the provocative acts with which Manasseh had provoked him. ²⁷So Yahweh said, "Judah, too, I shall remove from before my face, as I removed Israel. I will reject this city that I chose, Jerusalem, and the house of which I said, 'My name will be there.'"

²⁸The rest of Josiah's acts and all that he did: these things are indeed written down in the annals of the kings of Judah. ²⁹In his days Pharaoh Neco, king of Egypt, went up against the king of Assyria by the Euphrates River. King Josiah went to engage him, but [Neco] killed him at Megiddo when he saw him. ³⁰His staff transported him dead from Megiddo and brought him to Jerusalem, and buried him in his tomb. The people of the country got Jehoahaz son of Josiah, and anointed him and made him king instead of his father.

*[Verses 31–37 relate how Neco replaces him with his brother Jehoiakim; both kings are more like their earlier ancestors than like their father.]*

²⁴:¹In his days Nebuchadnezzar the king of Babylon came up, and Jehoiakim became his servant for three years, then turned and rebelled against him. ²Yahweh sent against him Chaldean, Aramean, Moabite, and Ammonite raiders. He sent them against Judah to destroy it, in accordance with Yahweh's word that he spoke by means of his servants the prophets. ³Indeed, it was at Yahweh's command that it happened to Judah, to remove them from before his face because of Manasseh's offenses, in accordance with all that he had done, ⁴and also the innocent blood that he had shed. He had filled Jerusalem with innocent blood, and Yahweh was not willing to pardon. ⁵The rest of Jehoiakim's acts and all that he did: these things are indeed written down in the annals of the kings of Judah. ⁶Jehoiakim slept with is ancestors and his son Jehoiachin became king instead of him. . . . ⁸Jehoiachin was eighteen years old when he became king; he reigned three months in Jerusalem. His mother's name was Nehushta daughter of Elnathan, from Jerusalem. ⁹He did what was displeasing in Yahweh's eyes, in accordance with all that his father did. ¹⁰At that time the subordinates of Nebuchadnezzar king of Babylon went up to Jerusalem and the city came under siege. ¹¹Nebuchadnezzar

king of Babylon came to the city while his subordinates were besieging it, [12]and Jehoiachin king of Judah came out to the king of Babylon, he, his mother, his staff, his commanders, and his officers.

*[Verses 13–16 relate how Nebuchadnezzar took the king and the rest of the Judahite leadership into exile in Babylon, along with the valuables from the temple.]*

The first time I visited the United States, I came to give a week's guest lectures in a seminary. People must have thought the lectures were OK, because they were then interested in offering me a job, but it wasn't a moment when I could think about such a move. It was just as well, because a couple of years later there was a coup in the seminary, and the president was given the sack. The goals and principles he had worked for were abandoned. I was very grateful that when I resigned as principal of my seminary and came to the United States, I could rejoice in the appointment of my successor, because I knew she fundamentally shared my vision.

Josiah's experience was more like the one of that seminary president in the United States. It's odd, really, because his immediate successor was his own son, as was the next king of Judah. But then, the politics kept changing. Indeed, the very factors that initially facilitated Josiah's reformation were eventually involved in bringing about his death. In 611 the **Babylonians** took the **Assyrian** capital and sounded the death knell for the Assyrian empire, though this did not establish what would happen next. An attenuated Assyrian empire continued to exist, and the Egyptians would be interested in trying to ensure that Babylon did not simply replace Assyria as master over Egypt. It seems that Pharaoh Neco therefore set off to intervene in events as they were unfolding to the northeast, and that Josiah in turn tried to intervene in Neco's expedition, though we are not clear what his game plan was. Whatever it was, it came unstuck, and he lost his life (the battle took place at Megiddo, at the pass between the Mediterranean and Israel's central plain, the place that generates the name Ar-mageddon, "Mount Megiddo"). Second Chronicles 35 is clear that this involved an act of disobedience to God. Huldah had promised that Josiah would die in peace. Perhaps he has forfeited the promise by his disobedience. Or perhaps he is fortunate not to see the eventual conflict between Babylon and Judah, and to see the fall of Judah.

His son Jehoahaz's three-month reign is enough to displease God, which might simply be a conventional summary or might point to his maintaining his father's anti-Egyptian stance. Alternatively, it might be the first sign that "the people of the country" who put him on the throne were less deeply affected by Josiah's religious commitments than one would like to have thought. While 2 Kings is not specific about people serving other gods in these last years of the Judahite state, Jeremiah and Ezekiel are specific about it.

Jehoahaz certainly displeases the Egyptians, who replace him by his brother, whom they perhaps think they can control better. Perhaps they are right. They could hardly blame Jehoiakim for submitting to Babylonian authority when the Babylonian king, Nebuchadnezzar, comes knocking on Judah's door (with a battering ram). He does rebel against Babylon three years later. By this time Egypt is in any case a spent force, and it will be three or four centuries before it takes a serious interest in Judah again. Jehoiakim is in turn succeeded by his son Jehoiachin, who also displeases both God and the Babylonians and is deposed by the imperial power after three months and replaced by another of Josiah's sons.

Second Kings knows that the people who must pay for wrongdoing are the people who do the wrongdoing. Yet it reveals in a story such as that of Jeroboam and Abijah (1 Kings 13) its recognition that life doesn't work out neatly in this way, as we ourselves know. What applies to the family also applies to the nation. An op-ed piece I read a little while ago noted how the twenty years after the Second World War saw the United States making progress in seeing that the whole nation had adequate jobs, food, homes, education, medical care, and social security, but that subsequent policies (and the Vietnam war) slowed or reversed much of this development. People alive today are thus paying the price for decisions taken by the previous generation or two. In Judah's history, the ending of the nation's life (of which we will read in 2 Kings 25) might seem an enigma after Josiah's magnificent reformation. The disparity between the story's enthusiasm for Josiah and the thinness of the long-term results of his work has been an important factor in the generating of theories that there have been at least two editions of Second Kings, the first coming from Josiah's time, the second from after the fall of Jerusalem.

On reflection, humanly or sociologically speaking, Josiah's failure is not so surprising. It takes a lot to change a culture, particularly in a context where cultural change happens very slowly. England in the sixteenth century switched several times between a Protestant reformation and Catholic counterreformation; whichever you identify with, you can see that lasting change is slow to happen.

Second Kings puts the point theologically. In this connection, too, there are limits to what Josiah's reformation could achieve. There is a sense in which repentance changes everything; it restores the relationship between people and God. There are limits, however, to the sense in which it cleans the slate. A murderer who repents does not then get pardoned and freed from prison. This would make too little of the offense. Theologically as well as sociologically, the repentance in which Josiah leads the people does not simply clean the slate. It is significant that 2 Kings speaks not of God's unwillingness to forgive but of God's unwillingness to pardon. When I forgive someone, I "carry" the wrong they did to me (the Hebrew word commonly translated "forgive" is the ordinary word for "carry"). When we talk about pardon, we are talking about the remission of wrongdoing that was done to other people, not to one's self, about someone's ignoring objective standards of right and wrong. Manasseh had filled Jerusalem with innocent blood that is still crying out from the ground. Perhaps his action still could not be pardoned.

## 2 KINGS 24:17–25:30

### Is It the End, or Is There Hope?

[17]The king of Babylon made Mattaniah, [Jehoiachin's] uncle, king instead of him, and changed his name to Zedekiah. [18]Zedekiah was twenty-one years old when he became king. He reigned eleven years in Jerusalem. His mother's name

was Hamutal. [19]He did what was displeasing in Yahweh's eyes in accordance with all that Jehoiakim had done, [20]because Yahweh's anger was against Jerusalem and Judah until he threw them out of his presence.

So Zedekiah rebelled against the king of Babylon. [25:1]In the ninth year of [Zedekiah's] reign, on the tenth day of the tenth month, Nebuchadnezzar the king of Babylon came against Jerusalem, he and all his forces. He camped against it and built siege works around it. [2]The city came under siege until the eleventh year of King Zedekiah. [3]On the ninth day of the month the famine had become overwhelming in the city. There was no food for the people of the country. [4]The city broke open, and all the men in the army [left] by night through the gate between the double wall by the king's garden, while the Chaldeans were all round the city. So [the king] went by the road to the steppe, [5]but the Chaldean forces pursued the king and overtook him in the Jericho steppes when all his forces had scattered from him. [6]They captured the king and took him up to the king of Babylon at Riblah and pronounced a decision about him. [7]Zedekiah's sons they slaughtered before his eyes, the eyes of Zedekiah were gouged out, and he was bound with bronze chains and taken to Babylon.

[8]On the seventh day of the fifth month (it was the nineteenth year of Nebuchadnezzar, king of Babylon) Nebuzaradan, the chief of the guards, servant of the king of Babylon, came to Jerusalem [9]and set fire to Yahweh's house, the king's house, and all the houses in Jerusalem. Every house of an important person he set on fire. [10]The walls around Jerusalem, all the Chaldean forces with the chief of the guards broke down. [11]The rest of the people who were left in the city and the people who had submitted to the king of Babylon (the rest of the population), Nebuzaradan, the chief of the guards, took into exile, [12]but the chief of the guards left some of the poor people in the country as vinedressers and farm workers.

*[Verses 13–26 describe how the Babylonians destroyed things in the temple in order to take to Babylon materials of value and how they appointed a man called Gedaliah as governor, who was then killed by loyalists.]*

[27]In the thirty-seventh year of the exile of Jehoiachin, king of Judah, on the twenty-seventh day of the twelfth month,

Ewil-merodach, king of Babylon, in the year he became king, released Jehoiachin king of Judah from prison. [28]He spoke positively with him and gave him a seat above the seat of the kings who were with him in Babylon. [29]He changed his prison clothes and ate with him regularly for his whole life. [30]His provision was given him as a regular provision from the king, an amount for each day, for his whole life.

On the morning of September 11, 2001, I was sitting on my patio when one of my neighbors passed and told me that a plane had flown into one of the Twin Towers in New York. I went indoors and watched transfixed for a while (I didn't even sit down) as the television replayed the scene time after time, including the moment when another plane flew into the second tower. My sense of mesmerized horror from three thousand miles away was nothing compared with that of people in New York and New Jersey who gave their eye-witness descriptions of what happened, sometimes knowing that their loved ones were in the buildings as they fell.

One senses something of that transfixed horror as one reads the last chapter of 2 Kings. Paradoxically, it comes out through the narrating of the story in a rather matter-of-fact fashion, as if by someone who is still in shock from what they have seen. The account tells us nothing of the dreadfulness of siege, but we know something of its implications from what we have read in 2 Kings 6 (the book of Lamentations tells us that women were eating their babies on this occasion, too). Typically, one might suspect, the leadership tries to look after its own skin, but it fails. Matter-of-factly, again, the narrator describes how the **Babylonians** kill the two sons of the king (who is himself about thirty) and how that is the last sight his eyes ever behold because the Babylonians then blind him, perhaps by searing his eyes with hot metal. As far as they are concerned, he is a traitor. He must pay for his treachery to show people what happens to traitors, and he must be disabled so that it is unlikely that he will ever be put on the throne again; and neither will his sons. The chapter goes on to detail what happened to the bronze columns in the temple, the equipment used for sacrificing, and the decorative work in the building, all that made the house of God beautiful and functional for worship. It relates how there seems to be no end to the community's stupidity. The Babylonians install a form of local government over what is left of the country after its devastation and the transporting of its leadership, and some Judahites kill them as collaborators. But they then realize they have eliminated any prospect of having a future in the country themselves, and they escape for their lives.

All this stands under the solemn words that introduce this final chapter: "**Yahweh**'s anger was against Jerusalem and Judah until he threw them out of his presence." Maybe these words even embrace the words that immediately follow: "so Zedekiah rebelled against the king of Babylon," implying that the very rebellion that Zedekiah undertook for what he thought were good political reasons was actually an outworking of God's decision to bring judgment on the city. The note about God's anger is actually the last sentence in chapter 24. The account of the rebellion and the siege and its aftermath contains no mention of God. It unfolds as a series of human decisions by people such as Zedekiah, Nebuchadnezzar, Nebuzaradan, and Gedaliah's murderers. God is missing from the story, having withdrawn from the city. Yet behind the scenes God's will is being implemented.

If the chapter ended with the flight of Gedaliah's murderers, it would leave the audience leaving the movie theater in a quiet and somber mood. Admittedly there is a sense in which this would be a misleading reaction. The Old Testament knows that when you have betrayed God (never mind Babylon), all you can do is cast yourself on God's mercy. Christians often think that Israelites thought that the way you get right with God is by offering sacrifices. Perhaps there were Israelites who thought so, but this is not what the **Torah** told them. Sacrifices can deal with taboos such as skin disorders of the kind we have considered in 1 and 2 Kings, but they can't deal with deliberate religious or moral waywardness. When you have come to your senses about such waywardness, all you can do is plead for God's mercy. One way of looking at 1 and 2 Kings is to see it as a telling of Israel's story that invites the people to acknowledge the books' truth and in doing so throw themselves on that mercy. Paradoxically, then, whether 2 Kings ends in hopelessness or in hope depends on how people react to it. If they affirm its truth, they open up the possibility of hope. They do not guarantee it. But they open up the possibility.

The books' last paragraph hints at hope in a different way. Remember Jehoiachin, Zedekiah's predecessor as king? He was Zedekiah's nephew, but he was only three years younger than his uncle. The Babylonians had taken Jehoiachin off to Babylon ten years before the fall of the city, so for a while there are two **exiled** kings of Judah in Babylon. Fast-forward a quarter of a century from the final fall of Jerusalem, to 562. We don't know if Zedekiah is still alive. Nebuchadnezzar is dead. When a U.S. president leaves office, he sometimes pardons people of wrongdoings. Middle Eastern kings did that when they came to power; it was a way of showing that the administration was new and of showing what its priorities and principles might be. So Ewil-merodach pardons Jehoiachin and gives him rather a senior status in the Babylonian court.

Second Kings continues to make no mention of God's being behind the scenes of this event. It was a political act by the new Babylonian king. But maybe, just maybe, it is a sign of hope. First and Second Kings has referred several times to the way God has reserved dominion in Jerusalem for David. Having made a promise to David along those lines, God has been keeping it. Might the promise still have life in it? It's just possible that this elevation of Jehoiachin is a sign that it has.

The author of 2 Kings doesn't know what will happen next. This is the very end of the gargantuan story that runs from Genesis to 2 Kings. At the end of each book so far, you can turn over to see what happens next. When you turn over the page at the end of 2 Kings, it doesn't work. We are not merely at the end of a season of this series; we're at the end of the entire series. It would turn out that the elevation of Jehoiachin in itself led nowhere, but the hope it could suggest was real. There is a sense in which the book of Ezra continues the story in 2 Kings, and it shows you how God stayed faithful.

# GLOSSARY

**aide**

A supernatural agent through whom God appears and works in the world. Standard English translations call them "angels," but this term suggests ethereal figures with wings, wearing diaphanous white dresses. Aides are humanlike figures; hence it is possible to give them hospitality without realizing that this is who they are (Hebrews 13). They have no wings; hence their need of a stairway or ramp between heaven and earth (Genesis 28). They appear in order to act or speak on God's behalf and represent God so fully that they can speak as if they are God (Judges 6). They thus bring the reality of God's presence, action, and voice without bringing such a real presence that it would electrocute mere mortals or shatter their hearing. That can be a reassurance when Israel is rebellious and God's presence might indeed be a threat (Exodus 32–33), but aides can themselves implement God's punishment as well as God's blessing (Exodus 12; 2 Samuel 24).

**altar**

The word altar usually refers to a structure for offering a sacrifice by burning it (the word comes from the word for sacrifice), made of earth or stone. An altar might be relatively small, like a table, and the person making the offering would stand in front of it. Or it might be higher and larger, like a platform, and the person making the offering would climb onto it. The word can also refer to a smaller stand for burning incense in association with worship.

**Amorites**

The term is used in several ways. It can denote one of the original ethnic groups in **Canaan**, especially east of the Jordan. It can denote the people of Canaan as a whole. Outside the Old Testament it denotes a people living over a wider area of Mesopotamia. "Amorites" is thus a little like the word "America," which commonly refers to the United

States but can denote a much broader area of the continent of which the United States is part.

## Aram, Arameans

In some contexts, the Arameans are a people spread over a wider area of the Middle East, and Aramaic is a widely used international language that eventually replaced Hebrew as the language of the **Judahites**. But in a narrower sense, in 1 and 2 Kings Aram is the country to the northeast of Israel, approximately the area of modern Syria. Like Syria, it is a much bigger country than Israel.

## Asherah

The word is used both to signify the name of a deity and the name of an aid to worship (the two meanings come close together in 1 Kings 14–15). In Canaanite religion and elsewhere, Asherah was a particular goddess, but the name came to be used in the plural as a general term for a goddess. As a word for an aid to worship, it denotes something that can be "erected," "planted," and "burned," which suggests a treelike column or pillar that represented and suggested the presence of the deity.

## Assyria, Assyrians

The first great Middle Eastern superpower, the Assyrians spread their empire westward into Syria-Palestine in the eighth century, the time of Amos and Isaiah, and made **Ephraim** part of their empire. When Ephraim kept trying to assert independence, they invaded, and in 722 they destroyed Ephraim's capital at Samaria, transported many of its people, and settled people from other parts of their empire in their place. They also invaded **Judah** and devastated much of the country but did not take Jerusalem. Prophets such as Amos and Isaiah describe how God was thus using Assyria as a means of disciplining Israel.

## authority

People such as Eli, Samuel, Samuel's sons, and the kings "exercise authority" over Israel and for Israel. The Hebrew word for someone who exercises such authority, *shopet*, is traditionally translated *judge*, but such leadership is wider than this term implies. In the book called Judges, these leaders are people who have no official position, like the later kings, but who arise and exercise initiative in a way that brings the people deliverance from the trouble they get into. It is a king's job to exercise authority in accordance with faithfulness to God and people.

## Babylon, Babylonians

A minor power in the context of Israel's early history, in Jeremiah's time Babylon succeeded Assyria as the region's superpower and remained that for nearly a century until conquered by **Persi**a. Prophets such as Jeremiah describe how God was using the Babylonians as a means of disciplining **Judah**. They took Jerusalem and transported many of its people in 587. Their creation stories, law codes, and more philosophical writings help us understand aspects of the Old Testament's equivalent writings, while their astrological religion forms background to aspects of polemic in the Prophets.

## Canaan, Canaanites

As the biblical terms for the country of Israel as a whole and for its indigenous peoples, *Canaanites* is not so much the name for a particular ethnic group as a shorthand term for all the peoples native to the country. See also **Amorites**.

## cherubs

These are not baby angelic figures (as that word may suggest in modern usage) but awesome winged creatures that transport **Yahweh**, who sits on a throne above them. There were statues of them in the temple standing guard over the **covenant chest**; they thus pointed to the presence of Yahweh there, enthroned invisibly above them.

## chest

The **covenant** chest is a box a bit more than a yard or meter long and half a yard or meter wide and high. The King James Bible refers to it as an "ark," but the word means a box, though it only occasionally designates chests used for other purposes. It is the *covenant* chest because it contains the stone tablets inscribed with the Ten Commandments, key expectations God laid down in connection with establishing the Sinai Covenant. It is regularly kept in the sanctuary, but there is a sense in which it symbolizes God's presence (given that Israel has no images to do so), and in that capacity the Israelites sometimes carry it with them as a symbol of God's presence with them. It can also be referred to as the

"Declaration Chest," with the same meaning: the tablets declare God's covenant expectations.

## covenant

The Hebrew word *berit* covers covenants, treaties, and contracts, but these are all ways in which people make a formal commitment about something, and I have used the word *covenant* for all three. Where you have a legal system to which people can appeal, contracts assume a system for resolving disputes and administering justice that can be used if people do not keep their commitments. In contrast, a covenantal relationship does not presuppose an enforceable legal framework of that kind, but a covenant does involve some formal procedure that confirms the seriousness of the solemn commitment one party makes to another. Thus the Old Testament often speaks of *sealing* a covenant, literally of *cutting* it (the background lies in the kind of formal procedure described in Genesis 15 and Jeremiah 34:18–20, though such an actual procedure would hardly be required every time someone made a covenantal commitment). People make covenants sometimes *to* other people, sometimes *with* other people. One implies something more one-sided; the other, something more mutual.

## devote, devotion

Devoting something to God means giving it over to God irrevocably. Translations use words such as "annihilated" or "destroyed," and that is often the implication, but it does not convey the word's distinctive significance. You could devote land, or an animal such as a donkey, and in effect Hannah devotes Samuel; the donkey or the human being then belongs to God and is committed to God's service. In effect the Israelites devoted many **Canaanites** to God's service in this way; they became people who chopped wood and drew water for the **altar**, its offerings, and the rites of the sanctuary. Devoting people to God by killing them as a kind of sacrifice was a practice known from other peoples that Israel takes over on its own initiative but which God eventually validates. Israel knows this is how war works in its world; it assumes it is to operate the same way, and God goes along with that.

## disciples of the prophets

Literally, these are the "sons of the prophets." First and Second Kings mentions communities of such prophets in various places in Ephraim in the time of Elijah and Elisha. They lived together and apparently made their services available to people who needed guidance from God on some matter. They would be dependent on donations from people who sought their help in this way; the stories indicate that this made them vulnerable to poverty.

## Ephraim, Ephraimites

After Saul's death, the Israelite clans split into two groups for a while. Politically, the bigger of the two groups, comprising the northern and eastern clans, kept the name **Israel**, with the much smaller southern group being called **Judah**. This can be confusing because Israel is still also the name of the people as a whole as the people of God. So the name Israel is open to being used in both these connections. After David and Solomon's reigns, the nation of Israel split into these two peoples more permanently, and again the northern group of clans kept the name **Israel**. The northern state can then, however, also be referred to by the name of Ephraim, one of its central clans, so I use this term to refer to the northern clans in the time of David and in that later context to try to reduce the confusion.

## exile

At the end of the seventh century **Babylon** became the major power in **Judah's** world, but Judah was inclined to resist its authority. As part of a successful campaign to get Judah to submit to it, in 597 and in 587 BC the Babylonians transported many people from Jerusalem to Babylon, particularly people in leadership positions, such as members of the royal family and the court, priests, and prophets. These people were compelled to live in Babylonia for the next fifty years or so. Throughout this period, people back in Judah were also under Babylonian authority, so they were not physically in exile but were living in the exile as a period of time.

## Greece

In 336 BC Greek forces under Alexander the Great took control of the Persian Empire, but after Alexander's death in 333 his empire split up. The largest part, to the north and east of Palestine, was ruled by one of his generals, Seleucus, and his successors. Judah was under its control for much of the next two centuries, though it was at the extreme southwestern border of this empire and sometimes came under the control of the Ptolemaic Empire in Egypt, ruled by successors of another of Alexander's officers.

## high place

Traditional religion in villages and towns in Canaan would center on a place of worship at the highest point in the village, possibly elevated by a platform. Here members of the community would bring their offerings and pray, for instance in connection with the birth of children and with the harvest. When the population of a village or city became Israelite, the nature of this worship would be expected to change so that it was **Yahweh** who was worshiped there, but in practice it commonly continued to work by the traditions of the past. Either it would still involve the worship of deities other than Yahweh, or it would involve Canaanite-style worship practices such as the use of images—or the sacrifice of children—even if people saw themselves as worshiping Yahweh. Some kings who are faithful to Yahweh let the high places continue to function without compromising their commitment to Yahweh, but in light of the abuse of the high places and the eventual development of a conviction that they should simply be abolished, 1 and 2 Kings feel ambivalent about them and manifest some unease about the way faithful kings allow them to continue in use.

## Israel

Originally, Israel was the new name God gave Abraham's grandson, Jacob. His twelve sons were then forefathers of the twelve clans that comprise the people Israel. In the time of Saul, David, and Solomon these twelve clans became more of a political entity; Israel was both the people of God and a nation or state like other nations or states. After Solomon's day, this one state split into two, **Ephraim** and **Judah**. Ephraim was far bigger and often continued to be referred to as Israel. So if one is thinking of the people of God, Judah is part of Israel. If one is thinking politically, Judah is not part of Israel, but once Ephraim has gone out of existence, for practical purposes Judah *is* Israel, as the people of God.

## Judah, Judahites

One of the twelve sons of Jacob, then the clan that traces its ancestry to him, then the dominant clan in the southern of the two states after the time of Solomon. Later, as a **Persian** province or colony, it was known as Yehud.

196

## man of God

In English usage "man of God" (or "woman of God") suggests someone of deep prayer life and clear moral commitment. The equivalent Hebrew expression has different significance. It suggests someone with extraordinary and rather frightening power and insight. A man of God knows things you might not want him to know and can do things you might not want him to do, though he also knows and does things that constitute good news. He knows and does such things not because of his deep spirituality (though he may be a deeply spiritual person) but because God takes hold of him and gives him the capacity to know and do them, simply because God decides to do so. He is a man who represents God in quite a strong sense. God makes him someone who stands for God in the world and who indicates this fact by the capacities he exercises.

## Master

The Hebrew word is *baal*, an ordinary word for a master or lord or owner, but also a word used to describe a **Canaanite** god. Its use thus parallels the use of the word *Lord* to describe **Yahweh**. So like *Lord*, in effect *Master* can be a proper name, as it is treated in translations when they transliterate the word as *Baal*. The Old Testament generally uses *Master* for a Canaanite god and *Lord* for the real God, Yahweh, to make the difference clear. Like other ancient peoples, the Canaanites acknowledged a number of gods, and strictly the Master was simply one of them, though he was one of the most prominent, but the Old Testament also uses the plural *Masters* (*Baals*) to refer to Canaanite gods in general.

## peace

The word *shalom* can suggest peace after there has been conflict, but it often points to a richer notion, to the idea of fullness of life. The KJV sometimes translates it "welfare," and modern translations use words such as "well-being" or "prosperity." It suggests that everything is going well for you.

## Persia, Persians

The third Middle Eastern superpower, after **Assyria** and **Babylon**. Under the leadership of Cyrus the Great, they took control of the **Babylonian** empire in 539 BC. Isaiah 40–55 sees God's hand in raising up

Cyrus as the means of restoring **Judah** after the **exile**. Judah and surrounding peoples such as Samaria, Ammon, and Ashdod were Persian provinces or colonies. The Persians stayed in power for two centuries until defeated by **Greece**.

### Philistia, Philistines

The Philistines were people who came from across the Mediterranean to settle in **Canaan** at the same time as the Israelites were establishing themselves there, so that the two peoples formed an accidental pincer movement on the existent inhabitants of the country and became each other's rivals for control of the area.

### Phoenicia, Phoenicians

Phoenicia is the area on the Mediterranean coast to the northeast of Israel, centering on the area of modern Lebanon but including part of modern Syria and part of ancient and modern Israel. It was not so much a state as a collection of city-states, among which were Tyre and Sidon. While these city-states could be at war with one another, they were aware of a common ethnicity and a common religion, which they also shared (along with their language) with the **Canaanites**. In other words, the Phoenicians were Canaanites who lived farther north than Canaan itself. Their distinguishing feature was that they were a great trading people.

### sackcloth

Sackcloth does not suggest something uncomfortable; it refers to the humble cloth from which ordinary people's garments were made. It stands in contrast to impressive clothes or the kind of clothes in which important people would appear in public.

### secondary wife

Translations use the word *concubine* to describe people such as some of the wives of the kings, but the Hebrew term does not suggest they were not properly married. Being a secondary wife rather means that a woman has a different status from other wives. It perhaps implies that her sons had fewer or no inheritance rights. It may be that a wealthy or powerful man could have several wives with full rights and several secondary wives, or just one of each, or just the former, or even just a secondary wife.

## Sheol

One of the Hebrew names for the place where we go when we die; it is also referred to as the Pit. In the New Testament it is called Hades. It is not a place of punishment or suffering but simply a resting place for everyone, a kind of nonphysical analogue to the tomb as the resting place for our bodies.

## Torah

The Hebrew word for the first five books of the Bible. They are often referred to as the "Law," but this gives a misleading impression. Genesis is nothing like "law," and even Exodus to Deuteronomy are not "legalistic" books. The word *torah* means "teaching," which gives a clearer impression of the nature of the Torah. Often the Torah gives us more than one account of an event (such as God's commission of Moses), so that when the early church told the story of Jesus in different ways in different contexts and according to the insights of the different Gospel writers, it was following the precedent whereby Israel told its stories more than once in different contexts. Whereas Samuel–Kings and Chronicles keep the versions separate, as would happen with the Gospels, in the Torah the versions were combined.

## Yahweh

In most English Bibles, the word "LORD" often comes in all capitals, as sometimes does the word "GOD" in similar format. These represent the name of God, Yahweh. In later Old Testament times, Israelites stopped using the name Yahweh and started to refer to Yahweh as "the Lord." There may be two reasons. They wanted other people to recognize that Yahweh was the one true God, but this strange foreign-sounding name could give the impression that Yahweh was just Israel's tribal god, and "the Lord" was a term anyone could recognize. In addition, they did not want to fall foul of the warning in the Ten Commandments about misusing Yahweh's name. Translations into other languages then followed suit in substituting an expression such as "the Lord" for the name Yahweh. The downsides are that it obscures the fact that God wanted to be known by name, that often the text refers to Yahweh and not some other (so-called) god or lord, and that it gives the impression that God is much more "lordly" and patriarchal than actually God is. (The form "Jehovah" is not a real word but a mixture of the consonants of Yahweh and the vowels of the word for "Lord," to remind people in reading Scripture that they should say "the Lord," not the actual name.)

## Yahweh Armies

This title for God usually appears in English Bibles as "the LORD of Hosts," but it is a more puzzling expression than that implies. The word for Lord is actually the name of God, **Yahweh**, and the word for Hosts is the regular Hebrew word for armies; it is the word that appears on the back of an Israeli military truck. So more literally the expression means "Yahweh [of] Armies," which is just as odd in Hebrew as "Goldingay of Armies" would be. Yet in general terms its likely implication is clear; it suggests that Yahweh is the embodiment of or controller of all war-making power, in heaven or on earth.